New Worlds for Old

THE APOCALYPTIC IMAGINATION, SCIENCE FICTION, AND AMERICAN LITERATURE

David Ketterer

I stand for the reform of municipal morals and the plain ten commandments. New worlds for old. Union of all, jew moslem and gentile. Three acres and a cow for all children of nature. . . . Electric dishscrubbers. Tuberculosis, lunacy, war and mendicancy must now cease.

—Bloom, in *Ulysses*

ANCHOR BOOKS

Anchor Press/Doubleday
Garden City, New York
1974

The Anchor Books edition is the first publication of *New Worlds for Old: The Apocalyptic Imagination, Science Fiction, and American Literature.*

Anchor Books edition: 1974

New Worlds for Old is available in a hard-cover edition from Indiana University Press.

ISBN: 0-385-00470-2
Library of Congress Catalog Card Number 72–96278
Copyright © 1974 by David Ketterer
All Rights Reserved
Printed in the United States of America
First Edition

To
my parents
and my wife, Jacqueline

I was like one set afloat upon a stormy sea and hanging his safety upon a plank; night was closing upon him, and an unexpected surge had torn him from his hold and overwhelmed him forever.

Brockden Brown, *Wieland*

In my mind, all had broken loose, habits of feeling, associations of thought, ideas of persons and things, all had dissolved and lost coherence and were seething together in apparently irretrievable chaos.

Edward Bellamy, *Looking Backward*

Down in the depths of me I had a feeling that I stood on the edge of a precipice. It was as though I were about to see a new and awful revelation of life. And not I alone. My whole world was turning over.

Jack London, *The Iron Heel*

All the known noon world loses its old staples and everything drops apart.

Brian Aldiss, *Barefoot in the Head*

It seemed to him that the world had lost its solidity, that he was tumbling through its substance toward the core, floating free, unable to check himself.

Robert Silverberg, *Tower of Glass*

Contents

PART THREE: THE PRESENT WORLD
                IN OTHER TERMS

PREFACE

One of the gaps in scholarship that this study proposes to fill—the lack of a relatively sophisticated critical appreciation and theoretical understanding of science fiction, particularly its contemporary manifestations—is presently highlighted by a growing academic interest in the subject. This interest is in response not just to students' demands for a "relevant" curriculum but also to the evidence that science fiction is in a state of expansion and, to some degree, appears to be closing with "mainstream" literature. I believe that this "new" affinity, thanks to the recent work of Brian Aldiss, J. G. Ballard, Lawrence Durrell, Kurt Vonnegut, Jr., and others, allows us to see science fiction in a truer perspective than was earlier possible. For the previous fifty or so years, science fiction, owing in great part to the efforts of Hugo Gernsback, has been artificially divorced from the literary mainstream. The form of accepted literature to which science fiction is specifically related, I have identified as "apocalyptic." Although typified by much American literature, apocalyptic literature as I define it should be understood as also drawing upon surrealism, metaphysical poetry, the pastoral tradition, Brecht's theory of estrangement, the work of Franz Kafka, the poetry of the romantics, particularly William Blake, and the phenomenological novel, among other possibilities.

An awareness of this larger context will hopefully encourage critics of science fiction to approach the genre in an explicatory manner comparable in detail and rigor to that presently reserved for non-science-fictional manifestations of the apocalyptic. At present, most such critics are content to rehash plot outlines, to exclaim over the ultimately banal expression of consciousness-expanding

"ideas," and to set up chronologies. If more teachers of
literature are to be convinced that science fiction is a viable area of study, it must be demonstrated to them that
a novel such as *The Martian Chronicles* can open up to
intense critical scrutiny just as *Moby-Dick* can. There
exists no book-length treatment of science fiction, such as
that which I attempted in the following pages, given
to the sustained explication of contemporary texts rather
than the work of Verne and Wells. In the case of such
texts, I have aimed at conveying a sense of the specifically
literary subtleties involved. The critical strategy I have
adopted involves the comparative, hopefully mutually illuminating consideration of science-fictional and non-science-fictional or "classic" manifestations of the apocalyptic
imagination. Because science fiction gives uniquely direct
expression to all the basic themes of the apocalyptic imagination, to set a classic apocalyptic work against a work
of science fiction that treats the same theme is to immediately clarify the extent to which the mainstream work
is apocalyptic, and at the same time, often, to reveal science-fictional elements in that work. Conversely while the
classic work assumes a science-fictional coloration, it
should be possible to appreciate classic stylistic and technical excellences in the similarly apocalyptic work of science fiction.

All my major examples of non-science-fictional literature
are drawn from American literature. It is my secondary
intention to emphasize the considerable concordance that
exists between all science fiction and the characteristics of
American literature generally and the American experience. The particularly American nature of science fiction
is virtually unexplored territory. It is true, of course, that
science fiction does exist and flourish in other major in-
dustrialized countries, but in terms of bulk and subject
matter, modern science fiction is as endemically American
as the "Western." This second omission is especially remarkable in view of all the critical attention that has been
focused on American literature in the past thirty or so
years and the consequent establishment of the romance

as the pre-eminent form. Although science fiction derives from the romance, its existence as a significant aspect of American literature has been largely ignored.

My approach to these two areas depends upon a detailed examination of the term "apocalyptic" as a critical counter. Since the word is as fashionable and relevant to our times as it is carelessly and inconsistently employed in critical discourse, there is a real need to examine its descriptive validity and usefulness. It is hoped, finally, that a definition of science fiction in terms of the apocalyptic imagination is not only a contribution to an understanding of science fiction and American literature but also a contribution to literary theory.

Acknowledgments

Parts of this book have previously been published, with some variations, as articles. An article entitled "New Worlds for Old: The Apocalyptic Imagination, Science Fiction, and American Literature," which appeared in *Mosaic* (1971), corresponds to the material in Part One of this book. Chapter 4 ("*The Left Hand of Darkness*: Ursula K. LeGuin's Archetypal 'Winter-Journey'") appeared with the same title in the *Riverside Quarterly* (1973). Chapter 5 ("Utopian Fantasy as Millennial Motive and Science-Fictional Motif") appeared with the same title in *Studies in the Literary Imagination* (1973). Chapter 8 ("*Solaris* and the Illegitimate Suns of Science Fiction") appeared with the same title in *Foundation* (1972) and *Extrapolation* (1972). A German translation of the same piece was published some months earlier in *Quarber Merkur* (1972). Chapter 9 ("Epoch-Eclipse and Apocalypse: Special 'Effects' in *A Connecticut Yankee*") appeared with the same title in *PMLA* (1973).

The academic consciousness in Montreal regarding science fiction has been considerably raised thanks to the coincidental presence of two science-fiction critics, Robert M. Philmus and Darko Suvin, at institutions neighboring my own, and I myself have benefited particularly from their proximity. I am particularly grateful to Robert Philmus for his careful reading of my final manuscript. Darko Suvin also read the final manuscript and commented helpfully on individual chapters, but I am most indebted to him for suggesting texts and for the stimulus provided by his theoretical formulations concerning the nature of science fiction. There exist considerable areas of agreement between Darko Suvin's definitions and my own, but where occasions for disagreement have arisen, he has prompted me to explore more deeply a number of areas I might otherwise have slighted. I am also grateful to the students in my graduate course in science fiction and American literature at what is now Concordia University during the period 1970 to 1972 for their critical response to my presentation of many of the ideas developed in the following pages.

A number of people have been involved in typing from my often challenging script, especially Mrs. Sheila Hoppe, who prepared the final manuscript with diligence and initiative. My colleague Professor David Sheps drew my attention to the passage in *Ulysses* that figures as an epigraph to the book. Thanks are also due to Ken Norris, my research assistant, who hunted up elusive footnotes and checked quotations. But, for the kinds of assistance that cannot be specified, I am most indebted to Jacki, my wife, who, in this enterprise, was my proofreader, and frequently my typist.

Part One: New Worlds for Old

I. THE APOCALYPTIC IMAGINATION, SCIENCE FICTION, AND AMERICAN LITERATURE

Biblical material has been particularly suggestive as an "open sesame" or interpretive index to American literature. It is now a critical commonplace to appropriate the Genesis story and talk about a hypothetical American Adam inhabiting, at least initially, an unfallen Eden in the New World.[1] Less often noted, but increasingly significant as a structure for the American experience, is the Book of Exodus. The metamorphosis of the Israelite metaphor in, for example, Melville's *Israel Potter*, Faulkner's *Go Down Moses*, and Bellow's (Moses) *Herzog* would seem to indicate that Exodus provides a convenient paradigm of a fallen America with the Promised Land as an elusive goal. Although the Wandering Jew role would seem to apply specifically to the black American, the current temptation to equate the situation of any supposedly disadvantaged group with that of the "nigger" has converted the figure of the alienated Jew into an image of the American Everyman. America's fall from grace and expulsion from Eden, imaginatively associated with the curse of slavery, may be taken, figuratively, as completed by the American Civil War. Since that time, American literature has not lacked its redeemer figures—most obviously the various J.C.s, ranging from Stephen Crane's Jim Conklin to Faulkner's

[1] *The American Adam: Innocence, Tragedy, and Tradition in the Nineteenth Century*, by R. W. B. Lewis (Chicago, 1951), remains the standard treatment of this theme. The underlying influence of Puritan thought processes, explored by Charles Feidelson, Jr., in *Symbolism and American Literature* (Chicago, 1953), goes some way toward explaining the prevalence of biblical tropes in American literature.

Joe Christmas. Their careers do not effect any immediate or lasting regeneration, and perhaps rightly so, since it is the Second Coming of Christ that is to usher in the establishment of heaven upon earth—so John of Patmos, or John the Divine, tells us in his Revelation, or Apocalypse. This book will explore, among other matters, some of the less obvious ways in which the Apocalypse may be relevant to an understanding of American literature.

Naturally enough, shades of the Apocalypse have colored literature at least from Chaucer onward (I am thinking of the ironic invocation to chaos at the end of "The Nun's Priest's Tale"), and American literature is no exception (Nathanael West's *The Day of the Locust* is the most obvious example). It is a legitimate topic of unavoidable universal concern, particularly today, when fictive intimations of catastrophe gain credibility from the existence of nuclear weapons. For the first time, man has it in his power to be the instigator of a do-it-yourself apocalypse. On the popular level, warnings find expression in such songs as Barrie McGuire's "Eve of Destruction" (1965) and Mama Cass's "California Earthquake" (1968). Furthermore, interpreters of the American scene, to judge from such titles as Stanley Edgar Hyman's *The Promised End* (1963) and Leslie Fiedler's *Waiting for the End* (1964), would seem to endorse the validity and relevance of the apocalyptic vision. James Baldwin, in a book entitled *The Fire Next Time* (1963), looks to the coming holocaust as a consequence of the injustice suffered by the black man at the hands of his white oppressors.

However, of more immediate interest are the expanded connotations that cling to recent usage of the word "apocalypse" in critical jargon. As a result of the writings of D. H. Lawrence, George Snell, Northrop Frye, R. W. B. Lewis, Ihab Hassan, and Frank Kermode, the word apocalypse now often functions as a somewhat Delphic critical counter. It is perhaps a moot question as to whether such usage is of any real worth or just another flashy and confusing tag popularized by attention-seeking critics. After all, apocalyptic is a heady word. But before reviewing the various theoretical applications of the term apocalypse, there may be some point, possibly as a check to critical irresponsibility, in recalling the word's origins.

The Greek word *apokalupsis,* which produces the English word apocalypse and an alternative title for the Book of Revelation, implies "an unveiling, either (a) of future events, or (b) of the unseen realms of heaven and hell."[2] John's Apocalypse, although the fullest and most convenient for my purposes, is only the best known of many such works. Certain images and allusions in the Apocalypse, many of which are pre-Christian and go back to the Judaic tradition and before, have gained a freewheeling currency outside their original context. Consequently, the following brief and selective summary of the narrative drift of the book may help place these particular elements.

John, in exile on the island of Patmos, experiences a vision of a white-haired Christ, whose "voice was like the sound of rushing waters" (1:15). (Usher's house, it may be recalled, falls to "a long tumultuous shouting sound like the voice of a thousand waters,"[3] and Herman Melville's *The Confidence-Man* opens with the advent of the flaxen-haired, lamblike man in his white fur hat.) Christ tells John to convey warnings of doom to the seven churches of Asia. God, in the vision that follows, hands Christ a scroll, fastened by seven seals, that holds the secrets of the future. A series of calamities ensue consequent upon the breaking of the seals one by one. These include wars, both of a limited and a global nature, famine, and death (represented by the four horsemen of the Apocalypse) and climax with falling stars and geological disturbances. As in the Genesis story, sinners implore the mountains to fall on them and thus hide them from the eyes of God.

[2] See the introductory material to *The Revelation of John,* ed. by T. F. Glasson (Cambridge, Eng., 1965), p. 1. Quotations from the biblical text may be located in this edition.
[3] *The Complete Works of Edgar Allan Poe,* 17 vols., ed. by James A. Harrison (New York, 1902), Vol. III, p. 297.

This is one of several details that suggest that the Apocalypse is in part a recapitulation of many of the memorable moments in the Bible.

As a result of the breaking of the seventh seal, there appear seven trumpets for seven angels, which, when blown, herald seven more assorted disasters. The plague of locusts with human faces, summoned by the fifth trumpet, might be instanced as an imagistic high point. After the blast of the seventh trumpet, follows the attenuated appearance—a little predictable by now—of the seven bowls of wrath, containing a variety of plagues reminiscent of the plagues visited on the Egyptians in Exodus. This accounts generally for what takes place in Chapters 8 to 16.

Between the blowing of the seventh trumpet and the appearance of the bowls of wrath, occurs the period of the Great Tribulation: the reign of the Antichrist, which goes on for three and a half years, the second half of the week of years preceding the end. The Antichrist confers his power upon a horrendous beast (representing Nero), which rises from the sea. Then a second beast emerges marked with the number 666, "which represents a man's name" (13:18).[4] After the afflictions suffered as a consequence of the seven bowls of wrath, Babylon, or Rome, is introduced, personified as a great whore, who is to be destroyed by the beast on which she rides, namely Nero, whereupon Christ returns to earth to defeat the two beasts at the battle of Armageddon.

Satan is bound in order to allow for the millennium, the thousand-year epoch of the messianic kingdom upon earth. At the end of this period, the brief loosening of Satan accounts for the last and worst apostasy, and the attack of the "hosts of Gog and Magog" (20:8) on Je-

---

[4] Glasson explains, "The most widely accepted interpretation is that the number stands for Nero Caesar. If these two names are written in Hebrew, the numerical value comes to 666. Any name may be turned into a number by taking the first letter of the alphabet for 1, the second for 2 and so on; and after 100 the other hundreds follow" (p. 83).

rusalem. Following their defeat and the destruction of the world by fire, the Last Judgment takes place. It is perhaps worth noting, in view of the popular equation of the apocalyptic with the catastrophic, that the literal destruction of the world is not described. We are told, ". . . there was no longer any sea" (21:1), because sea is equated with the chaos that has now ended. The new heaven and the new earth make their appearance. The "new Jerusalem, coming down out of heaven from God, made ready like a bride adorned for her husband" (21:2), is to be contrasted with the city of Babylon, presented as a whore.

As a result of this résumé of John's Apocalypse, four observations might be made that shed some light on the potential of the word apocalyptic as a critical term. First, it is readily apparent that the word has both a negative and a positive charge: there is a necessary correlation between the destruction of the world and the establishment of the New Jerusalem. Secondly, the prophetic side of John's work is compromised to the extent that he is governed by a historical context. He writes as a reaction to the persecuting Roman Empire.[5] Consequently, the visionary aspect of his work is radically undercut by an indirect satiric bitterness and possibly a sense of paranoia. Thirdly, because of the book's self-conscious use of echoes from other parts of the Bible, it functions as a kind of recapitulative coda, an often incoherent microcosm of everything preceding it—namely the more intellectually available biblical macrocosm. Or, alternatively, the promissory aspect of the Bible is set in a final, celestial context that presumably vindicates its meaning. Fourthly, the scope and grandeur of the Apocalypse necessitate a diminution of the human element. Clearly, then, the term

[5] The possibility that the Book of Revelation has more to say about the past than about the future is the subject of H. Bellamy's rather science-fictional exegesis *The Book of Revelation Is History* (London, 1942). It is really a figurative record of that time when the moon fell on the Earth, and another, captured moon took its place!

apocalyptic allows for a dialectic, conflict, or tension of
oppositions—and a dialectic, conflict, or tension of opposites is the stuff of literature. It is my contention that there
are a group of American writers who have produced what
may be called apocalyptic literature, because they are
concerned with the particular antitheses that that word
suggests. These antitheses may be viewed as one aspect
of a larger American literary dialectic, such as that abrupt
oscillation between the pragmatic or the material and the
speculative or the transcendental; or, to put it extremely
and modishly, between violence and the hallucinogenic
ethic.

A brief consideration of some recent critical usages of
the term apocalyptic may help to elucidate the elements
in tension. To my knowledge, George Snell was the first
critic to cordon off a group of American writers and call
them apocalyptic: namely Charles Brockden Brown, Edgar Allan Poe, Ambrose Bierce, Lafcadio Hearn, Herman
Melville, and William Faulkner.[6] In my view, his grouping is valid, but unfortunately he makes no attempt to
define his sense of the word apocalyptic. I shall turn now
to those writers who have struggled with the problem of
definition. Since the tendency has been to emphasize independently either the negative or the positive charges of
the word, the critics concerned may be conveniently divided into two groups.

Among those commentators who have emphasized the
negative charge, D. H. Lawrence's view is of particular
interest because he is in many ways an apocalyptic writer
himself as well as an interpreter of American literature.
Indeed Lawrence's assertion that American literature is
secretive and cabalistic implies one point of similarity with
apocalyptic writing. Toward the end of his life, Lawrence
undertook an exegesis of the Book of Revelation in a work
entitled *Apocalypse* (1932). He sees the Revelation quite
simply as the product of the spiteful wish fulfillment of the
underprivileged, an expression of frustrated power lust.

[6] See *The Shapers of American Fiction, 1798–1947* (New
York, 1947), pp. 32–104.

Presumably, then, bitterness and a sense of persecution, such as that which encouraged the Pilgrim Fathers to sail for America, should characterize the writer of apocalyptic literature.

The writer who is bitter and paranoid will, likely as not, turn to satire. And satire, as defined by Alvin Kernan in *The Plot of Satire*, may be understood as an apocalyptic mode, particularly when viewed in terms of his analysis of the "mob tendency" in *The Day of the Locust*.[7] The end result of satire, best illustrated perhaps by Pope's *Dunciad*, is to reveal that "thy dread Empire, CHAOS! is restored."[8] R. W. B. Lewis, in a long groundbreaking essay entitled "Days of Wrath and Laughter,"[9] concentrates on the contemporary manifestation of comic apocalyptic writing—related, of course, to satire—which he traces back to Nathanael West. By exploiting a comic perspective, says Lewis, novelists such as "Ralph Ellison and John Barth and Joseph Heller and Thomas Pynchon have made the day of doom the great saturnalia of our time."[10] One has only to think of the conclusion to *Dr. Strangelove*.

The purely negative usage has been taken furthest by Ihab Hassan in *The Literature of Silence*.[11] Hassan seems to make an equation between apocalyptic literature and what he calls the literature of silence—of which Henry Miller and Samuel Beckett are exemplars. Apocalyptic or

[7] *The Plot of Satire* (New Haven, Conn., 1965), *passim*. See R. W. B. Lewis' statement in *The Poetry of Hart Crane: A Critical Study* (Princeton, N.J., 1967): "Great satire, Kernan implies, is almost by definition apocalyptic . . ." (p. 382).
[8] *The Twickenham Edition of the Poems of Alexander Pope* (London, 1943), p. 409.
[9] See *Trials of the Word: Essays in American Literature and the Humanistic Tradition* (New Haven, Conn., 1965), pp. 184–235.
[10] Ibid., p. 185.
[11] *The Literature of Silence* (New York, 1967). See also Hassan's further exploration of the same concept in *The Dismemberment of Orpheus: Towards a Postmodernist Literature* (New York, 1971).

silent literature, in Hassan's vague terms, involves a sense
of outrage at the void and an expression of the nullity or
chaotic fragmentation of human experience. The ultimate
critical negative extension of the word apocalyptic, then,
connotes chaos or non-meaning. Apparently Hassan sees
very little evidence of the visionary side to the coin.

It was during the Romantic period in English literary
history, in the 1790s, that a positive apocalyptic charge
came to the fore. The American and French revolutions
were interpreted as the premillennial upheavals prophesied
in the Apocalypse. R. W. B. Lewis writes: "For the English imagination of the decade, in short, the word 'apocalypse' meant not a vision of horror but of dazzling splen-
dor, not of catastrophe but of the epochal and triumphant
social transformation that catastrophe led to."[12] In the
subsequent period of disillusionment, many writers (particularly William Blake, whose philosophical formulations
anticipate not only the work of Poe but many other
American practitioners of the apocalyptic imagination)
were bent upon portraying what M. H. Abrams has
termed "apocalypses of imagination" that celebrate a com-
pensatory grand new world.[13]

Northrop Frye's theoretical formulations in his *Anatomy
of Criticism* derive, as he has admitted, from his study of
Blake, and I assume that, as a consequence, he uses the
word apocalyptic only in the positive sense. Frye states:
"By an apocalypse I mean primarily the imaginative conception of the whole of nature as the content of an infinite and eternal living body, which if not human, is
closer to being human than to being inanimate."[14] The
perception of our conversion to this reality, Frye relates

[12] *Trials of the Word*, p. 200.
[13] M. H. Abrams, "English Romanticism: The Spirit of the
Age," in *Romanticism Reconsidered*, edited by Northrop Frye
(New York, 1963), pp. 53–60. An analogous term, "the
apocalypse of the mind," is used by Emerson in *Nature*. See
The Complete Works of Ralph Waldo Emerson, 12 vols.,
Centenary Edition (New York, 1903–4), Vol. I, p. 48.
[14] *Anatomy of Criticism*, (Princeton, N.J., 1957), p. 119.

to the alchemical principle whereby base metal is turned
into gold.[15] Playing the animal, vegetable, and mineral
game, Frye reveals three basic images of the apocalyptic
world: the mineral image of the heavenly city of Jerusalem, the vegetable image of the Arcadian garden, and the
animal imagery of the sheepfold and pastoral existence—
to be opposed to his basic images of the demonic world:
seas and dark cities, forests and wastelands, and beasts.
My sense of the word apocalyptic, as inclusive of Frye's
demonic world, implies that all literature is, in an imagistic, archetypal sense, apocalyptic. Obviously if the word is
to be of any use as a category, some sort of distinction
must be drawn between a delimited use of the word and
its wider possibilities.

The ultimate extension of the positive implications of
the term apocalyptic has been provided by Frank Kermode in his difficult book *The Sense of an Ending*.[16] The
title can mean either the apprehension of a conclusion,
or the meaning or purpose of a conclusion. Kermode
points out that throughout recorded time man has always
thought of his own age as the dark before the dawn.[17]

[15] Ibid., p. 148. The possible relationship between alchemy
and apocalypse is explored by Louis Pauwels and Jacques
Bergier in *The Dawn of Magic*, trans. by Rollo Myers (London, 1963): "The real aim of the alchemist's activities, which
are perhaps the remains of a very old science belonging to a
civilization long extinct, is the transformation of the alchemist
himself, his accession to a higher state of consciousness. The
material results are only a pledge of the final result which is
spiritual. Everything is orientated towards his deification, his
fusion with the divine energy, the fixed centre from which all
material energies emanate" (p. 73). And perhaps it is not
irrelevant to talk about the alchemy of art, as does Ben Jonson
in *The Alchemist*.
[16] *The Sense of an Ending: Studies in the Theory of Fiction*
(New York, 1967).
[17] Frequently, chiliastic hopes have provided an incentive
and structure for revolution, as Norman Cohn makes plain in
The Pursuit of the Millennium (New York, 1957). Millennial
expectations, naturally enough, tend to gain in intensity as a

We, in turn, think of our own times as apocalyptic because all times have been thought of as apocalyptic.
Kermode's explanation respects directly the historical bias
of apocalyptic thinking. Unlike the mystic, who attempts
to break through material reality, the apocalyptic arrives
at his revelation through an understanding of the true
significance of events in the historical world. Kermode
argues that man's sense of meaning depends upon dura-
tion and also upon his understanding of both a beginning
and an ending to things. McLuhan notwithstanding, Kermode would insist that man is a hopelessly linear creature.
We can appreciate time only in terms of spatial sequences—the hiatus between a tick and a tock. Any kind
of meaning depends upon the assumption of two fixed
points: a starting point and an ending point; in terms of
the meaning of human existence, a Genesis and an Apocalypse. Literature, says Kermode, provides an idealized
version of life's meaning and is to be distinguished from
life, because a book, however elliptical and abstruse, has
a first page and a last page. The literary technique of
peripeteia is equivalent to the historical experience of
misinterpreting the date for the end of the world. In this
teleological sense, for Kermode, all literature is apocalyptic.

An adequate definition of the apocalyptic imagination

---

given century draws to its close. For example, as already
noted, the optimistic apocalyptic imagination came to the fore
at the end of the eighteenth century in England. A related
phenomenon, examined by Jay Martin in *Harvests of Change:
American Literature 1865–1914* (Englewood Cliffs, N.J.,
1967), occurs in American literature as the nineteenth century
draws toward its close. Note that, although the perfect world
described by Edward Bellamy in *Looking Backward* (1887)
is set in the year 2000, the essential transformation involved is
supposed to have occurred at the very beginning of the
twentieth century. And very incidentally, it is surely not without significance that Charles Manson, key figure in the Sharon
Tate murder case, was able to control and galvanize his followers with promises of an apocalyptic revolution colored by his
reading of Robert Heinlein's science-fictional work *Stranger in
a Strange Land* (1961).

must depend upon combining my fractured survey above. In so doing, we discover a series of related tensions to be implicit in the term—tensions analogous to the four aspects of Revelation, mentioned earlier as bearing particularly on a possible critical usage. The destruction of an old world, generally of mind, is set against the writer's establishment of a new world, again generally of mind. Secondly, satire comes up against a prophetic mysticism to provide a form of "judgment." Thirdly, the creation of purpose and meaning (see Kermode) collides with the possibility of non-meaning and chaos (see Hassan). And fourthly, all the commentators I have cited at least imply that apocalyptic literature involves a certain magnitude or breadth of vision which militates against an interest in detailed characterization. If apocalyptic literature can be talked about in terms of its involvement with the dialectic to be derived from these opposites, it is apparent that such a literature must question the fundamental epistemological assumptions of the human situation. It will be a literature of ideas, as is the case with American literature.

Apocalyptic literature should be distinguished from mimetic literature on the one hand, and fantastic literature on the other. While mimetic literature addresses itself to reproductions of the "real" world, fantastic literature involves the creation of escapist worlds that, existing in an incredible relationship to the "real" world, do not impinge destructively on that world. *Apocalyptic literature is concerned with the creation of other worlds which exist, on the literal level, in a credible relationship (whether on the basis of rational extrapolation and analogy or of religious belief) with the "real" world, thereby causing a metaphorical destruction of that "real" world in the reader's head.* The apocalyptic imagination may finally be defined in terms of its philosophical preoccupation with that moment of juxtaposition and consequent transformation or transfiguration when an old world of mind discovers a believable new world of mind, which either nullifies and destroys the old system entirely or, less likely, makes it part of a larger design. "The Fall of the House of

Usher" provides a pictorial paradigm of that agonized juxtaposition. A limited world of fragile order maintains itself, precariously at best, over a threatening and unknown context. I would suggest that the successive collapse of meaning and structural coherence, of which we are today painfully aware, has long been a concern of the American imagination. But the fulfillment of the apocalyptic imagination demands that the destructive chaos give way finally to a new order.

1. Science Fiction

I

If, at its most exalted level, apocalyptic literature is religious, the concerns of such a literature, at its most popular level, find expression in the gothic mode and especially in science fiction. Clearly, the introduction of the other, the *outré*, whether in terms of supernatural manifestations or creatures from outer space, is going to upset man's conception of his own situation and prompt him to relate his existence to a broader framework. It is the particular function of all worthwhile science fiction to explore the philosophical consequences of any such radical disorientation.

The apocalyptic imagination, I submit, finds its purest outlet in science fiction. And in so far as science fiction concerns itself with the "sense of an ending," Kermode's understanding of the apocalyptic impulse acquires a new relevance.[1] Indeed while W. H. Auden talks about detective fiction in terms of the "phantasy of being returned to the Garden of Eden," Leslie Fiedler adduces that the dream of apocalypse is the myth of science fiction, "the myth of the end of man, of the transcendence or transformation of the human—a vision quite different from that of the extinction of our species by the Bomb, which

[1] The title of Stephen and Lois Rose's book *The Shattered Ring: Science Fiction and the Quest for Meaning* (Richmond, Va., 1970), but nothing else about it, is suggestive here. More suggestive is a footnote R. W. B. Lewis includes in *Trials of the Word*: "The huge contribution of science fiction to modern apocalyptic literature would be very much worth investigating . . ." (p. 193).

seems stereotype rather than archetype. . . ."[2] When Frye speaks of "the Flood archetype," the cosmic disaster, as characteristic of science fiction, he is insufficiently sensitive to the subsequent transformation.[3]

For the reader, an apocalyptic transformation results from the creation of a new condition, based upon a process of extrapolation and analogy, whereby man's horizons —temporal, spatial, scientific, and ultimately philosophic— are abruptly expanded. Science-fiction stories may be roughly grouped into three categories, depending upon the basis of the extrapolation involved. A writer may extrapolate the future consequences of present circumstances, in which case he will probably produce sociological science fiction within the "utopia"/dystopia range.[4] Secondly, and this is a frequently related category, typified by much of H. G. Wells' work, he may extrapolate the consequences following the modification of an existent condition.[5] This modification, as Kingsley Amis notes,

[2] W. H. Auden, "The Guilty Vicarage," *Harper's Magazine*, CXCVI (May 1948), p. 412. Leslie A. Fiedler, "The New Mutants," *Partisan Review*, XXXII (fall 1965), p. 508.

[3] *Anatomy of Criticism*, p. 203. It is, of course, true that a good many science-fictional ideas derive, however unconsciously, from a rationalistic appropriation of archetypes in the Book of Revelation. For example, the image of an insect with a human head, which figures in the film *The Fly*, has some affinity with the apocalyptic plague of locusts with human faces. Certainly the various monsters that science-fiction films have envisaged as devastating the globe are generically connected with the beasts of the Apocalypse.

[4] See, for example, John Brunner's Hugo-award winner *Stand on Zanzibar* (New York, 1969), in which one of the protagonists, Donald Hogan, prior to his very literal transformation, finds himself "suspended between the wreck of former convictions and the solidification of new ones . . ." (p. 198).

[5] See, for example, Fritz Leiber's *The Wanderer* (New York, 1964), which details the consequences when a new planet comes literally within human ken. As an epigraph for his book, Leiber quotes a passage from the Apocalypse and extracts from Blake's *The Tyger*. The relationship I am implying is explicit in the title of another of Leiber's books, *The Green*

NEW WORLDS FOR OLD

frequently takes the form "of some innovation in science
or pseudo-science or pseudo-technology" or "some change
or disturbance or local anomaly in physical conditions."[6]
Thirdly, the most philosophically oriented science fiction,
extrapolating on what we know in the context of our vaster
ignorance, comes up with a startling *donnée*, or rationale,
that puts humanity in a radically new perspective. In the
second and third categories, the element of analogy be-

Millennium (New York, 1953). Ecologists are presently teaching us that we live in a closed system of multiple and delicate
checks and balances. The implication is that we must be as
sensitive to our environment as, ideally, literary critics should
be to the closed systems of works of art. A major change in
ecological factors, particularly the increase of pollution, right
now appears to provide a particularly plausible means by
which the biblical Apocalypse may take place. Science-fiction
writers like Leiber, who predicate an apocalyptic transformation as a result of one significant alteration, are, whether they
recognize it or not, dealing in matters of ecology. One science-
fiction writer who *is* aware of this fact is Frank Herbert, who
dedicates his Hugo-award-winning novel about a desert planet,
Dune (New York, 1965), to "the dryland ecologists." See
also George R. Stewart's *Earth Abides* (New York, 1949),
which features an ecologist as hero. It should be apparent
from this sketchy account that the notion of an ecological
apocalypse enforces the connections I am making among
the biblical Apocalypse, the science-fictional philosophical
apocalypse, and the value of the concept of a philosophical
apocalypse to critical and aesthetic theory. Edgar Allan Poe's
awareness, incidentally, of the "reciprocity of adaptation" is
illuminating in this context. See *The Complete Works of Edgar
Allan Poe*, Vol. XVI, p. 9.
[6] *New Maps of Hell* (New York, 1960), pp. 18, 24. The
effect of science is pre-eminent. J. O. Bailey, in *Pilgrims
Through Space and Time: Trends and Patterns in Scientific
and Utopian Fiction* (New York, 1947), notes, ". . . the First
Men of Stapledon's *Last and First Men* (London, 1930) think
of science as a religion, not merely because 'it was through science that men had gained some insight into the nature of the
physical world, but rather because the application of scientific
principles had revolutionized their material circumstance'" (p.
296).

comes increasingly evident. Needless to say, the three categories overlap, and distinction depends upon emphasis.

In spite of an over-all emphasis on ideas in science fiction, the author's extrapolative structures rarely lend themselves to overt allegorical ends, because of the danger of jeopardizing the illusion of a surface verisimilitude.[7] What all science fiction aims at is destroying old assumptions and suggesting a new, and often visionary, reality. The extent to which science fiction is satiric is particularly apparent in the dystopias treated by Mark R. Hillegas.[8] As for the other side of the coin, Samuel R. Delany writes:

> The vision . . . that sf tries for seems to me very close
> to the vision of poetry, particularly poetry as it con-
> cerned the nineteenth century Symbolists. No matter
> how disciplined its creation, to move into an unreal
> world demands a brush with mysticism. Virtually all
> the classics of speculative fiction are mystical.[9]

But the mysticism must never exceed the bounds of plausibility, or the work's satiric edge will be blunted. The technique of extrapolation demands a commitment to logic.[10]

[7] C. S. Lewis' allegorical trilogy *Out of the Silent Planet, Voyage to Venus, That Hideous Strength* (London, 1938, 1943, 1946), is a mix of fantasy and science fiction.

[8] *The Future as Nightmare: H. G. Wells and the Anti-Utopians* (New York, 1967), *passim.* In so far as academic criticism has grappled with an understanding of science fiction as a genre, the tendency has been to consider its satiric aspects. See Robert M. Philmus, *Into the Unknown: The Evolution of Science Fiction from Godwin to H. G. Wells* (Berkeley and Los Angeles, 1970), for a recent example.

[9] "About Five Thousand One Hundred and Seventy-Five Words," *Extrapolation: A Science Fiction Newsletter,* X (May 1969), p. 63.

[10] The plausibility issue points to an important distinction between science fiction and fantasy, hinging on what Delany calls the "level of subjunctivity," ibid., pp. 61–64. H. Bruce

In detailing some examples, I am going to confine myself to my third science-fiction category, in which a startling rationale is involved, because I find the third type the most significant as an expression of the philosophical sense of the apocalyptic imagination and because this category has not previously been isolated by critics of the genre. One American example is provided by H. P. Lovecraft's stories, which, oscillating uncertainly between the gothic and science fiction, are held together by a mythology that takes as its starting point the assumption that man is only the latest of a series of beings who have inhabited the Earth. Among the earlier denizens were a race who discovered the secret of time travel. Lovecraft's mythology is quite complicated in all its ramifications, but what he basically suggests is that many ghostly phenomena may be explained as the materializations of Earth's early time travelers. I shall have more to say about Lovecraft toward the conclusion of this study. The same goes for another American writer, Kurt Vonnegut, Jr., who, in *The Sirens of Titan* (1959), tells us that eons ago a spaceship containing a robotlike alien crash-landed on one of the moons of Saturn. It turns out that the history of humanity has been manipulated by related aliens from a distant galaxy, in order to allow for that time when a spaceship from Earth reaches Titan "accidentally" carrying a piece of material that will function as a spare part! Arthur C. Clarke provides an English example of this species of science fiction in *2001: A Space Odyssey* (1968). It is speculated that we owe our present stage of evolution to the interference of spiritual beings while we were at the ape stage. But for the appearance of the mysterious slab, the human race would have died out in its infancy. The result of entertaining these revolutionary

---

Franklin distinguishes between types of fiction on a similar basis in *Future Perfect: American Science Fiction of the Nineteenth Century* (New York, 1966), p. 3. The lack of a plausible relationship between fantasy and the "real world" makes it impossible to speak about works of fantasy effecting a philosophical apocalypse.

notions is the sensation, however momentary, of a philosophical apocalypse.

II

I want now to suggest that certain characteristics of science fiction, particularly the philosophical apocalyptic kind, are present in American literature generally and, secondly, try to explain why. H. Bruce Franklin has done much of the groundwork in preparing his anthology *Future Perfect: American Science Fiction of the Nineteenth Century.* He concludes: "There was no major nineteenth-century American writer of fiction, and indeed few in the second rank, who did not write some science fiction or at least one utopian romance." "Rip van Winkle," he notes, "is a time-travel story," while other examples include Cooper's *The Monikins* (1835) and *The Crater* (1848), Melville's *Mardi*, Twain's *A Connecticut Yankee in King Arthur's Court*, and (less convincingly) Stephen Crane's *The Monster.*[11] The inclusion of the allegorical Hawthorne is also questionable, but Poe, Fitz-James O'Brien, Edward Bellamy, and Ambrose Bierce consistently wrote science fiction. It is only necessary to think of the affinity between Melville's Ahab and Jules Verne's Nemo and the degree to which *2001: A Space Odyssey* is indebted to *Moby-Dick* (particularly in basing metaphysical speculation on technology) to recognize the science-fictional element operational in the latter work.[12]

To speak more generally, characterization is generally slighted in American fiction in favor of the expression of ideas and metaphysical abstractions. The same bias is true of science fiction. A concern for the meaning of existence invariably reaches its limits with an awareness of

[11] Franklin, op. cit. p. x.
[12] Note also that Ray Bradbury wrote the script for the latest film version of *Moby-Dick* and the existence of Philip José Farmer's science-fiction sequel, *The Wind Whales of Ishmael* (New York, 1971).

cyclical process. In this connection it is interesting to relate the cyclical patterning of many science-fiction stories,
typified perhaps by H. G. Wells' *The Time Machine*, to
such American works as Irving's "Rip Van Winkle,"
Thoreau's *Walden*, Fitzgerald's *The Great Gatsby*, and
Hemingway's *The Sun Also Rises*, in which cyclical theory
is particularly pertinent. The fact that much "space opera"
science fiction is a displaced form of the "Western" is
indisputable, but there is also some relationship between
the mystical impulse of science fiction and American transcendentalism. Furthermore, like much science fiction,
American literature is notable for its prophetic character,
perhaps attributable to the American impetus toward
originality: sophisticated symbolic techniques in the novel,
and experimental methodology in poetry, developed in
America long before they became standardized in Europe.
The sharp juxtaposition in American literature, noted previously, of pragmatism and materialism with the transcendental and speculative is implicit in the term science
fiction and suggests something about the paradoxical nature of the genre that is lost in terms like "speculative
fiction" or "speculative fabulation."[13]

Then there is the quality of wonder, which Tony Tanner, in *The Reign of Wonder* (1965), finds in American
literature. However, it is even more characteristic of science fiction, as is apparent from the title of Damon
Knight's book on the subject, *In Search of Wonder*
(1967). Delany talks about a "sense of wonder" and
"these violet nets of wonder called speculative fiction."[14]
And as an epigraph to *The Martian Chronicles* (1950),
Ray Bradbury has these lines: "'It is good to renew one's

[13] I would speculate that dissatisfaction with the term science
fiction is less a reflection of doubt concerning its descriptive
appropriateness than the result of a desire to disassociate from
that body of literature called science fiction the aura of op-
probrium frequently engendered by the term. Note that science-fiction works of obvious literary merit, such as *Brave New
World* and *1984* are not generally thought of as science fiction.
[14] Op. cit., p. 63.

sense of wonder,' said the philosopher. 'Space travel has
again made children of us all.' "

III

The question remains: why should many of the characteristics of science fiction be in alignment with many of
the features that distinguish American literature? In large
measure, the answer lies in the fact that science fiction
derives from the romance, which, thanks largely to Richard Chase, we now recognize as the basic form of the
American novel.[15] Works that we call science fiction were
originally called "scientific romances." Actually all popular
escapist literature—the gothic horror story, romantic fiction, the Western, detective and thriller fiction, pornog-
raphy and science fiction—derives from the romance, and
given the prevalence of the romance in American literature, it is not surprising that all forms of the popularized
romance have flourished with particular intensity in America. Both Fiedler and Harry Levin have argued that it is
the gothic offshoot of the romance that best expresses the
American imagination.[16] No one, to my knowledge, has
examined in detail the extent to which science fiction has
functioned as an outlet for the American writer, although
Fiedler, in defining science fiction as a neogothic form,
includes it in his thesis.

If biblical myth has provided American writers with a
way of ordering their subject matter, the romance, par-

[15] See *The American Novel and Its Tradition* (New York,
1957).
[16] See Harry Levin, *The Power of Blackness* (New York,
1958), and Leslie A. Fiedler, *Love and Death in the American
Novel* (New York, 1960). Fiedler considers science fiction only
in the revised edition (1967), pp. 500, 502. Certainly the
evasion of heterosexual relationships, which Fiedler observes in
American literature, is also notable in science fiction, which is
generally characterized by an extreme purity of subject matter—unless, of course, one wants to see science fiction as dis-
guising fantasies of a return to the womb!

ticularly the gothic *and* science-fictional offshoots, has provided the characteristic mode. My point is that most of the reasons adduced by Chase to explain the prominence of the romance—in particular its latitude, its being in Hawthorne's terms "a neutral territory, somewhere between the real world and fairy-land," and its suitability as an expression of the incongruity of the American situation —also explain the existence of science fiction and science-fictional elements in American literature.[17]

But there are other factors, which relate specifically to science fiction. To some degree, surely, the lack of a usable past must have encouraged American writers to look to the future for their myths. After all, America has always been a land of promises. Indeed America, with its surrealistic skyscrapers, provides one alternative blueprint of the future for the rest of the world. The notion of the American Adam is common enough. Less common is the recognition that the idea of a second Adam, or a second Eve for that matter, is generally the province of science fiction. What usually happens is that, after the nuclear holocaust, two survivors see themselves as the progenitors of a new world.[18] "Utopias" and dystopias are regular science-fiction fodder, and, as A. N. Kaul argues in *The American Vision* (1963), fodder for the American imagination, which is obsessed with dreams of a utopia. American society is, in fact, a projected utopia that now seems to have turned into a dystopia. Note also that the area beyond the frontier and the Indian once represented that unknown and alien exotic so beloved of science fiction. In a sense, the exploration of space has supplied America with a further outlet for its tradition of frontiersmanship. America's fall from grace, Leo Marx suggests in *The Machine in the Garden*, may have something to do with the industrial revolution and the growth of technology.[19]

[17] *The Centenary Edition of the Works of Nathaniel Hawthorne* (Columbus, Ohio, 1962), p. 36.
[18] See, for example, my concluding remarks on Ray Bradbury's *The Martian Chronicles* in the next chapter.
[19] See *The Machine in the Garden: Technology and the Pastoral Ideal in America* (Fair Lawn, N.J., 1964). Incidentally, it

And, as the term science fiction implies, to some people it has seemed that the genre derives its subject matter from scientific advances. Certainly science fiction flourished in the throes of the industrial revolution. But the tremendous contemporaneous influence of Charles Darwin should also be appreciated, both upon "mainstream" American literature and also upon the opening up of a temporal and cyclical canvas directly amenable only to science fiction.

In general terms, the proliferation of science fiction is a response to abruptly changing social conditions. During times of stability, when change neither happens nor is expected, or happens so gradually as to be barely noticeable, writers are unlikely to spend time describing the future condition of society, because there is no reason to expect any significant difference. With the nineteenth century, things speeded up, and now change is a constant and unnerving factor in our daily lives. If we are to live rationally, and not just for the moment, some attempt must be made to anticipate future situations. Hence writers are drawn to science fiction; it is an outgrowth and an expression of crisis. Thus Robert Heinlein attests to the value of science fiction: "We cannot drive safely by looking only in the rear-view mirror [shades of McLuhan]; it is more urgent to watch the road ahead."[20] The analogy is imperfect,

---

is interesting to note that, in *The Tempest*, which Marx relates to the pastoral attraction of North America (pp. 35–72), Kingsley Amis finds science-fictional prototypes: scientist and attractive daughter, "an early mutant" in the shape of Caliban, while Ariel functions as an "anthropomorphised mobile scanner" (*New Maps of Hell*, p. 30). Can we then speak of *The Tempest* as a science-fiction vision of America?

[20] See *The Science Fiction Novel*, ed. by Basil Davenport (Chicago, 1959), p. 54. Alvin Toffler's argument in *Future Shock* (New York, 1970) is particularly relevant to my point here. The changes that the conventions of science fiction have undergone in this century are themselves evidence of the form's success as a preparatory aid. For example, it would be interesting to fix the point in time at which any science-fiction

but Heinlein's point is sound enough, although science fiction is not primarily valuable as prediction. Rather, it teaches adaptability and elasticity of mind in the face of change.

A final and most important explanation of the science-fictional elements in American literature is the realization that the discovery and colonization of America are imaginatively equivalent to the conquest of space and the future colonization of, say, the moon or Mars. Since the colonization of other worlds belongs to the realm of science fiction, one might indeed expect to discover that certain aspects of American literature have something in common with science fiction. The essential element that they have in common, I see as the apocalyptic imagination.

---

writer was no longer compelled, for reasons of verisimilitude, to always begin his story in the present and then describe, usually in some detail, how his adventurers come to arrive at some far epoch in time or some distant planet. Edgar Allan Poe's *Mellonta Tauta* (1849), on the other hand, to take the earliest example I can think of and a very isolated one it is too, opens directly in the alien environment. As the result of a similar process, plus our present technological reality, science-fiction writers may take the scientific and technological aspects of their speculation more and more for granted. Thus it is that the gap between science fiction and mainstream literature is beginning to close. Part of the reality that "naturalistic" fiction now details must be scientific.

2. A Prophecy of America, the Moon, and Mars

I

The discovery of America did in fact what the best science-fiction stories attempt to do in imagination; the American perspective provided a radical reorientation of man's perceptions and his understanding, and it placed man in a new context, with the result that a previously accepted, stable reality was cast abruptly into question. Science fiction is particularly valuable for its ability to disorientate, making the form particularly at home in today's era of multimedia. The American experience has provided science fiction with its major analogical model. Why else, for example, does one frequently come across the image of space travelers as "pilgrims," if not, in part, because of the potent example of the Pilgrim Fathers?[1] The only historical equivalent to the discovery of America is the event, in July 1969, of man's setting foot on the moon. As William Blake recognized, the emergence of America brought about an apocalypse of mind, the discovery of a new world of mind—similar to the philosophical apocalypse that Norman Mailer sees as following in the wake of Apollo 11. In order to illustrate the apocalyptic potential of both events, it may be worthwhile briefly to set Blake's *America, a Prophecy* against Mailer's *Of a Fire on the Moon.*

America, a Prophecy is Blake's characteristically veiled analysis of the American Revolution in terms of the bibli-

[1] It appears to me that science fiction is best understood in relationship to various such analogies. The pastoral tradition, metaphysical poetry, Darwin and Darwinistic theory, Brecht's theory of estrangement, surrealism, and phenomenology also work well as analogical models for science fiction.

cal Apocalypse. The apocalypse, for Blake, will come
about as a result of the correction of man's erratic and
imprisoned perceptions. Blake understands that truth is
relative, that what a person sees depends upon his particular sense ratio. When sense ratios change, for whatever
reason, the world of sense changes too: an old perception
of the world dies and a new perception of the world is
born. Similarly if a man should move "his dwelling-place,
his heavens also move" (p. 126).[2] Blake sees the discovery
and realization of American independence as effecting the
ultimate change, the final correcting or cleansing of the
gates of perception. Thus Blake gives poetic backing to the
belief, still advanced by the Mormons, that America will
bring about the new world of the Apocalypse. Certainly
Columbus saw his role in this light: "God made me the
messenger of the new heaven and the new earth, of which
He spoke in the Apocalypse by St. John . . . and He
showed me the spot where to find it."[3] American place
names bear witness to the same faith. It was hoped that
such locations as New York, New England, and New
Hampshire might be new in the ideal sense of the *New*
Jerusalem. Salem is a contraction of Jerusalem, and an
actual New Jerusalem exists in Ohio. In *America, a Prophecy*, which incidentally illustrates the combination of satire
and vision that I have noted as one of the qualities of the
apocalyptic, the American Revolution is seen as an indication of the coming fall of Babylon, or England. The King
of England, George III, who represents the spirit of
English tyranny, the limitations of reason, or Blake's Urizen, is presented as "A dragon form clashing his scales at
midnight" (p. 51), the Nero of the Apocalypse.

The various plagues and disasters directed at America

[2] All parenthetical references to Blake's work may be located
in *The Poetry and Prose of William Blake*, ed. by David V.
Erdman (New York, 1965).
[3] Cited in Charles Sanford, *The Quest for Paradise: Europe
and the American Moral Imagination* (Urbana, Ill., 1961),
p. 40.

but that recoil upon England as a kind of judgment are recognizable from the Book of Revelation. In accordance with Blake's system, final revelation comes about as a result of the improvement of sensual enjoyment or the freeing of "red Orc," the spirit of organic life. Eventually the advancing flames of desire consume the five fallen senses so as to restore men to their unfallen potential represented by the lost city of Atlantis. Mentioned earlier in the poem, Atlantis, a New Jerusalem, subsequently rises from the sea as also in Hart Crane's *The Bridge*. As Blake adapted the legend, "In the Golden Age before the Fall, humanity or Albion dwelt at peace in its Paradise or Atlantis. The Fall produced a chaotic world and the central symbol of chaos is water. . . . The Altantic Ocean, then, symbolizes the fallen world . . . the 'Sea of Time and Space.' The rise of a new civilization of English origin in America indicates the reintegrating of Atlantis, the disappearance of the Atlantic Ocean, and the return of the Golden Age."[4]

The command module of Apollo 11 was named Columbia in order to draw attention to a parallel between the landing on the moon and Christopher Columbus setting foot on the shores of America. In *Of a Fire on the Moon*, Norman Mailer speculates that the exploration of space will, like the discovery of America, cause a philosophical apocalypse.[5] "Are you ever worried, Dr. Gilruth," Mailer

---

[4] Northrop Frye, *Fearful Symmetry: A Study of William Blake* (Princeton, N.J., 1947), p. 206. For their over-all interpretations of Blake, see also Harold Bloom, *Blake's Apocalypse* (New York, 1963), and Thomas J. J. Altizer, *The New Apocalypse: The Radical Christian Vision of William Blake* (East Lansing, Mich., 1967). The false world of perception associated with the white, leprous figure of Urizen, which Orc is responsible for destroying, may, according to Altizer (pp. 160–63), provide an illuminating gloss on the nature of the White Whale which Ahab pursues so desperately. In this connection note the reference in *America, a Prophecy* to the "Whale in the Southsea, drinking my soul away" (p. 51).

[5] *Of a Fire on the Moon* (Boston and Toronto, 1970). Parenthetical references within the text are to this edition.

asks the uncomprehending director of the Manned Space-craft Center, "that landing on the moon may result in all sorts of psychic disturbances for us here on earth?" (pp. 16–17). Such are the possibilities that Aquarius, as Mailer styles himself, entertains: "This emergence of a ship to travel the ether, thrust across a vacuum, was no event he could measure by any philosophy he had been able to put together in his brain" (p. 55). Since the world that the possibility of space travel opens up is quite new to Aquarius, ". . . the interior of the VAB [vehicle assembly building at Cape Kennedy] was the antechamber of a new Creation" (p. 55). Unlike the exhausted western frontier, but still in the American tradition, a new "frontier was open and would never close" (p. 59). So, in a speech that Aquarius describes as "quietly apocalyptic" (p. 77), Wernher von Braun states, ". . . we are expanding the mind of man" (p. 76). The manned moon landing "will cause a new element to sweep across the face of this good earth and to invade the thoughts of all men" (p. 77). Aquarius affirms that "a species of apocalypse was upon us" (p. 456).[6] But, and this is the burden of the entire book, what will be the nature of the new element, benign or malevolent? Apocalypses are destructive before they can be creative.

In effecting a philosophical apocalypse, it is to be expected, the conquest of heavenly bodies will alter human psychology. Consequently Aquarius (the new Mailer) ponders the possibility that "the Psychology of Astronauts" may provide some advance indication of the way we are headed, "for they were either the end of the old or the

[6] At this point in time it is virtually impossible for us to observe consequences that are sufficiently radical to merit the description apocalyptic. However, the British astronomer Fred Hoyle had drawn attention to the likelihood that the beginning of our current interest in ecology seems to be coincident with man's landing on the moon and hence the result of a new objectivity. Note also Bellow's recent title *Mr. Sammler's Planet* (New York, 1970) and the lunar-obsessed perspective of Sammler.

first of the new men, and one would have nothing to
measure them by until the lines of the new psychology
had begun to be drawn" (p. 49). We have heard mention
of "new men" before. As an answer to the question, "What
is an American," J. Hector St. John (Crèvecoeur) writes:
"The American is a new man, who acts upon new principles; he must therefore entertain new ideas, and form
new opinions."[7] There would appear to be some analogy
between Armstrong's boyhood dream, in which "he was
able to hover over the ground if he held his breath"
(p. 45), and the American dream. In deep accord with
"the most soul destroying and apocalyptic of centuries"
(p. 47), Aquarius finds that "the astronauts had person-
alities of unequaled banality and apocalyptic dignity"
(p. 47), a reflection of the staggering glory and yet
strange blandness of their accomplishment.

In an enterprise of man and machine, the human and
the mechanical are not easily distinguished. Consequently
Aquarius speculates at length about "the Psychology of
Machines." On the assumption that the conquest of space
will transform all aspects of human ecology, Aquarius
snatches at every possibility. The book ends with Aquarius
pondering a moon rock. Perhaps Le Monde Invisible, a
picture by René Magritte of a rock in a living room,
provides a clue: "It was as if Magritte has listened to the
ending of one world with its comfortable chairs in the
parlor, and heard the intrusion of a new world, silent as
the windowless stone which grew in the room, and knowing not quite what he had painted, had painted his
warning nonetheless. Now the world of the future was a
dead rock, and the rock was in the room" (p. 134). For
the black professor in the room where Aquarius at that
moment stands, the future may be just that bleak. Does
this WASP accomplishment, a feat of cold numerological
efficiency, at the expense of the black man's sense of soul,
imply a diseased imbalance, the encroachment of a cancer
cell in the body of the universe?

[7] Letters from an American Farmer (London, 1782). See the
Signet edition (New York, 1963), p. 64.

Then again, if the event is comparable with the birth of Christ, as some people believe, perhaps the biblical Apocalypse, with its description of the Second Coming of Christ, may be a veiled account of what is happening now. Under the influence of this conception and perhaps also *2001: A Space Odyssey*, Aquarius, at his most extravagant, hypothesizes, "If God finally was the embodiment of a vision which might cease to exist in the hostilities of the larger universe . . . then it was legitimate to see all of human history as a cradle which had nurtured a baby which had now taken its first step. . . . If it were so, then the flight of Apollo 11 was a first revelation of the real intent of History" (pp. 150–51). But this line of reasoning takes a final twist to the recognition "that eschatology had conceivably been turned on its head" (p. 151). If Earthmen are to function as the aggressive vehicles and embattled defenders of God's vision, then courage, expeditious judgment, and speed are the Christian virtues, and "Hell's Angels were possibly nearer to God than the war against poverty" (p. 151). The face of the future at every turn resembles that of Janus.

II

In order to cement this comparison between the apocalyptic potential of the eventual colonization of new worlds in space and the colonization of the New World on Earth, I can do no better than glance at a science-fiction novel that, on one level, talks about the colonization of Mars in terms of the colonization of America. I am referring to Ray Bradbury's *The Martian Chronicles*. The Martians with their "fair, brownish skin" (p. 642),[8] like the American Indians, are ousted from their cities and become virtually extinct. The identification is made quite apparent when one of the Earthmen says: "I've got some Cherokee blood

8 All parenthetical references to *The Martian Chronicles* may be located in the Bantam paperback edition (1954).

in me. My grandfather told me lots of things about Oklahoma Territory. If there's a Martian around, I'm all for him" (p. 59). Most of the Martians have died of an Earthman's disease: chicken pox (H. G. Wells' Martians, it will be recalled, in *The War of the Worlds,* also fall foul of our bacteria). Those who remain exist in a state of degradation comparable to that of the American Indian. One of their sympathizers asks: "How would you feel if a Martian vomited stale liquor on the White House floor?" (p. 64).

Ironically, the Earthmen are likened to the Pilgrim Fathers. It is noted, "After all, like the Pilgrims these people came here to escape Earth" (p. 39). "They came because they were afraid or unafraid, because they were happy or unhappy, because they felt like Pilgrims or did not feel like Pilgrims" (p. 72). A comparison with the early American settler is also implicit in this passage:

Mars was a distant shore, and the men spread upon it in waves. Each wave different, and each wave stronger. The first wave carried with it men accustomed to spaces and coldness and being alone, the coyote and cattlemen, with no fat on them, with faces the years had worn the flesh off, with eyes like nailheads, and hands like the material of old gloves ready to touch anything. Mars could do nothing to them, for they were bred to plains and prairies as open as the Martian fields. . . . And among the second men, were men who looked, by their eyes, as if they were on their way to God . . . (p. 87).

One of them plants trees on Mars and in so doing recalls "Johnny Appleseed walking across America planting apple trees" (p. 74). Other colonists erect settlements that are carbon copies of American towns, down to the local hot-dog stand. In one case, "It was as if, in many ways, a great earthquake had shaken loose the roots and cellars of an Iowa town, and then, in an instant, a whirlwind twister of Oz-like proportions had carried the entire town off to Mars to set it down without a bump . . ." (p. 88).

It is also quite apparent that Bradbury sees his semi-allegorical colonization of Mars in terms of a philosophical apocalypse. Earth is referred to as a "frame of reference" (p. 65), a hypothetical system of "logic, common sense, good government, peace and responsibility" (p. 173). The new, Martian perspective provides a new context. As one convert puts it: "I've got what amounts to a religion, now. It's learning how to breathe all over again. And how to lie in the sun getting a tan, letting the sun work into you. And how to hear music and how to read a book" (p. 68). The way in which the mind constructs its own reality is made literally evident on Mars; the Martians are able to metamorphosize themselves and the environment to fulfill the Earthmen's subconscious wishes by means of some sort of telepathic hallucination. The extreme degree to which reality is a state of mind is further dramatically demonstrated in one poignant episode strikingly similar in idea to Philip Wylie's *The Disappearance* (1951). An Earthman and a Martian meet, but, because of their differing mental contexts, discern one another only as shadowy ectoplasms:

"I can see through you," said Thomas.
"And I through you!" said the Martian, stepping back (p. 82).

They exist in different mental dimensions, like the men and women in Wylie's book.

Nor are the more literal trappings of the Apocalypse lacking. Man's spaceships descend on Mars like an apocalyptic plague of locusts:

The rockets set the bony meadows afire, turned rock to lava, turned wood to charcoal, transmitted water to steam, made sand and silica into green glass which lay like shattered mirrors reflecting the invasion, all about. The rockets came like drums, beating in the night. The rockets came like locusts, swarming and settling in blooms of rosy smoke (p. 78).

Just as the locusts in the Apocalypse are summoned at the blast of the fifth trumpet, so the departure of man's

locust rockets (those carrying the Negroes, anyway) is
"as if a whole city had walked here with hands full, at
which time a great bronze trumpet had sounded, the
articles had been relinquished to the quiet dust, and one
and all the inhabitants of the earth had fled straight up
into the blue heavens" (p. 101).

Earth is literally destroyed: "It caught fire" (p. 143).
In the final story, an Earthman says: "I'm burning a way
of life, just like that way of life is being burned clean of
Earth right now" (p. 179). "The fire leaped up to emphasize his telling. And then all the papers were gone except
one [a map of Earth, which is soon to follow]. All
the laws and beliefs of Earth were burnt into small hot
ashes which soon would be carried off in a wind"
(p. 180). I have stated "The Fall of the House of
Usher" provides a pictorial paradigm of the apocalyptic
imagination, and appropriately it is recalled by Bradbury
in the chapter entitled "Usher II," which follows the chapter entitled "The Naming of Names," suggestive of a new
creation.

The new world the apocalypse is to usher in occurs,
rightly enough, at the turn of the present century. Bradbury even has a Simeon-like figure awaiting the Second
Coming in the shape of Hathaway, who waits twenty
years for a spaceship from Earth. The Earthmen who
experience this return to paradise are, in actuality, the
new Martians. They include the familiar new Adam and
new Eve motif. In disentangling this biblical structure in
Bradbury's book, in many ways I have dislocated or reversed the chronology of the fable. The evocation of a
new world precedes the destruction of the old world—
correctly, because the notion of apocalypse behind *The
Martian Chronicles* is predominantly a philosophical one,
and the philosophical apocalypse differs from the biblical
variety in reversing the apparently natural order.[9]

[9] Other works of science fiction that use the American experi-
ence as a direct analogical model might include *When Worlds
Collide* (New York, 1932, 1933), by Philip Wylie and Edwin
Balmer (see my discussion of this novel in Chapter 6); *The*

III

It is my contention that the kind of philosophical apocalypse I have defined as an integral aspect of the American experience, while manifesting itself overtly in the displacements of science fiction, also, logically enough, is evident in a good deal of "mainstream" American literature. The writers, predominantly Puritan, of the early-colonial period—William Bradford, Jonathan Edwards, John Winthrop, Increase and Cotton Mather—provide ample evidence for an apocalyptic formulation of the New World concept.[10] An important if negative aspect of this formulation is the jeremiad tradition, described in detail by Sacvan Bercovitch.[11] Of the major American writers who might be thought of as mainline apocalyptics at some point and in some sense, Charles Brockden Brown, Herman Melville, Mark Twain, Nathanael West, and William Faulkner incline toward the negative consequences of world transformation, while a lesser number, including Edgar Allan Poe, Walt Whitman, and Hart Crane, attempt to keep the positive possibilities of their "new worlds" in mind. A list of American writers who, to a greater or lesser degree, can be brought under the apoca-

---

Judgment of Eve (New York, 1966), by Edgar Pangborn; and *Cities in Flight* (New York, 1970), by James Blish. Blish's tetralogy makes the new American spatial environment literally evident. We see major American cities against the background of outer space.

[10] For detailed analyses of the apocalyptic character of early American literature see Perry Miller, *Errand into the Wilderness* (Cambridge, Mass., 1956); Sanford, *The Quest for Paradise;* and the unpublished doctoral dissertation by Alethea Joy Bourne Gilsdorf, "The Puritan Apocalypse" (Yale University, 1965).

[11] See Sacvan Bercovitch, "Horologicals to Chronometricals: The Rhetoric of the Jeremiad," in Vol. III of the four-volume series *Literary Monographs* (Madison, Wis., 1967–71), pp. 1–124.

lyptic umbrella might include Washington Irving, Henry David Thoreau, Ralph Waldo Emerson, Emily Dickinson, James Fenimore Cooper, Nathaniel Hawthorne, Ambrose Bierce, Lafcadio Hearn, Jack London, and James Branch Cabell, and more recently, Henry Miller, Ralph Ellison, John Barth, Thomas Pynchon, Joseph Heller, and Hubert Selby.[12]

In writing about apocalyptic transformations, these writers are concerning themselves with the distinguishing feature of science fiction, and frequently their books contain science-fictional elements. Charles Brockden Brown's *Wieland; or, The Transformation,* for example, involves a philosophical apocalypse analogous to the American experience but which can be read as predicated upon the future development of the mind of man, one of the major themes of science fiction. This particular case will be argued in detail in Chapter 7. Not out of place, therefore, in this listing of mainstream, American, apocalyptic writers are those few writers of superior science fiction, Ray Bradbury, Kurt Vonnegut, Jr., and William Burroughs (particularly his *Nova Express*).

In its broadest sense, the apocalyptic imagination is an aspect of the writer's craft. Obviously, to a degree, the creating artist is performing an apocalyptic function. Thus Thoreau's *Walden* ultimately suggests, in the "artist of Kouroo" passage, that a work of art is apocalyptic because a kind of transcendence of temporal reality figures in the artistic process.[13] And what do we mean when we

12 See John R. May, *Towards a New Earth: Apocalypse in the American Novel* (Notre Dame, Ind., 1972). For a treatment of three American writers within the apocalyptic tradition, see the unpublished doctoral dissertation by Lakshmi Mani, "The Apocalypse in Cooper, Hawthorne, and Melville" (McGill University, 1972).

13 In the wake of Kermode's apocalyptic view of literature, theoretical criticism appears to be moving away from a spatialized approach to literature and toward an appreciation of the various temporal factors involved. The American writer's bifocal and therefore "apocalyptic" awareness of an immediate and an eternal present is the subject of John F. Lynen's *The*

say of a book that it may "set the world on fire" if not that it may cause a philosophical apocalypse? Immanuel Velikovsky's *Worlds in Collision* is hailed as a "literary earthquake"; its "world-shaking conclusions" "will have an explosive effect." In a general sense, too, there is a relationship between the over-all movement of tragedy (to the extent that it parallels the course of revolution) and the apocalyptic imagination. And then there are works like *Moby-Dick,* whose fictional "worlds" underwent radical alteration during composition, presumably as a result of some apocalyptic breakthrough on the part of the author. I would wish, however, to exclude such possible usages from my definition of a philosophical apocalypse, because the notion of a serious radical transformation of reality does not *consciously* and *continuously* inform the works concerned.

The criteria of continuance would exclude fictions that involve momentary epiphanies. An example might be the conclusion to *The Great Gatsby,* which, for that moment, places the action in a new and mythic context. *The Scarlet Letter* is a more complicated case. In a notebook entry for August 30, 1842, Hawthorne wrote, "We certainly need a new revelation—a new system—for there seems to be no life in the old one."[14] The ambiguous title of the final chapter, "The Revelation of the Scarlet Letter," implies that the letter is not only the object of disclosure but also the means of revelation. And what the "A" as apocalypse apparently reveals, sporadically and indirectly, is a sense of total relationship, a unity, but a unity that incorporates the chaotic instability of a wilderness experi-

---

Design of the Present: Essays on Time and Form in American Literature (New Haven, Conn., 1969). Lynen draws on Feidelson's analysis of the Puritan symbolizing process as an explanation.

14 *The American Notebooks,* ed. Randall Stewart (New Haven, Conn., 1932), p. 165. Several of Hawthorne's tales, such as "Earth's Holocaust" (1843) and "The New Adam and New Eve" (1842), a postcatastrophe tale, are overtly apocalyptic in character.

enced literally by Dimmesdale and metaphysically by the reader, who is asked to entertain the possibility that, in a bewildering heavenly context, love and hate amount, at bottom, to the same thing—that Chillingworth may be a better man than Dimmesdale. What I am essentially talking about is, of course, a form of a collective rather than individual epiphany, but an epiphany that is on such a total, lasting, and literal scale that the force of the revelation frequently invites that it be concretely rendered by means of apocalyptic imagery. Sometimes in such cases what might appear to be objective scenes of world destruction are more meaningfully viewed in metaphoric terms.

Allowing for the various tensions already enumerated, a valid critical usage of the term "apocalypse" would, then, depend upon an external distinction between it and a usage either so general and vague as to be inclusive of all literature, or so limited and momentary as to invite confusion with the term "epiphany." It would, however, incorporate internal distinctions, based on the nature of the apocalyptic world consciously and continually envisaged. I would separate transcendental or visionary new worlds, which exist outside time and space, from new worlds, often *satiric*, that exist inside time and space. This latter category consists primarily of "utopias," which exploit the premillennial theory of catastrophe (the good times will occur before everything goes up in smoke), and dystopias, which exploit the postmillennial theory of catastrophe (we all die first). Both these types of other worlds should be distinguished from the philosophical kind of writing, with which this book is particularly concerned, which reveals the *present* world in new or other terms—this form coinciding with my earlier, third science-fiction category. This last grouping may be further divided depending upon whether the startling rationale involved is based essentially upon our ignorance about the nature of man, as in the case of *Wieland* (parapsychology) and, to cite a "straight" science-fictional example, Theodore Sturgeon's *More Than Human;* upon our ignorance about the nature of material reality, as in the case of *The Mysterious Stranger* (reality is a dream) and the science-fictional, dimensional romance *Flatland* by E. A. Abbott; or upon our ignorance about the nature of an outside manipulator, as in the case of *The Confidence-Man* (God is Satan) and Vonnegut's "straight" science-fictional novel *The Sirens of Titan*. I would submit that all works that can be legitimately described as apocalyptic fit somewhere within this framework. Unless the word apocalypse is to lose its meaning entirely, I would urge that usage of the term as a critical counter be limited by this framework.

Part Two: Other Worlds

II. OTHER WORLDS OUT OF SPACE AND TIME

Few, presumably, would dispute the application of the label apocalyptic to those writers—and other artists—whose works tend toward the expression of a visionary reality, the sense of other worlds out of space and time. For example, within the British tradition, Milton, Blake, Shelley, Wordsworth, most of the romantics in fact, D. H. Lawrence, Joseph Conrad, and some of the more serious practitioners of gothic and supernatural fiction might be described, to a greater or lesser degree, as apocalyptic. The apocalyptic aspect of many of these writers has been the subject of various critical studies. In this context, a book entitled *The Apocalyptic Vision in "Paradise Lost,"* by Leland Ryken, is of particular interest.[1] Ryken is primarily concerned with the techniques Milton uses to convey the impression of an ideal apocalyptic reality. Ryken follows Frye's distinction between the demonic and the apocalyptic, between a system of imagistic archetypes associated with things hellish and a polarized system of archetypes with heavenly associations. Accordingly, Ryken deals with Heaven and Eden, but he does not treat Hell. However, the Apocalypse, in the conventional religious sense, will involve the revelation of the unseen worlds of both Heaven and Hell. By the apocalyptic, Frye would appear to intend the paradisal. Because of Frye's influence, this limited positive critical usage of apocalyptic has become standardized in a way that the more popular relationship between apocalypse and chaos or conflagration has not. It does of course happen that, with a few exceptions, visionary apocalyptics are much more interested in

[1] See *The Apocalyptic Vision in "Paradise Lost"* (Ithaca, N.Y., 1970).

aligning themselves with a heavenly reality than with a hellish one.

Of American writers, Edgar Allan Poe is the apocalyptic par excellence. The reality he seeks, described in the poem "Dream-Land" as "Out of SPACE—out of TIME," makes him at home in the present section of my argument, but, as I shall indicate in the following chapter, Poe's work can be viewed as an illustration of virtually all aspects of the apocalyptic imagination. Although Poe was perhaps more successful, more genuine even, in his ambitions, the entire American transcendentalist movement is a manifestation, biased toward the positive pole, of the visionary apocalyptic imagination. Aside from Poe, the major visionary apocalyptics in American literature are Thoreau, Emerson, Lafcadio Hearn, and Henry Miller, and among poets, Walt Whitman, Emily Dickinson, Hart Crane, and William Carlos Williams. I am omitting a good many American writers where it would be a matter of debate and lengthy analysis as to whether the expression of a spiritual reality should be regarded as epiphanic or apocalyptic. The same problem arises in connection with many works of science fiction.

There is a certain amount of resistance in some quarters to the admission of a mystical reality in works of science fiction. Darko Suvin, for example, would argue that the rational extrapolative and analogical technique of science fiction does not allow for the presentation of a mystical realm. Although Suvin will countenance "the treatment of religious beliefs or mythic material as historical material," he maintains that "all attempts to transplant the metaphysic orientation of mythology or religion into sf, in a crudely overt way such as in C. S. Lewis, van Vogt, or Zelazny, or in more covert ways in very many others, will result only in private pseudo-myths, in fragmentary fantasies or fairy tales." He goes on to give instances from Stapledon's *First and Last Men* (1930), and *A Canticle for Leibowitz* (1960), by Walter Miller, Jr., where "the ideological attraction to myth as world view and not as formal pattern got the best of the sf writer."[2] Suvin's distinction here would also require him to reject much of the work of Arthur C. Clarke, who is very much oriented in evolutionary terms toward the attainment of something equivalent to a metaphysical reality. It is because Suvin has done such useful work in separating science fiction from fantasy in the face of a seemingly growing number of people who prefer to speak only of the difference between realism and fantasy and who, when pressed, admit that all literature is fantasy, that I wish to correct his equating of mythic or religious world views and fantasy.

Indeed, in terms of Suvin's purist distinctions, no consistent work of science fiction could possibly exist. Any putative science-fiction book would turn out to be a mosaic of realistic, science-fictional, and fantasy elements. I would prefer to take the book in a contextual fashion, whereby the dominant element would inform the credibility level of the entire novel. However, in terms of the way in which I see science fiction, the possibility of a conflict between the element of religious mysticism and other extrapolative or analogical details does not amount to an inevitability. Certainly plausibility is the important characteristic of science fiction, but while this plausibility derives largely from an adherence to logical processes, it is not therefore inconsistent with other matters that are plausible because they are matters of religious belief. And surely the sublime majesty and immensity of the universe—the vision that science fiction continually invokes, of stars beyond number and distances without end—provides some kind of empirical basis for that awe traditionally associated with man's response to the idea of a God. Indeed the apparent infinity of the universe provides us with an analogy for eternity and some basis for confusing the heavens with Heaven. The truth, of course, is that the scientific outlook does not necessarily supplant the re-

---

[2] Quotations are taken from the manuscript version of Suvin's article "Science Fiction and the Genealogical Jungle," forthcoming in *Genre*, fall 1973.

ligious and that the concepts of science fiction and theology frequently coexist. In a three-part article entitled "The Mystic Renaissance: A Survey of F. Orlin Tremaine's 'Astounding Stories,'" Leland Sapiro provides ample evidence from the heyday of the pulps that the quest for mystical experience is a viable theme for science fiction.[3] Less directly, the Faust theme, which permeates the beginnings of modern science fiction with the warning that there are matters that man is not qualified to understand, implies the existence of a spiritual province where such matters rightfully belong.[4] More recently, the mystical concept of "grokking," in Heinlein's *Stranger in a Strange Land,* attests to the continuing cross-fertilization of mysticism and science fiction.

It is, then, hardly surprising that the pragmatic and scientific streak of many of the American transcendentalists should occasionally produce conceptions that are strikingly science-fictional, particularly in the case of Walt Whitman. For example, in *Song of Myself* Whitman relates his own gestation to the forces of universal creation:

Before I was born out of my mother generations guided me,

My embryo has never been torpid, nothing could overlay it.

For it the nebula cohered to an orb,

The long strata piled to rest it on,

[3] See *Riverside Quarterly,* II, 2 (June 1966), pp. 75–88; II, 3 (November 1966), pp. 156–70; II, 4 (March 1967), pp. 270–83.

[4] See again Leland Sapiro, "The Faustus Tradition in the Early Science Fiction Story," *Riverside Quarterly,* I, 1 (August 1964), pp. 3–18; I, 2 (November 1964), pp. 43–57; I, 3 (February 1965), pp. 118–25; and Robert M. Philmus, "Old Myths and New: Or Faustus Redivivus," in *Into the Unknown,* pp. 79–107. The complete lineage would highlight Prometheus, Daedalus, Faust, and Frankenstein.

Vast vegetables gave it sustenance,
Monstrous sauroids transplanted it in their mouths and
deposited it with care.[5]

This description transcends metaphor: we are to take
Whitman's statements in the widest context as factual.
Ray Bradbury knew what he was doing when he appropriated the title of one of Whitman's poems, "I Sing
the Body Electric," for his own 1970 collection of science-
fiction stories. And one particularly fine science-fiction
story, Isaac Asimov's "Nightfall" (1941), was directly inspired by an idea of Ralph Waldo Emerson. At the beginning of *Nature*, Emerson, after considering the stars as
evidence of sublimity, offers this startling idea: "If the
stars should appear one night in a thousand years, how
would men believe and adore; and preserve for many
generations the remembrance of the city of God which had
been shown."[6] Asimov quotes the entire passage as an
epigraph for a tale in which he constructs a planetary
system allowing for Emerson's eventuality.

To ease the transition here between the mystical tradition of science fiction and those closely related works of
science fiction that treat religious themes and problems, I
might mention a short story of A. C. Clarke entitled "The
Star" (1955). The celestial body in question is the star of
Bethlehem. Clarke accounts for its sudden visibility as a
result of the atomic incandescence that accompanies the
destruction of an otherwise invisible world. To separate
religious issues or beliefs from science fiction would severely impoverish the genre.[7] Whether the C. S. Lewis tril-

[5] See the *Reader's Edition of "Leaves of Grass,"* ed. by Harold
W. Blodgett and Sculley Bradley, in *The Collected Writings of
Walt Whitman*, fifteen vols. (New York, 1965), p. 81.
[6] See the twelve-volume Centenary Edition, *The Complete
Works of Ralph Waldo Emerson* (Boston and New York, 1903–
4, 1968), Vol. I, p. 7.
[7] For a treatment of the religious theme in science fiction, see
William Atheling, Jr., *Issues at Hand* (Chicago, 1964), pp.
49–70.

ogy should be taken as science fiction or fantasy depends upon whether the religious theme exists most credibly on a literal level, as in the case of *Paradise Lost*, an apocalyptic work, or on an allegorical level, as in the case of *The Faerie Queene*, a work of fantasy. A decision here and in the case of some of Bradbury's stories can ultimately be made only in the minds of individual readers. Certainly if the science-fictional plausibility of the trilogy is to be rejected because of its Christian religious ideology, the same must go for another excellent novel, *A Case of Conscience* (1959), by James Blish. In both cases, a world is quarantined for religious reasons. Lewis' "silent planet," Earth, is cut off from the rest of the solar system because, unlike Mars and Venus, it is a fallen world. Blish's world, Lithia, appears to be unfallen although its reptilian inhabitants know nothing of God. The protagonist, Father Ruiz-Sanchez, a Jesuit biologist, decides that the planet is a snare devised by Satan to prove that God need not exist, and hence he advocates the quarantine policy. Other works in which, to use Suvin's phrase, religious beliefs function "as historical material" would include Walter Miller, Jr.'s *A Canticle for Leibowitz*, in which a religious order preserves a fragment of a shopping list as revelatory of the world that existed before the nuclear holocaust, and Michael Moorcock's *Behold the Man* (1966), in which Christ turns out to be a time traveler.

The distinction in literature between a religious system as a world view and a religious system as simply subject matter can be a tricky one to make, and it is fortunate that it does not apply to the decision as to whether a particular work is science fiction or not. Science fiction is at home in all forms of the apocalyptic imagination, the transcendent visionary no less than the satirical or the philosophic. It is not surprising that, with the growing tendency to consider particular religious systems as similar in kind to mythology in seeking to map the same metaphysical reality, science fiction is now often assumed to be a species of mythology. As I shall attempt to indicate in the chapter devoted to Ursula K. LeGuin's *The Left Hand of*

Darkness, there is a dangerous irrelevance in pressing too close an identification between science fiction and specific mythological stories, but the all-at-oneness that the cyclical structure of myth attests to is obviously relevant to those works of science fiction which are oriented toward the mystic experience. My analysis in the following chapter of Poe's contribution to the visionary tradition of science fiction, and in Chapter 4 of LeGuin's use of cyclical myth to suggest unified awareness, is intended to anchor much of the foregoing theoretical material in specific but representative texts.

3. Edgar Allan Poe and the Visionary Tradition of Science Fiction

I

Even if the term had existed in Poe's time, it is doubtful that he would have thought of himself as a science-fiction writer. Actually he liked to think of himself as a poet. Yet, in 1926, when Hugo Gernsback articulated his sense of "scientifiction," he offered the work by Poe, Wells, and Verne as representative of the form: "By 'scientifiction' I mean the Jules Verne, H. G. Wells, and Edgar Allan Poe type of story—a charming romance intermingled with scientific fact and prophetic vision."[1] A circular logic would seem to dictate that an adequate description of Poe's fictive concerns must also be a description of science fiction. But this should be set against the fact that today Poe occupies a niche in the popular imagination not as a writer of science fiction but as a writer of horror stories, although that same imagination would fully credit the notion that Wells and Verne are writers of science fiction. Recent Poe scholarship, on the other hand, would seem to endorse an image of Poe as an American Blake, a composite of satirist and transcendental visionary. Gernsback's view is a minority critical opinion, but more recently Clarke Olney, Sam Moskowitz, and H. Bruce Franklin have sought to characterize all or aspects of Poe's writing as science fiction.[2]

[1] See the editorial to the first issue of *Amazing Stories* (April 1926).
[2] See Olney, "Edgar Allan Poe—Science Fiction Pioneer," *Georgia Review*, XII (winter 1958), pp. 416–21; Moskowitz, "The Prophetic Edgar Allan Poe," in *Explorers of the Infinite* (Cleveland and New York, 1963), pp. 46–61; and H. Bruce Franklin, "Edgar Allan Poe and Science Fiction," in *Future Perfect*, pp. 93–103.

Both Olney and Moskowitz credit Poe with contributing to the "nuts and bolts" kind of science fiction, in which the story line is often an excuse for presenting incredibly detailed descriptions of a futurist technology and hardware. They point to the length of explanatory material devoted to mechanical and physical principles in "A Descent into the Maelstrom," "The Balloon Hoax," and "Hans Pfaall." This "hard" science fiction is exemplified in the work of Jules Verne, who, as it happens, was very much influenced by Poe or rather by his carefully edited appreciation of Poe.[8] The whirlpool episode in *Twenty Thousand Leagues Under the Sea* (1870) derives from "A Descent into the Maelstrom"; "The Balloon Hoax" inspired both *Five Weeks in a Balloon* (1863) and *Voyage Around the World in Eighty Days* (1872), while the business of losing time in the latter work owes something to Poe's "Three Sundays in a Week." *From the Earth to the Moon* (1867) draws heavily on "The Unparalleled Adventures of One Hans Pfaall," and the hypnotism business in *Mathias Sandorf* (1885) appears to be taken from "The Facts in the Case of M. Valdemar." In addition, Verne provided Poe's supposedly incomplete *Narrative of A. Gordon Pym* with a materialistically extrapolated sequel entitled *The Sphinx of the Ice Fields* (1897). It was left to H. P. Lovecraft to write the rather more visionary-oriented sequel entitled *At the Mountains of Madness* (1931), which is somewhat more in sympathy with the tenor of Poe's novel. This distinction points to the way in which Verne single-mindedly separated the material speculation in Poe's work from the metaphysical. Consequently, because of the direct line between Poe and Verne, Poe's contribution to science fiction has been viewed in the distorted light provided by Verne's selective use of his themes. Olney's

[8] For Poe's influence on Verne, see Moskowitz, pp. 56, 75–76; *Jules Verne and His Work* (New York, 1966), by I. O. Evans, who treats *The Narrative of A. Gordon Pym* and "The Balloon Hoax" as science-fiction tales to which Verne was indebted, pp. 115–17, 155, *et passim;* and Monique Sprout, "The Influence of Poe on Jules Verne," *Revue de Littérature Comparée,* XLI (1967).

statement that Poe "was the first writer of science-centered fiction to base his stories firmly on a rational kind of extrapolation, avoiding the supernatural," echoed by Moskowitz's assertion that Poe established the precept whereby "every departure from norm must be explained *scientifically*," ignores the crucial fact that invariably the passages of pseudo science in Poe, aside from being for the most part cribbed, exist either in the interests of a direct hoax or else allow for the possibility that, on one level, the tale in question be conceived as a hoax.[4]

To see Poe's use of pseudo science within the context of a hoax and to see the hoax within the context of a philosophical framework based on the assumption that reality is a hoax, is severely to undercut any conception of Poe as a science-fiction writer in the Vernian mold. There is a fundamental difference between the effect of a Poe tale read on its own terms and the same tale considered as an aspect of the philosophical system provided by the entire corpus. Within this system, I believe that no single work of Poe's qualifies as what is generally understood as "straight" science fiction. The claims of those tales that come closest are vitiated either because they were conceived as hoaxes or dream experiences or because a science-fictional displacement device is actually a secondary means of endorsing what is basically a metaphysical statement. What remains are science-fictional *elements* only. But although the larger philosophical context detracts from the science-fictional emphasis of the most obvious claimants among Poe's work, there is a sense in which the larger context suggests the existence of a science-fictional quality coloring tales that, in isolation, would never be thought of as science fiction. It would seem that, while no single work of Poe's can be totally described as science fiction, virtually all of his creative work can be seen as marginally science fiction in one or more of four possible senses.

[4] Olney, p. 417; Moskowitz, p. 60.

II

The first of these senses may be deduced from the philosophical position that unites and makes intelligible all of Poe's work. It is Poe's basic assumption that man lives in an inevitable state of deception as a result of the subjective, idiopathic nature of his awareness, which is limited externally by his circumscribed place in space and time, and internally by his personal experience, eccentricities, and in particular his erratic, dissecting, and gullible reason. Time, space, and self are treated directly in many of the grotesque tales as providing the co-ordinates of man's deception. "The Devil in the Belfry" is perhaps the clearest example. This tale is concerned with the insular inhabitants of a Dutch village. The arrival of a representative from the larger universe, a French devil, throws the neatly enclosed system of village life awry. The devil causes utter consternation when he arranges that the Town Council clock strike thirteen, thus suggesting the existence of a state beyond the villagers' spatio-temporal continuum. Man fails in perceiving his segment of reality accurately, first because he cannot see it in relation to the whole, and second because he cannot help but see it in relation to himself. As a consequence, so-called "reality," like a grotesque gargoyle, is a fabrication composed of heterogeneous fragments, and the grotesque tales reveal in a variety of ways the illusory and deceptive nature of the material world.

There appear to be four basic types of grotesque tale: tales like "The Devil in the Belfry," which directly confront the deceptive nature of reality; a second group more particularly concerned with the deceptive, perverse nature of the self, doppelgänger tales such as "William Wilson" and "The Tell Tale Heart"; a third group, which treats deceptive practices on the part of others, as in "The Business Man" and "Diddling"; and a fourth group, Poe's hoaxes, such as "The Balloon Hoax" and "Hans Pfaall,"

which might be considered personal acts of deception designed to prove the existence of human gullibility in the
face of a reality that, by allegorical extension, is also a
hoax. Because all the grotesque tales are directed toward
the demonstration that reality is a lie, a tale describing an
act of chicanery should be seen in an analogical relationship to the illusory reality that man inhabits. It seems
likely that Poe's biographical circumstances encouraged
this fourfold vision of deception, since most of the known
facts of Poe's career, including the early disappearance of
his parents, the various pseudonyms he adopted, the
partly fictitious "Autobiography" he concocted, his paranoid search for plagiarism, his schizophrenic tendencies,
his death in the gutter (perhaps following rough usage
as a dummy voter), and the posthumous damaging forgeries of Rufus Wilmot Griswold, Poe's literary executor
by some perverse decision, might be arranged under the
same four categories into which the grotesques fall.

A clue to Poe's methodology for overcoming man's unhappy situation is lodged in this passage from an 1836
review of *The American in England*, by Lieutenant Sli-
dell:

> As the touches of a painting which to minute inspec-
> tion, are "confusion worse confounded," will not fail to
> start boldly out to the cursory glance of a connoisseur—
> or as a star may be seen more distinctly in a sidelong
> survey than in any direct gaze however penetrating and
> intense—so there are, not infrequently, times and meth-
> ods, in which, and by means of which a richer philoso-
> phy may be gathered on the surface of things than can
> be drawn up, even with great labor, *e profundis* (VIII,
> 215).[5]

The "cursory glance" and the "sidelong survey" are elsewhere referred to as the "half-closed eye." In elaborating
his definition of art, in the "Marginalia," as "the reproduc-

[5] All parenthetical references in this section are to *The Complete Works of Edgar Allan Poe*, seventeen vols., ed. by James
A. Harrison (New York, 1902).

tion of what the senses perceive in Nature through the veil of the soul," Poe continues, "We can, at any time, double the true beauty of an actual landscape by half closing our eyes as we look at it. The naked senses sometimes see too little—but then *always* they see too much" (XVI, 164). The effect of looking at the world through half-closed eyes is, of course, to blur the outlines, allowing everything to fuse into everything else—in fact to destroy the external universe as usually perceived, and such is Poe's means of eradicating the barriers erected by time, space, and self. With the destruction of the reasoned world, the true world of the imagination—and the half-closed eye, at least initially, is simply a metaphor for the imagination—can take over. The fused, fluid world that results denies all conventional sensory divisions, most significantly that between life and death, and thus allows for the reanimation of Ligeia, Morella, and anybody else in Poe's universe. Poe's fondness for synesthesia, paradox, oxymoron, indefiniteness, particularly as exemplified by music, and median states, are all obvious corollaries of the technical strategy of fusion whereby Poe communicates the vision of the half-closed eye. The same applies to his critical principles regarding length, the didactic heresy, plot construction, and unity of effect.

I offer the above account of Poe's philosophical rationale as further substantiation for the growing awareness in recent Poe scholarship that the horrific Mr. Poe is but a negative image of a writer who is more accurately understood as a visionary, a species of transcendentalist, an American Blake. Indeed, there are so many detailed similarities between the two writers that it is tempting to hypothesize that since Poe published his first volume in 1827, the year in which Blake died, we have a case of metempsychosis, or, to adapt a line from *Milton*, a case of Blake in Poe's left foot! But Poe should be distinguished from virtually all visionary writers including the transcendentalists and Blake because of the markedly "scientific" or science-fictional nature of his visionary reality.

Poe's preferred reality is not a spiritual realm but an alternative material dimension. In a letter to Lowell, dated

New York, July 2, 1844, Poe denies the existence of spirituality except as "unparticled matter, permeating and impelling all things." In his "rudimental" state, "Man, and other thinking beings [here we are directly in the realm of science fiction], are individualizations of the unparticled matter."

> What we call death is the painful metamorphosis. The stars are the habitations of rudimental beings. But for the necessity of the rudimental life, there would have been no worlds. At death, the worm is the butterfly—still material, but of a matter unrecognized by our organs—recognized, occasionally, perhaps, by the sleepwalker, directly—without organs—through the mesmeric medium. Thus a sleepwalker may see ghosts. Divested of the rudimental covering, the beings inhabit space. . . .[6]

And sure enough, in "Mesmeric Revelation," published the following month, a mesmerized subject, at the point of death, confirms the theoretical statements in Poe's letter. He explains that there is no such thing as spirit, only "infinitely rarefied matter" (V, 247), or, in the case of God, "unparticled matter" (V, 246), and goes on to repeat, almost verbatim, the analogy in Poe's letter. It should be apparent that, by positing the existence of "unparticled matter," Poe is seeking to dissolve the boundary that "rudimental" man assumes to exist between life and death. That "individualized" (V, 249) man sees only a void where matter actually exists, is simply a function of perceptual limitation. To emphasize this point, the mesmerized subject introduces a science-fictional analogy that appropriately defines the generic tenor of the entire account: "There are many things on the Earth, which would be nihility to the inhabitants of Venus—many things visible and tangible in Venus, which we could not be brought to appreciate as existing at all" (V, 253). The rationale in

[6] John Ward Ostrom, ed., *The Letters of Edgar Allan Poe*, two vols. (New York, 1948), vol. I, p. 256.

"Mesmeric Revelation" can be assumed as underlying all of Poe's creative work, and since this rationale is science-fictional, all of Poe's work can be regarded as marginally science-fictional. In providing a visionary reality out of space and time with a science-fictional rationale, Poe inaugurated that visionary tradition of science fiction that owes nothing to Jules Verne but that includes many of the masterpieces of the genre.

III

There is a second science-fictional aspect to Poe's underlying philosophical rationale, which makes possible the transition from our clogged and particled material state to an awareness of unparticled matter. It depends upon an understanding of Poe's use of the term "arabesque," which appears undefined in Poe's letters as early as May 1833 and in the title *Tales of the Grotesque and Arabesque* (1840). Although Poe's love of music makes the musical connotations of the term relevant, the repeated references to arabesque curtaining, coverings, and tapestries in Poe's tales makes this sense of the word pre-eminently important. An arabesque tapestry is so called because of its complexly interwoven, convoluted, and fluid design. The word arabesque, and the arabesque tapestries and fixtures that adorn the chambers in the tales, are symbolic of reality as viewed through the blurring, half-closed eye. Poe's preferred reality, frequently symbolized by the omni-color white, might, then, appropriately be designated "arabesque reality," and I would distinguish as arabesques those Poe tales directed toward such a state. Arabesque designs and décor are of paramount agential importance in Poe's efforts to melt away the rigid patterns imposed by man's limited perceptions. If, as Poe believed, the vague suggestiveness of music provides man's most immediate avenue to ideality, then an arabesque room or environment might be regarded as a more concrete or

permanent method of harnessing the transforming potential of an arabesque musical composition.

Perhaps the clearest representative example is the description of the stranger's room in "The Visionary—A Tale,"
published in January 1834:

> Rich draperies in every part of the room trembled to
> the vibration of low, melancholy music, whose unseen
> origin, undoubtedly lay in the recesses of the crimson
> trellis-work which tapestried the ceiling. The senses
> were oppressed by mingled and conflicting perfumes,
> reeking up from strange arabesque censers which
> seemed actually embued with a monstrous vitality, as
> their parti-colored flames writhed up and down, and
> around their extravagant proportions. The rays of the
> newly risen sun poured in upon the whole, through
> windows formed each of a single pane of crimson-
> tinted glass. Glancing to and fro, in a thousand reflec-
> tions, from curtains which rolled from their cornices
> like cataracts of molten silver, the beams of natural
> glory mingled at length fitfully with the artificial light
> and lay before me. A sense of dreamy and incoherent
> grandeur took possession of my soul, and I remained
> within the doorway speechless (II, 116 and 346).

In the revised and shortened version of this passage,
printed in 1840, under the new title "The Assignation,"
the adjective "convolute" is substituted for "arabesque,"
presumably as a synonym. In either case, all the characteristics of reality as apparent to the half-closed eye
are present in this passage. The static, distinct world becomes fluid and indistinct—even animate. Drapery moves,
perfumes mingle, as does the natural light with the artificial. The arabesque censers seem to be alive. The effect
is dizzying and kaleidoscopic. This is Poe's continuum
arabesque reality, the new dimension, if we would only
see it. In such a state the distinctions between fire and
water, light and dark, sight and sound disappear. The line

between life and death is similarly artificial, and thus the alchemy is complete.

The stranger, a one-time "decorist," explains the process to the amazed narrator as follows: "You behold around you, it is true, a medley of architectural embellishments. The chastity of Ionia is offended by antediluvian devices, and the sphynxes of Egypt are outstretched upon carpets of gold. Yet the effect is incongruous to the timid alone. *Proprieties of place, and especially of time, are the bugbears which terrify mankind from the contemplation of the magnificent*" (II, 123; my italics). In other words, by fusing what is conventionally kept apart, the stranger conquers death. He has made a suicide pact with the Marchesa, who is married to someone else, and, on hearing that she has fulfilled her part of the bargain, he drinks poison. The transition from conventional to arabesque reality is made specifically through the agency of the arabesque censers, with which he is in sympathy: "Like these Arabesque censers my spirit is writhing in fire, and the delirium of this scene is fashioning me for the wilder visions of the land of real dreams whither I am now rapidly departing" (II, 124).

The description of the chamber in "Ligeia" is particularly close to that of the stranger and plays a similarly "active" role. To enter such a room is to be utterly disoriented, to lose all sense of equilibrium. Perhaps our nearest equivalent is the experience of a psychedelic discothèque in full swing, where the effect of the revolving strobe lights and the alternating on/off illumination is to make the individual dancer hard to distinguish. As in "The Assignation," the room in "Ligeia" causes the dimensions of time and space to give way to a new dimension, which will allow Ligeia's return from the dead. The same applies to the arabesque design of "The Fall of the House of Usher." Wherever Poe seeks to fuse contraries or make fixed outlines fluctuate, he is invoking the arabesque state. In the landscape pieces, nature is artfully sculptured to allow for the same arabesque effects as Poe's interiors.

The dizzying sensation on entering an arabesque room may also be achieved by jumping off a cliff, and consequently Poe's falls—as in "Ms. Found in a Bottle," *The Narrative of A. Gordon Pym*, "A Descent into the Maelstrom," and "The Pit and the Pendulum"—are always fortunate. By way of the metaphorical extension of *falling* in love, women in Poe's tales also trigger arabesque awareness. Inevitably Poe does a better job of destroying the outlines of conventional reality than in revealing a transcendent reality. Nevertheless, in so far as Poe fails, he fails in attempting the impossible.

There is something pragmatic, almost scientific, about Poe's devices for escaping a conventional reality. Poe's theory is very close to the notion of a space-time warp, a favorite ploy of science-fiction writers who wish to transport their characters or material objects backward or forward in time or into a parallel universe or unfamiliar dimension. In walking from one room to another, a person may pass accidentally through such an intersection and find himself in a strange world. Alternatively a scientist may invent some form of mechanism to help bring about this transition. The second aspect of Poe's underlying rationale, like the first, implies that all of his creative work may be regarded as marginally science-fictional. In the case of other, non-science-fictional visionary writers, the experience of transcendental reality depends upon personal volition (an unreliable program of fasting or praying), or divine intervention. In Poe's case, as in science fiction, natural phenomena may effect the transition *accidentally*, and the conditions of such phenomena may be mechanically duplicated.

IV

It has recently become fashionable to take Poe's cosmological treatise *Eureka*, published in 1848, the year before his death, and use it as an introductory blueprint for his entire output.[7] In *Eureka*, it seems almost as if Poe is compensating for the death of Virginia, the only being who gave his life meaning, by solving the riddle of the universe itself—a final, futile, paranoid gesture. Yet Poe's cosmology, while firmly based on the scientific knowledge of his day, is weirdly anticipative of many subsequent astronomical theories, including the recent pulsating-universe theory.[8] Moreover, in a most subtle manner that it is not part of my present purpose to explicate, Poe protects himself against the possibility of being pinned down to a particular error by a complex skein of irony. Debatable concepts are inevitably couched either in ironic terms or in an ironic context, which makes Poe's precise meaning a hopelessly slippery thing to grasp. For the same ironic purpose, Poe makes use of the principle of reciprocity of adaptation as a way of equivocating the props of cause

[7] For the best such attempt, see Richard Wilbur, "Introduction" and "Notes" to *Poe: Complete Poems* (New York, 1959). See also Geoffrey Rans, *Edgar Allan Poe* (Edinburgh and London, 1965); Joseph J. Moldenhauer, "Murder as a Fine Art: Basic Connections between Poe's Aesthetics, Psychology, and Moral Vision," *PMLA*, LXXXIII (May 1968), pp. 284–97; and Louis Broussard, *The Measure of Poe* (Norman, Okla., 1969).

[8] Connections between *Eureka* and contemporary or subsequent science are made in the following studies: Frederick Drew Bond, "Poe as an Evolutionist," *Popular Science Monthly*, LXXI (September 1907), pp. 267–74; Margaret Alterton, *Origins of Poe's Critical Theory* (Iowa City, 1925), pp. 112–22, 132–69; George Norstadt, "Poe and Einstein," *Open Court*, XLIV (March 1930), pp. 173–80; Philip P. Wiener, "Poe's Logic and Metaphysic," *Personalist*, XIV (October 1933), pp. 268–74; Clayton Hoagland, "The Universe of *Eureka*: A Comparison of the Theories of Eddington and Poe," *Southern Literary Messenger*, N.S. I (May 1939), pp. 307–13; for Eddington's comments on *Eureka* see Arthur Hobson Quinn, *Edgar Allan Poe: A Critical Biography* (New York, 1941), pp. 555–56; Frederick W. Connor, "Poe's *Eureka*: The Problem of Mechanism," *Cosmic Optimism* (Gainsville, Fla., 1949), pp. 67–91; Haldeen Braddy, "Poe's Flight from Reality," *Texas Studies in Literature and Language*, I (autumn 1959), pp. 394–400.

and effect underlying his own argument or any argument
that might be mounted against him.

Poe's materialistic conception in *Eureka* of a repeatedly
expanding and contracting universal entity existing in a
present state of irradiated fragmentation, but subsequently
and ideally in a collapsed and arabesque unity, is similar
to ideas of an "Overmind" or "Oversoul," to use Emerson's
terms, in the science fiction of Olaf Stapledon, Arthur C.
Clarke, and others. This "influence," plus Poe's desire that
his cosmology be valued aesthetically as a "romance" or a
"poem" (XVI, 183) and that the laws of the universe be
considered as aspects of the "plot of God" (XIII, 46; XVI,
10), however devoid of character interest, suggest possible
lines of argument for describing *Eureka* as a strangely
pure and literal brand of science fiction. If Poe's tales
and poems can be interpreted as dramatizations of *Eureka*,
then they might all be viewed as a species of displaced
science fiction. H. Bruce Franklin assumes this argument
in his suggestion that *Eureka*, "Mesmeric Revelation"
(which anticipates some of the metaphysical argumentation of *Eureka*), and "The Fall of the House of Usher" be
envisaged as a continuum expressing a movement from
"science" to "fiction": "The three forms may be called pure
speculation, pure speculation in a dramatic frame, and
dramatized speculation."[9]

I cannot go along entirely with the argument for placing
the cart before the horse. All the evidence suggests that
Poe's position in *Eureka* is one he worked toward spas-
modically. Yet I am perfectly willing to concede that the
basic movement of *Eureka* does appear embryonically in
certain of the tales and that these tales are a displaced
form of literal science fiction. Franklin's "pure speculation
in a dramatic frame" category is exampled not just by
"Mesmeric Revelation" but also in "Mellonta Tauta" (the
discussion of the value of intuition over inductive and
deductive reason is reproduced in *Eureka*) and the postapocalyptic colloquies: "The Conversation of Eiros and
Charmion," "The Colloquy of Monos and Una," and "The

9 Franklin, pp. 101–2.

Power of Words." In all these pieces, many of the ideas in *Eureka* are presented directly. Maurice Beebe makes a particularly convincing case for relating "The Fall of the House of Usher" to the collapsing universe of *Eureka*.[10] And the centrifugal and centripetal currents of the *Eureka* cosmology can also be felt in the sea tales, especially *The Narrative of A. Gordon Pym* and, less distinctly, in "Ms. Found in a Bottle" and "A Descent into the Maelstrom."[11] The moment of *"bouleversement"* (II, 94) in "Hans Pfaall," when the gravity pull of Earth gives way to the gravity pull of the moon, may be compared to the overturning of the *Grampus* at the conclusion to the first half of *Pym*, and both events may be related to that moment in *Eureka* when the force of attraction (or gravity) overcomes the force of repulsion (or electricity), which at present serves to stabilize the dispersed universe. Paralleling the plot of the God-projected universe in Poe's cosmology, the narrative action in the detective tales, or, as Poe termed them, tales of ratiocination, seems intended as projective of Dupin's character. Dupin functions as a "detective god," who, in solving a crime, draws his fragmented universe into an ordered unity.[12]

There is a more generalized point, bearing on the science-fictional coloration of Poe's work, to be made about

[10] "The Universe of Roderick Usher," *The Personalist*, XXXVII (spring 1956), pp. 147–60. The sentience of all matter, as proposed in "Mesmeric Revelation" and *Eureka*, provides a science-fictional rationale for the sentience of Usher's house. See E. A. Robinson, "Order and Sentience in 'The Fall of the House of Usher,'" *PMLA* (March 1961), pp. 68–81.

[11] For connections between *Pym* and *Eureka*, see Charles O'Donnell, "From Earth to Ether: Poe's Flight into Space," *PMLA*, LXXVII (March 1962), pp. 85–91.

[12] On the relationship between the ratiocinative tales and *Eureka*, see Edward H. Davidson, *Poe: A Critical Study* (Cambridge, Mass., 1957), pp. 213–22; Robert Daniel, "Poe's Detective God," *Furioso*, VI (summer 1951), pp. 45–54; and Richard Wilbur, "The Poe Mystery Case," *The New York Review of Books*, IX (July 1967), pp. 16, 25–28.

the relationship between the ratiocinative tales and *Eureka*. These pieces represent the culmination of Poe's interest in cryptograms and problem solving, an interest that activates the intellectual faculties and, according to Poe's philosophical formulation as I have presently stated it, can only contribute to the web of deception. Thus scientific explanations of wondrous events invariably serve the interests of a hoax. In the arabesque tales, Poe's fondness for a hoax realism provides one level of meaning. It is Poe's intention that the alert reader be encouraged to maintain various alternative interpretations, psychological and realistic, supernatural and allegorical, in a state of suspension to create a fluid form. Thus the surface of such tales becomes the equivalent of a writhing arabesque tapestry. But *Eureka* is one rationalistic structure in which Poe seems to have believed, and in order to allow for this and his own highly developed analytic abilities and make coherent the role of the analytical faculty in the artistic process, he was compelled to modify his understanding of the place of reason in his system of things.

The solution, which Poe embodies allegorically in the tales of ratiocination, is simple enough. He proposes two types of reason: on the one hand, the systematized, plodding reason that makes for deception and is exemplified by the Prefect of Police; on the other, Dupin's dazzling analytic ability or intuition, which, bred from the combination of reason and imagination, discovers that arabesque Truth which is also Beauty. Thus, when Dupin recommends the perspective of the half-closed eye, we are to understand that it is intuition rather than just imagination that is called for:

> To look at a star by glances—to view it in a side-long way, by turning toward it the exterior portions of the *retina* (more susceptible of feeble impressions of light than the interior), is to behold the star distinctly—is to have the best appreciation of its lustre—a lustre which grows dim just in proportion as we turn our vision *fully* upon it. A greater number of rays actually fall upon the

eye in the latter case, but, in the former, there is the
more refined capacity for comprehension. By undue
profundity, we perplex and enfeeble thought; and it is
possible to make even Venus herself vanish from the
firmament by a scrutiny too sustained, too concentrated,
or too direct (IV, 166).

Our sense here that intuition and imagination are becoming almost synonymous terms is borne out by a further
reference to the half-closed eye in this item from "A Chapter of Suggestions" (1845): "That intuitive and seemingly
casual perception by which we often attain knowledge,
when reason herself falters and abandons the effort, appears to resemble the sudden glancing at a star, by which
we see it more clearly than by a direct gaze; or the half-
closing the eyes in looking at a plot of grass the more fully
to appreciate the intensity of its green" (XIV, 189–90).
At one time, the half-closed-eye image was equated only
with the imagination.

There exists a contradiction in what I have hitherto said
about the science-fictional rationales underlying Poe's
corpus and his antipathy toward reason. The extrapolative
and analogical techniques of science fiction depend very
much upon reason. By redefining the half-closed-eye metaphor to allow for reason, Poe legitimizes the intellectual
element characteristic of all his work but previously only
doubtfully acknowledged. And in so doing, he goes some
way toward legitimizing my argument for considering
certain aspects of his philosophical or cosmological framework science-fictional. There is another contradiction, less
easily reconciled, between "The Assignation" and "The
Fall of the House of Usher," between the concept of an
individual arriving at arabesque reality via the equivalent
of a space-time warp but in the context of the present,
and the future collective achievement of the same(?) arabesque state when the universe has collapsed into unity.
It is possible to weave complicated arguments about temporal paradoxes, the relationship between the individual

microcosm and the universal macrocosm, or the relationship between psychology, allegory, and reality, but in "Ms. Found in a Bottle," "The Conversation of Eiros and Charmion," and the poem "The City in the Sea," Poe suggests a solution that, in theological terms, is surprisingly orthodox. These pieces, in different ways, suppose a period of time between the individual transition, whether by death or some agential mechanism, and the universal collapse. In other words, there are gradations of arabesque reality in the movement of the universe from its particled to its unparticled state, and we are given to suppose some form of coarse-grained arabesque limbo existing in the relatively unparticled, or "etherized" (to use the terminology of *Eureka*) condition in the spaces between the hard-packed heavenly bodies. We are to assume that the stranger/decorist, the Marchesa, Ligeia, and others are transported by various agential mechanisms, artificial or natural, to the intermediate, arabesque realm.

v

A survey of the specifically science-fictional elements in Poe's work will serve to bring this analysis to a conclusion. I speak of "elements" because, as I have intimated, even in those tales which critics have categorized as genuine science fiction, there is some crucial feature that militates against the descriptive comprehensiveness of the label. Although a goodly number of Poe's fictional pieces and even some of his poems do contain plot ideas and futuristic scientific inventions that figure in works of "straight" science fiction, in Poe's context they function primarily as details or elements in a whole of somewhat different character, whether it be a dream, a hoax, a fantasy, or a disguised metaphysical treatise. It is nevertheless true that the pieces that combine such elements with one or more of the underlying rationales described above do come closest to contemporary notions of science fiction.

Three of Poe's poems merit some consideration here.

Al Aaraaf takes its title from a "wandering star" Poe equates with that discovered by the Danish astronomer Tycho Brahe. Poe presents the planet, temporarily illuminated by the light of the four suns of the constellation Cassiopeia, as an aesthetic realm inhabited by lesser angels and exceptional mortals such as (Michael)Angelo, whose business it is to mediate between heaven and the many worlds of God's universe. There is some doubt as to whether or not Earth is literally destroyed by fire after the close passage of Al Aaraaf has dislodged Earth from its orbit. Since the entire poem appears to be an allegory illustrating Poe's conviction that didactic truth and passion are destructive of poetic beauty, it would seem that the fiery apocalypse should be taken metaphorically as a means of underlining the philosophical apocalypse that Angelo experiences following his death. Mention might appropriately be made here of one of Poe's poetic metaphysical pieces, "The Conversation of Eiros and Charmion," which involves a postapocalyptic discussion between two angels. We are informed that the end of the world occurred when a passing comet deprived Earth's atmosphere of nitrogen, causing it to ignite. Perhaps H. G. Wells' tale "The Star" (1897) or his novel *In the Days of the Comet* (1906) owes something to Poe's piece. In Wells' novel, a passing comet, albeit in a different manner from Poe's comet, also effects Man's transformation. Scientific explanations of Earth's demise are not offered in the two other postapocalyptic metaphysical pieces, "The Colloquy of Monos and Una" and "The Power of Words." However, Poe's first metaphysical piece, "Shadow—A Parable" (September 1835), is of some science-fictional relevance, since it appears to make analogical use of the supplanting of the Ptolemaic system of astronomy by the Copernican.[13]

But to return to the poetry, "The City in the Sea" (published in various forms in 1831 and 1845) is vaguely science-fictional, given its relation to myths of sunken cities

[13] Joseph M. De Falco, "The Sources of Terror in Poe's 'Shadow—A Parable,'" *Studies in Short Fiction*, VI (fall 1969), pp. 643–48.

such as Atlantis and Gomorrah. A third poem, *Ulalume* (1847, 1849), is also relevant, because it makes use of astrology. In this poem, Venus has just emerged from the constellation of the Lion. "Shadow—A Parable" contains one reference to the ill disposition of the stars: "Now had arrived the alternation of that seven hundredth and ninety-fourth year when, at the entrance of Aries, the planet Jupiter is conjoined with the red ring of the terrible Saturnus" (II, 147). Aside from astrology, Poe knew something of the pseudo sciences of phrenology, graphology, mesmerism, and alchemy. There is an obvious consequential development between such speculative or pseudo-scientific speculation and science fiction. Phrenology and graphology have little science-fictional application beyond indicating Poe's mental disposition, but his use of mesmerism, which he seems to have valued as a "scientific" means of putting his belief in an alternate reality to the test, is of much greater interest. Doris V. Falk, in a fine article entitled "Poe and the Power of Animal Magnetism," distinguishes mesmerism from mere hypnotism and thereby enhances the science-fictional credibility of the three mesmeric tales.[14] Mesmerism, or "animal magnetism," draws upon a physical fluid similar to electricity that permeates the universe and that, in *Eureka*, is called "ether" (XVI, 305–6), the stuff of Poe's material, intermediate, arabesque reality. In both "A Tale of the Ragged Mountains" and "The Facts in the Case of M. Valdemar," a mesmerist is able to preserve life beyond the point of apparent death thanks to his influence with this vital fluid. These mesmeric tales appear to come very close to pure science fiction. However, it may be that they should be understood primarily as hoaxes and only secondarily as a compromised form of science fiction.[15] In two letters, Poe maintains that "The Facts in the Case of M. Valdemar"

[14] See "Poe and the Power of Animal Magnetism," *PMLA*, LXXXIV (May 1969), pp. 536–46.
[15] See G. R. Thompson, "Is Poe's 'A Tale of the Ragged Mountains' a Hoax?" *Studies in Short Fiction*, VI (summer 1969), pp. 454–60.

was intended as a hoax. "Mesmeric Revelation" (August 1844), as indicated previously, is basically a vehicle for Poe's cosmological and metaphysical theory. The science-fictional element is a means toward a non-fictional end. Poe's use of mesmerism is, however, of a generalized science-fictional importance, because it further serves to define the material nature of Poe's visionary reality.

It is in the admitted hoax "Von Kempelen and His Discovery" that Poe's interest in alchemy comes into full play. As a result of Von Kempelen's success in turning lead into gold, gold becomes no more valuable than lead. This material transformation seems to be analogous to that larger material transformation of reality which is Poe's constant concern. There is some evidence of this metaphorical use of alchemy in "The Gold Bug" and "The Fall of the House of Usher."[16] Once again, but for Poe's intention to write a hoax, "Von Kempelen and His Discovery" might be considered as an unqualified science-fiction story of the marvelous-discovery type. Kempelen is a science-fictional type, and it should be noted that the Automaton Chess Player, probed by Poe in "Maelzel's Chess Player," was invented by Baron Kempelen. This example of Poe's analytical skill bears some slight relevance to the robot theme in science fiction, but rather more to Poe's compulsive desire to hoax his readers. Poe's demonstration that the Chess Player was not a machine but depended upon the agency of someone concealed within the box on which the chessboard rested, appears to have been lifted from an analysis by Sir David Brewster in his *Letters on Natural Magic*.[17] A rather different admixture of the mechanical and the human in Poe's burlesque "The Man That Was Used Up," in which a

[16] See Barton Levi St. Armand's two articles "Poe's 'Sober Mystification': The Uses of Alchemy in 'The Gold Bug,'" *Poe Studies*, IV (June 1971), pp. 1–7; and "Usher Unveiled: Poe and the Metaphysic of Gnosticism," *Poe Studies*, V (June 1972), pp. 1–8.

[17] See W. K. Wimsatt, Jr., "Poe and the Chess Automaton," *American Literature*, XI (May 1939), pp. 138–51.

general maintains his impressive appearance thanks to
artificial limbs and other mechanical contrivances, might
be loosely related to the androids and cyborgs of science
fiction.

To move from Poe's knowledge of the speculative sciences to scientific speculation is to confront those oceanic
voyages that seem ultimately oriented toward an inner
Earth and those sky voyages that seem ultimately oriented
toward outer space. Or are we once more talking about
the centripetal and centrifugal patterns of *Eureka*? The
sea tales are often misleadingly related to science fiction
because the mass of factual ballast abets a sense of verisimilitude and credibility that biased critics divorce from
Poe's hoax intentions. A rather more convincing argument
for relating the sea tales to science fiction might be
mounted on the evidence that, in these tales, Poe is making use of Symmes' "holes at the pole" theory, which is
referred to at the conclusion of "Ms. Found in a Bottle," to
account for the whirlpool in that tale. The maelstrom, in
the second sea tale, might be explained similarly. If so,
the "Discovery" (II, 10), toward which the narrator in
"Ms. Found in a Bottle" is headed, might be of an interior world within a hollow Earth, like that depicted in
Captain Adam Seaborn's (John Cleves Symmes) *Symzonia* (1820). Although J. O. Bailey's belief that *The
Narrative of A. Gordon Pym* is incomplete appears now to
be inaccurate, his suggestion that the conclusion of the
novel allows the reader to infer the discovery of an inner
world along the lines of *Symzonia* but to be called *Pym-
zonia* is not implausible.[18] The story of the exploration of
this inner world belongs to Edgar Rice Burroughs, Arthur
Conan Doyle, and, of course, Jules Verne.

Poe's three tales involving extraordinary balloon voyages
might all be construed as science fiction, especially for
their time, except that they were all conceived as hoaxes
and might most appropriately be described as "send-

[18] See J. O. Bailey, "Sources for Poe's *Arthur Gordon Pym*,
'Hans Pfaall,' and Other Pieces," *PMLA* LVII (January 1964),
pp. 513–35.

ups."[19] Another tale and not a hoax, "The Angel of the Odd," includes an episode with a manned balloon. The least of the three balloon voyage tales, "The Balloon Hoax," describing with much scientific detail a trans-Atlantic crossing by a balloon, was Poe's most successful hoax. Printed in *The* [New York] *Sun*, the same paper that had previously carried Locke's famous "Moon-Hoax," this hoax was similarly successful. Less immediately successful as a hoax, the lengthy tale from which Poe believed Locke had plagiarized his "Moon-Hoax" was entitled "The Unparalleled Adventures of One Hans Pfaall." This account of a journey to the moon by balloon would appear to be the most overtly science-fictional of Poe's tales. Joseph Adderley's (George Tucker) *A Voyage to the Moon* (1827), Sir John Herschel's *A Treatise on Astronomy* (1834), and Abraham Rees's *Cyclopedia* (1819) provided Poe with much of the scientific information he needed to make Pfaall's trip convincing reading.[20] As I have argued in detail elsewhere, this tale is not quite the straightforward hoax it is usually taken to be.[21] The satiric attack on the limitations of human knowledge as exemplified by the opening description of the Dutch burghers, who are clearly related to the insular villagers in "The Devil in the Belfry," is inconsistent unless the account of the moon voyage is not the hoax many of the burghers assume it to be: "Some of the over-wise even made themselves ridiculous by decrying the whole business as nothing better than a hoax. But hoax with these

[19] This is Daniel Hoffman's term. See his "Send-ups," *The London Magazine* (January 1970), pp. 30–36, republished in revised form in *Poe Poe Poe Poe Poe Poe Poe* (New York, 1972), pp. 153–60.
[20] See Bailey; M. N. Posey, "Notes on Poe's 'Hans Pfaall,'" *Modern Language Notes*, XLV (December 1930), pp. 501–7; and William H. Gravely, Jr., "A Note on the Composition of Poe's 'Hans Pfaall,'" *Poe Newsletter*, III (June 1970), pp. 2–5.
[21] See David Ketterer, "Poe's Usage of the Hoax and the Unity of 'Hans Pfaall,'" *Criticism*, XIII (fall 1971), pp. 377–85.

sort of people, is, I believe, a general term for all matters
above their comprehension" (II, 102). It would seem,
then, that readers who take Pfaall's adventures as a simple
hoax are allying themselves with these overrationalistic
Dutchmen in excluding an extrasensory reality. A careful
reading of the tale will reveal that Pfaall died along with
his three creditors in the unexpectedly powerful explosion
at take-off. The voyage is, then, a disguised account of
Pfaall's transference from conventional reality to arabesque
reality, and the tale is not literally about a trip to the
moon, not literally science fiction, and not a direct hoax.
Poe's hoax consists in making his readers believe the tale
to be a hoax. However, although "Hans Pfaall" is not
straight science fiction, it may be considered science-
fictional, because of its reliance on the three materialistic
rationales concerning arabesque reality. As I have previously indicated, the moment of *"bouleversement"* (II, 94)
may be related to the dynamics of the universe in *Eureka*.

Hans Pfaall leaves Earth on "the first of April" (II, 54),
and the newspaper balloon the people of Rotterdam see
resembles "a huge fool's-cap turned upside down" (II, 44;
note the pun). "Mellonta Tauta" consists of a diary-form
epistle written by a muddleheaded woman named Pundita
and beginning on April 1, 2848. It is worth noting that a
coincidentally high number of Poe's hoaxes, including
"Maelzel's Chess Player," "A Tale of the Ragged Mountains," "The Balloon Hoax," "Some Words with a
Mummy," and "Von Kempelen and His Discovery," although published in different years, all made their initial
appearance in April. "Mellonta Tauta" might best be considered as one of the three tales that experiment with the
theme of time displacement. "The Thousand and Second
Tale of Scheherazade," "Some Words with a Mummy,"
and "Mellonta Tauta" demonstrate the inaccuracy of past
conceptions of the future, present conceptions of the past,
and future conceptions of the present, respectively. Appropriate to this theme of human illusion, all three tales
contain elements destructive to their air of realism and

verisimilitude and hence to any categorization of these tales as outright time-centered science fiction. "Scheherazade" is based on fantasy, albeit a corrected fantasy; "Some Words with a Mummy" appears to be a dream experience resulting from strain and indigestion; and "Mellonta Tauta" is a hoax.

But science-fictional *elements* are certainly present. Scheherazade's account of the further adventures of Sinbad includes descriptions of a manned balloon, the "Voltaic pile" (VI, 99), Maelzel's Automaton Chess Player, and other nineteenth-century technological marvels, all of which Sinbad misunderstands and Scheherazade's auditor, the king, dismisses as nonsense. In "Some Words with a Mummy," a voltaic pile, which may be assumed to utilize some electrical connection with mesmerism or animal magnetism, is used to revivify an Egyptian mummy. The mummy informs the astonished company that the ancient Egyptians had not only anticipated much nineteenth-century knowledge but, among other things, had also discovered the secrets of suspended animation. The future world of "Mellonta Tauta" (the title comes from the Greek for "these things are in the near future") is something like a Wellsian dystopia. Pundita and her husband, Pundit, are flying in their balloon. Much of Pundita's letter, in standard "utopian" fashion, sets the marvels and revelations of the future against the primitive standards and knowledge of the past. But this tale is of particular science-fictional interest because it may well be the first temporal-displacement "utopia" to open directly in a future environment with no such verifying convention as a frame narrative describing the transition to "utopia" from the author's present world. The letter Pundita corks in a bottle and throws overboard is, by some temporal paradox, discovered in 1848, and the part in which she sings the praises of intuition, then used in place of inductive and deductive reasoning (a faith somewhat undercut by her husband's complete misinterpretation of past history and certain nineteenth-century artifacts), finds its way into

Eureka, thus enhancing the science-fictional quality of that larger work.

VI

Nevertheless, although there may be moon beings mentioned in "Mellonta Tauta" and voltaic piles in "Scheherazade" and "Some Words with a Mummy," the essentially unreal context in which they appear militates against designating these tales *primarily* as science fiction, since a straight-faced illusion of credibility is a mandatory aspect of the genre. The same goes for the other tales, which various critics have described as works of science fiction. But if the science-fiction label can be applied to Poe only in a marginal sense, there is no such doubt about the label apocalyptic.

Although, as I have argued, there are different senses of the apocalyptic, in practice my three broad categories invariably overlap. Writers who are most satisfactorily described as apocalyptic will inhabit all three areas. This is true in the case of Edgar Allan Poe, who is America's paradigm apocalyptic writer. Although Poe's arabesque condition is a visionary realm outside of space and time, he belongs also in the company of those writers who interpret the present world in other terms, because of the scientific manner in which he dramatically redefines material reality. At the same time, Poe's satirical attack on conventional reality, the future world of "Mellonta Tauta," and his concern with the end of the world in *Eureka* and the pieces that may be affiliated with it, give him some claims in the area of other worlds in space and time. A philosophical apocalyptic in the broadest natural, moral, and metaphysical sense, Poe is primarily a visionary apocalyptic, but he also deserves consideration as a satiric and philosophical apocalyptic in the narrower sense. One consequence of this range is the connection Poe welds between science-fictional rationales and elements on the one hand and transcendental reality on the other. In Poe's case, the science-fiction writer is subservient to the transcendental visionary. In the case of other writers, such as Ursula K. LeGuin, for whom Poe paves the way, a transcendental reality serves the larger context of science fiction.

4. The Left Hand of Darkness: *Ursula K. LeGuin's Archetypal "Winter-Journey"*

I

As distinct from the general recognition that a relationship exists between mythology and any form of literature, science-fiction criticism has recently made much of science fiction as a peculiarly significant vehicle for myth. Unfortunately this idea is being taken rather too literally by a growing number of science-fiction writers, with the result that their work, far from being the articulation of a "new mythology," to use a current critical cliché, consists essentially of the sterile revamping of the old.[1] It is not of course totally erroneous to speak of science fiction as a "new mythology," but what I wish to deplore is the lack of particularity that generally accompanies such assertions. New-mythology critics are curiously loath to offer specific examples, although possible exhibits are certainly at hand. There is for instance what might be called the "terminal beach" myth, to appropriate Ballard's title, the notion being that, just as, in Darwin's view, the transposition of life from the sea to the land allowed for the genesis of humanity, so the end of man might appropriately be envisaged as taking place "on the beach," to utilize Nevil Shute's title. H. G. Wells is perhaps the originator of this "myth." His time traveler's glimpses of Earth's end are from "a sloping beach," while, in a short story entitled "The Star" (1897), the destruction that follows in the wake of that errant body is depicted as follows: "Every-

[1] See, for example, the 1968 MLA forum involving Bruce Franklin, Darko Suvin, Isaac Asimov, and Frederick Pohl, entitled "Science Fiction: The New Mythology," the tape of which is transcribed in *Extrapolation*, X (May 1969), pp. 69–115.

where the waters were pouring off the land, leaving mud-silted ruins, and the earth littered like a storm-worn beach with all that had floated, and the dead bodies of the men and brutes, its children."[2]

In Northrop Frye's formulation, the mythic basis of any fiction, aside from the occasional reworkings of an O'Neill or a Sartre, should exist irrespective of an author's intentions and in a severely displaced relationship to the story line.[3] In science-fiction novels such as *The Einstein Intersection* (1967) and *Nova* (1968), by Samuel R. Delany, and some of Roger Zelazny's work, there is no doubt as to the author's conscious awareness of his mythic source material and very little attempt at displacement aside from matters of environment. Inevitably in such fictions the logic of plot development is at the service of a mythic structure, and suffers accordingly. *The Left Hand of Darkness*, by Ursula K. LeGuin, the 1969 Hugo *and* Nebula Award winner, is a further case in point. But something is gained here, because, to a degree, this work functions as a science-fiction novel about the writing of a science-fiction novel and is particularly informative for that reason. Since the various fictional genres can be meaningfully defined in relation to basic myths or to segments of myth, the mythic concern of LeGuin's novel, in spite of its attendant deleterious effects on the narrative, does have its point.

As I have argued, science fiction is concerned with effecting what might be termed an epistemological or philosophical apocalypse. A new world destroys an old world. Given that this apocalyptic transformation involves the mythic structure of death and rebirth, for which the cycle of the seasons is the model, we can speculate as to why Gethen, the new world in *The Left Hand of Darkness*, enjoys such an inhospitable climate that the place is known, in English, as Winter. At the same time perhaps we can hypothesize some connection with Frye's "mythos of winter," by which he distinguishes the duplicitous

[2] See *The Works of H. G. Wells*, Atlantic Edition (London, 1924, 1925), for *The Time Machine* (1895), Vol. I, p. 105; for "The Star," Vol. X, p. 569.
[3] See *Anatomy of Criticism, passim.*

modes of irony and satire, as opposed to the unitary,
"apocalyptic" mode of romance. Science fiction draws
very much on the combination of satire and romance, and
the concepts of unity and duality are, as I shall indicate,
central to the theme of LeGuin's book.

II

The Left Hand of Darkness tells a story set in the distant future. Genly Ai has spent two unprofitable years in
the nation of Karhide, on the planet Gethen, his mission
being to persuade Gethen to join the Ekumen, a loose
confederation of eighty or so worlds. Because of a political dispute over the desirability of joining the Ekumen
and doubt as to its very existence, Ai's Gethenian friend,
Estraven, one time senior councilor to Argaven XV, the
mad king of Karhide, is exiled and replaced in office by his
opponent, Tibe. The king gives Ai the impression that
Estraven has been exiled not for promoting the Ekumen's
cause, as officially stated, but for working against it.

His faith in Estraven undermined and otherwise generally frustrated, Ai tries his cause elsewhere within the
Great Continent, which is divided between Karhide and
the rival nation of Orgoreyn, to the northwest. At this point
Estraven has already begun his exile, in Orgoreyn. The
central portion of the narrative chronicles, in more or less
alternating chapters, the respective yet linked careers of
Ai and Estraven in Orgoreyn. Ai has the more eventful
time. He crosses over at a disputed border area known
as the Sinoth Valley, and his first night's sleep in Orgoreyn
is interrupted by a raid from Karhide that leaves Ai without his passport (an inspector having kept it for the night)
to join a group of refugees from the raid, who, also lacking
identification papers, are incarcerated in a windowless
cellar. The machinations of Shusgis, First Commensal Dis-
trict Commissioner of Entry-Roads and Ports, extricate
Genly from this predicament and bring him to the Commissioner's home in Mishnory, the largest city on Gethen.

In Mishnory, Genly runs into Estraven, from whom he learns something of the danger of his situation. Apparently Shusgis is a representative of the Domination faction, which is opposed to the Free Trade faction. In short, Shusgis is opposed to the Envoy's mission, and is actually an agent of the Sarf, a police organization that controls the Free Trade faction. Consequently Genly is imprisoned again, this time at the Pulefen Farm and Resettlement Agency, in the frigid northwest of Orgoreyn.

With the help of Estraven, who has, to a degree, controlled Genly's progress (he plays a part in arranging that Genly feel disposed to leave Karhide when the king begins to favor an unfriendly faction), the Envoy escapes. The concluding third of the book traces their tortuous journey "north through the mountains, east across the Gobrin, and down to the border at Guthen Bay" (p. 191)[4] —the Gobrin being the notorious ice sheet and the border being that fronting on Karhide. Estraven had sent word to King Argaven of the Envoy's arrest on the assumption that Argaven, ignoring Tibe's advice, would inquire and would be falsely informed by Mishnory of Genly's unfortunate death. Estraven later believes that, on discovering Genly's presence in North Karhide, Argaven, now aware of Orgoreyn's duplicitous treatment of the Envoy, would be sympathetic to Genly's mission and enable him to safely call down his star ship, which has all the time been circling Gethen. Except that Estraven, a traitor in his own country, is shot attempting to cross the border back into Orgoreyn, everything, however unlikely, happens as planned: Gethen joins the Ekumen.

III

That an "intelligible" summary of the often arbitrary action of LeGuin's novel is possible without any mention of

[4] All parenthetical references are to the Ace paperback edition of *The Left Hand of Darkness* (New York, 1969).

what it is that makes the Gethenians especially distinctive, especially alien—namely their unique form of bisexuality—argues against the book's structural integrity. The truth of the situation appears to be that Gethenian sexuality, like Gethen's climate, has less to do with the surface plot than with the underlying mythic pattern of destruction or division and creation or unity. Making sense of the novel, and this is its essential weakness, depends upon an act of dislocation on the part of the reader and seeing what should be implicit as explicit, seeing the way in which the mythic structure rigorously, almost mechanically, determines the various turns of the plot. The Gethenians alternate between periods of twenty-one or twenty-two days when they are sexually neuter, neither male nor female, and six-day periods of *kemmer*, when they become sexually active and take on sexual identity. When a Gethenian in kemmer has located a partner in a similar condition, intercourse is possible. During the successive phases of kemmer, one of the parties will develop male sexual organs and the other, female, depending upon how they react to one another. It is therefore possible for any Gethenian to become pregnant. Incest, except between generations, is allowed, with minor restrictions.[5]

It is proposed that, as a result of their ambisexuality, Gethenians are much less prone to the dualistic perception that conceivably is related to the permanent male/female split that characterizes most other forms of humanity: "There is no division of humanity into strong and weak halves, protective/protected, dominant/submissive, owner/ chattel, active/passive" (pp. 93–94). Commenting on the Orgota (i.e., of Orgoreyn) word translated as "commensal," "commensality," for almost any form of group organization, Genly remarks on "this curious lack of distinction between the general and specific applications of the word, in the use of it for both the whole and the part, the state and the individual, in this imprecision is its precisest

[5] Hermaphroditic beings have, of course, appeared in science fiction before, most notably perhaps in Theodore Sturgeon's *Venus Plus X* (New York, 1960). See my discussion in Chapter 5.

meaning" (p. 107). As one of the Handdarata Foretellers (whom Genly consults at one point), Estraven is "less aware of the gap between men and beasts, being more occupied with the likenesses, the links, the whole of which living things are a part." Genly concludes, "You're isolated, and undivided. Perhaps you are as obsessed with wholeness as we are with dualism" (p. 222).

This Gethenian peculiarity is epitomized by the book's title, which is extracted from "Tormer's Lay":

Light is the left hand of darkness
and darkness the right hand of light (p. 222).

Here is capsulized the destruction of unity and the re-emergence of unity out of a disparate duality, a movement implicit in the thesis-antithesis-synthesis structural arrangement of the book and a movement basic to my theoretical definition of science fiction. From the Gethenian point of view, a unified Gethenian reality is destroyed by the knowledge of the much larger reality of the Ekumen confederation prior to being incorporated in that larger unity. Likewise, the reader's terrestrial vision is destroyed and then reintegrated to the extent that, during the reading process, he accepts the world of Gethen with its aberrant sexuality and the apocalyptic suggestion that both Gethen and Terran civilization were experiments by superior beings on the planet Hain. LeGuin's book effects a philosophical apocalypse in the three ways that science fiction can: by presenting a radically different image of man, by pointing to the existence of a previously unsuspected outside manipulator, and thirdly, as a consequence, by radically altering man's vision of human reality. The sense of mystical unity that "Tormer's Lay" initially suggests suffers an interim disorientation because of the paradoxical equation of the concrete with the abstract and the reversed correlation of light with the left hand, given the sinister associations of left, and of darkness with the right hand. But, almost immediately, the traditional association between the female and the left and between the female and primal darkness helps reintegrate the breach.

IV

The state of division that Genly brings to Gethen is dramatized by means of a series of widening objective correlatives. Estraven, the first alien to whom we are introduced, is presented twice by Genly as "the person on my left" (pp. 10, 11), hence somewhat apart and unfamiliar. The king of Karhide, being mad, is presumably divorced from his true self and thus a symbol of disorder and chaos. Hence the efficacy of deception and the rise of Tibe to power, Tibe who is spoken of as possessing the non-Gethenian trick of hate. Of course the major analogy for the state of duality, division, and destruction resides in this piece of information from Estraven: "You know that Karhide and Orgoreyn have a dispute concerning a stretch of our border in the high North Fall near Sassinoth" (p. 20). We are told, "If civilization has an opposite, it is war" (p. 101), with the implication that we infer the opposition between order and chaos. In normal times war is unknown in Gethen, perhaps because of the lack of continuous sexual differentiation. It is hypothesized that war may "be a purely masculine displacement-activity, a vast Rape" (p. 95).

In Orgoreyn both Genly and Estraven are in exile, a condition of separation, Genly from his kind and Estraven from his homeland, although, in some ways, faction-ridden Orgoreyn is a mirror image of Karhide just as Gethen is an inverted image of Earth. As Estraven is approaching the shore of Orgoreyn, he observes, "Darkness lay behind my back, before the boat, and into darkness I must row" (p. 78). For Genly the experience in Orgoreyn is also that of darkness, darkness betokening the destruction of reality, death and chaos. The raid that issues from an unspecified border town of Karhide appears to be a dream. After supper in Siuwensin, Genly "fell asleep in that utter country silence that makes your ears ring. I slept an hour and woke in the grip of a nightmare about explosions, invasions, murder, and conflagration." This is the moment of apocalypse.

Although Genly has mentioned waking, he continues to speak of what is happening as a dream: "It was a particularly bad dream, the kind in which you run down a strange street in the dark with a lot of people who have no faces, while houses go up in flame behind you, and children scream" (p. 108). From this moment until Genly's revival or rebirth from his mock death (arranged by Estraven to aid the escape from Orgoreyn), unreal in a literal sense but real in a symbolic sense, the reader cannot be totally sure that everything is not a dream. But this intervening loss of a stable reality, one of the more subtle aspects of the book, is exactly appropriate as an analogy for the destructive effect the apocalyptic transformations of science fiction have on conventional reality. Thus it is that *The Left Hand of Darkness* may be viewed as a sciencefiction novel about the theoretical definition of science fiction.

In his "dream," Genly is incarcerated with a group of refugees in a windowless "vast stone semi-cellar": "The door shut, it was perfectly dark: no light" (p. 109). Genly is metaphorically "in the dark" for most of the time in Orgoreyn, as witness his ambiguous description of Mishnory, the capital city: "It was not built for sunlight. It was built for winter" (pp. 112–13). Yet, at the same time, Genly felt as if he had "come out of a dark age" (p. 113) in Karhide. This sense of unreality is subsequently confirmed by Genly's description of the buildings of central Mishnory: "Their corners were vague, their façades streaked, dewed, smeared. There was something fluid, insubstantial, in the very heaviness of this city built of monoliths, this monolithic state which called the part and the whole by the same name" (p. 141).

Later, confined in a windowless truck on his way to Pulefen Farm, Genly begins to understand the chaotic nature of Orgoreyn:

It was the second time I had been locked in the dark with uncomplaining, unhopeful people of Orgoreyn. I knew now the sign I had been given my first night in

this country. I had ignored that black cellar and gone
looking for the substance of Orgoreyn above ground, in
daylight. No wonder nothing had seemed real (p. 160).

Genly is suffering the sense of dislocated confusion attendant upon his awareness of a new world—the lack of
co-ordinate points: "One's magnetic and directional sub-
stances are all wrong on other planets; when the intellect
won't or can't compensate for that wrongness, the result is
a profound bewilderment, a feeling that everything, literally, has come loose" (p. 161). This is, of course, also a
description of the apocalyptic sense of disorientation that
the reader of science fiction experiences and that is perhaps the major reason why he reads the stuff. This experience is not unique to science fiction; it is just more
purely expressed in the science-fiction form. Indeed the
repeated references to the truck as a "steel box" (pp.
161, 166), "our box" (p. 164), and "existence in the steel
box" (p. 165) are surely reminiscent of Private Henry
Fleming's experiences, in a sense apocalyptic, in *The Red
Badge of Courage,* as a member of an army that is referred to as a directionless "moving box."[6] And it is surely
not accidental that Estraven's first job on arrival in Orgoreyn involves running "a machine which fits together and
heatbonds pieces of plastic to form little transparent boxes"
(p. 145), symbols presumably of unconscious contain-
ment, isolation, alienation, separation, and hence destruction and chaos. As a final analogy to the import of dualism,
the mock death of Genly and the deaths of Estraven and
of King Argaven's son all betoken the destruction of an old
world of mind in the face of a radically new vision.

v

The extent to which the mythic pattern of death and
rebirth underlies the action of the novel is reinforced by

6 See *Stephen Crane: An Omnibus,* ed. by R. W. Stallman
(New York, 1952), p. 248.

the "myths" injected into the book in relation to various aspects of the plot. The myth of the "Place inside the Blizzard" (pp. 26–30), in which two brothers, one then dead, who had vowed kemmering to one another, are momentarily reunited, bears on the later action. Hode, the dead brother, seized the other, Gethenen, "by the left hand," which, as a consequence, was frozen and subsequently amputated. The Place inside the Blizzard is clearly a mystic point where life and death may be united. It subsequently transpires that Estraven had vowed kemmering to his now-dead brother although, as Estraven reflects, his "shadow followed me" (p. 76). Later, as anticipated (p. 192), Estraven and Genly find themselves "inside the blizzard" (p. 246), a kind of still point. This mythic configuration culminates at the novel's conclusion, when Genly is introduced to Sorve Harth, the child of the two brothers, now both dead. Thus life and death are one, an intuition rather clumsily underscored by the book's final lines, Sorve's question to Genly regarding Estraven: "Will you tell us how he died?—Will you tell us about the other worlds out among the stars—the other kinds of men, the other lives?" (p. 283).

Estraven, in fact, has a family history of bringing unity out of discord through "treachery," as is indicated in the Romeo-and-Juliet-like mythic story of "Estraven the Traitor" (pp. 120–25). The matching hands of two mortal enemies make for a reconciliation. This is the myth Estraven re-enacts with Genly. Although they are aliens to each other, they become as one, particularly when Estraven exhibits a capacity for telepathic communication or "bespeaking" (p. 238), as it is appropriately termed. In this way, the mind expansion attendant upon the awareness of a new reality is made both metaphoric and literal. Why speak of telepathic communication as the "Last Art" (p. 240) if not to insinuate the possibility of an apocalypse of mind? And although it is not possible to communicate telepathically anything other than the truth, Estraven believes at one point that it is his dead brother Arek bespeaking him rather than Genly.

Later, as a consequence of this telepathic awareness, Genly, hearing Estraven's words, believes that he himself spoke them. This is a confusion that the reader is made to share, since, although most of the story is told from Genly's point of view, several chapters, without warning, are narrated from Estraven's perspective. Genly explains: "The story is not all mine, nor told by me alone. Indeed I am not sure whose story it is; you can judge better. But it is all one, and if at moments the facts seem to alter with an altered voice, why then you can choose the fact you like best; yet none of them are false, and it is all one story" (p. 7). What confusion exists is designed to augment the impression of unity. There is a similar gain in Chapter 7, "The Question of Sex," where LeGuin plays on the reader's expectations by delaying, until the end of the chapter, the revelation that the anthropological notes by Ong Tot Oppong are the work of a woman.

Unity of awareness is also enjoyed by the Handdarata Foretellers, who are introduced in the chapter of injected myth called "The Nineteenth Day" (pp. 46–49), which illustrates the rather vague nature of their prophecies, a vagueness Genly recognizes when he consults them. The Foretellers are controlled by Faxe the Weaver, who brings the various disparate and chaotic forces together like "the suspension-points of a spiderweb" (p. 66). Indeed the weaving imagery, which permeates the book and may be related to the triangular netlike structure created by the relationship of unity to duality, finds its nucleus here. Genly feels himself "hung in the center of a spiderweb woven of silence" (p. 64), "a point or figure in the pattern, in the web" (p. 67). The act of putting together a novel and creating an aesthetic unity can be imaged as a weaving process. Thus Genly speaks of forgetting "how I meant to weave the story" (p. 174). Estraven, making his way to rescue Genly from Pulefen Farm, travels by caravan "weaving from town to town" (p. 178). Traveling between two volcanoes, Drumner and Dremegole, the hissing sound of Drumner, which is in eruption, "fills all the interstices of one's being" (p. 215). These "interstices" may be seen as objectified by the "crevasses" (pp. 215, 219, 248, 251) or "crevassed area" (pp. 233, 251) to which repeated references are made during the journey across the ice; objectified also by the indirect, crisscross path that Genly and Estraven travel, invariably turning "east-northeast by compass" (p. 223) or "a little south of east" (p. 247) and almost never directly north, south, east, or west. On a larger scale, what is referred to as the "shifgrethor" relationship in Gethenian society appears to be a theoretical network or unformulated pattern of right behavior, rather similar in fact to that web of worlds known as the Ekumen, which is not so much a "body politic, but a body mystic" (p. 245) modeled on the process of evolution. In view of the importance of webbed relationships to the awareness of a new unity, it is in no way accidental that Faxe the Weaver, at the end of the book, is likely to take Tibe's place as the Prime Minister of Karhide.

VI

The Left Hand of Darkness, which begins with a chapter entitled "A Parade in Erhenrang" and ends with chapters entitled "Homecoming" and "A Fool's Errand," is primarily concerned with the journey from Karhide to Orgoreyn, "One Way" or "Another Way," and back to Karhide following "The Escape" from Pulefen Farm. Physically the journey describes a jagged clockwise circle. I mention its being clockwise because the book, beginning and ending in late spring, covers a temporal cycle. What is being dramatized is the ultimate unity of space and time. Since Gethen is known as the planet Winter, when Genly speaks of his and Estraven's "winter-journey" (p. 259) it is intended that the reader infer the identification of space and time—it is a journey across and through Winter with, as I have intimated, all the associations of Frye's mythos of winter. The period of death and destruction here symbolized by winter is occasioned by the conjunc-

tion of an old and a new world of mind, the basic concern
of science fiction.

The journey to and across the ice is replete with imagery suggestive of the forces of creation. Two injections
of Gethenian myth point the way. "On Time and Darkness" (pp. 155–57) explains that "Meshe [note the net im-
plications] is the Center of Time" (p. 155), Meshe being
the founder of the Yomesh cult, which broke from the
Handdarata. Genly experiences something of this insight
traveling by truck with a group of prisoners to Pulefen
Farm: "We drew together and merged into one entity oc-
cupying one space" (p. 163). One member of the group
dies. It is significant that just before Estraven's death,
Genly is "taken by fits of shuddering like those I had experienced in the prison-truck crossing Orgoreyn" (p. 267).
Once again it should be apparent that all the narrative action illustrates the two basic structures of division/duality
and unity. The sense of temporal unity at Meshe is perhaps the inspiration for the Gethenian method of number-
ing the year backward and forward from the present year,
which is consequently always at the center.

"An Orgota Creation Myth" provides a second pointer.
We are told, "In the beginning there was nothing but ice
and the sun," a notation that explains the landscape
through which Genly and Estraven have just passed. The
previous chapter ends with a reference to "the veiled sun,
the ice" (p. 224). In the process of reaching the blindingly
white Gobrin Glacier, white with all the implications of
fusion and unity that the color holds for Poe at the polar
conclusion of his *Narrative of A. Gordon Pym*, Genly and
Estraven have made their way between the two volcanoes
of Drumner and Dremegole, Drumner in eruption. The
impression is of "the dirty chaos of a world in the process of making itself" (p. 216). The creation myth concludes with a reference to Meshe, "the middle of time"
(p. 226), which explains the environment of the next
chapter. On the Gobrin Glacier, Genly feels himself and
Estraven to be "at the center of all things" (p. 227). It
is "On the Ice" (pp. 227–47) that Genly truly comes to

OTHER WORLDS 89

recognize Estraven as both man and woman. "Until then I had rejected him, refused him his own reality" (p. 234). The telepathic experience and the experience "Inside the Blizzard" follows his understanding. This mutual understanding, which is equivalent to a rebirth, is symbolized by changes in the environment as "that bland blind nothingness about us began to flow and writhe" (p. 247) and the incident in which Genly "delivers" Estraven from a crevasse into which he falls to emerge with a vision of "Blue—all blue—Towers in the Depths" (p. 250). The crevasses become the cracks in an eggshell, with Genly and Estraven both inside and outside.

This unifying sense of a microcosm and macrocosm is dramatized by the arrival of the Ekumen star ship. It is as if the world view of the Ekumen and that of Gethen are collapsed together. Genly plans his call to the ship with a consciousness of setting "the keystone in the arch" (p. 272). One thinks perhaps of Hart Crane's bridge or the bridge on Jupiter in the first volume of Blish's *Cities in Flight* but more particularly of the keystone ceremony with which *The Left Hand of Darkness* opens, which is now seen for its symbolic significance. From among the stars, which have earlier been likened to "far cities" (p. 106), the approaching ship is quite literally "one star descending" (p. 278); I say literally because it represents "the coming of a new world, a new mankind" (p. 280). For the reader, a metaphorical conflation of Earth and Gethen has already taken place encouraged by King Argaven's initially disconcerting reference to Gethenians as "human beings here on earth" (p. 40) and by Estraven's similar reference to Gethen as "this earth" (p. 87). In addition Genly points out, "Fundamentally Terra and Gethen are very much alike. All the inhabited worlds are" (p. 118).

My point has been that LeGuin's use of duality and unity as mythically connotative of destruction and creation is in fact a way of talking about the relationship between new and old worlds of mind and that this relationship is at the theoretical basis of science fiction. As such, *The Left*

Hand of Darkness is a skillfully integrated, perhaps I should say woven, piece of work, although my criticism that the plot is unfortunately subordinate to the overly conscious use of mythic material remains. The world of the novel, like the snowbound ecology of Gethen and the snowy metaphors it gives rise to, is developed with a consistency that at least equals Frank Herbert's sandbound world of *Dune*. Mention of "a snow-worm" (p. 212) recalls the sand-worms of *Dune* (1965), which figure so prominently in the plot of that novel. But LeGuin's single and singular reference is perhaps indicative of that loss of dramatic surface incident compelled by her rigorous adherence to a mythic design insufficiently displaced. To use a repeated Gethenian image of unity, the wheel of LeGuin's plot turns rather too inexorably and predictably in its seasonal and mythic groove.

III. OTHER WORLDS IN SPACE AND TIME

As a general principle, it is a foolish enterprise to define any term in such a way as to contradict commonly accepted usage. In the case of the word apocalyptic, understood as a critical term, a basic congruency should exist between my specialized definition and the sense that a majority of critics would accept. I have defined as apocalyptic any work of fiction concerned with presenting a radically different world or version of reality that exists in a credible relationship with the world or reality verified by empiricism and common experience—the world or reality the author may assume his reader to bring to a reading of his work. My use of the adjective "credible" rather than the narrower qualifier "rational" is based on the assumption that an act of faith and an act of reason may be equally and inextricably involved in the acceptance of any unseen world that is, in some sense, concordant with the known world. Yet while few, I believe, would quarrel with my usage of apocalyptic in the previous section of this study as descriptive of visionary reality, a rather larger number might question my application of the term to the alternative, unseen, secular realities of science fiction. I would argue that the interests of important areas of consistency here overrule the area of differentiation and that visionary worlds and science-fictional worlds should be understood as performing essentially the same apocalyptic function.

Religion, mysticism, and science fiction concern themselves—in different ways, to be sure—with the same ground, the unknown. The shared object of desire is the revelation of a genuine, hitherto hidden, reality. David Norman Samuelson's doctoral dissertation, "Studies in the

Contemporary American and British Science Fiction
Novel," includes a comparison between Auden's analysis
of Eden regained in the detective novel and the science-
fiction story, "where innocence seems to be assumed from
the first, the victory over nature or unreason is a temporary
thing, reversible by time, and the fundamental achievement is a hard-won beachhead in the territory of the real
enemy, the unknown."[1] In Philip José Farmer's *To Your
Scattered Bodies Go* Richard Burton explains his purpose
to the other resurrectees on the Riverworld: "I will tell
you that we are setting sail because the Unknown exists
and we would make it Known."[2] If the unknown reality,
when known, is to be radically and convincingly different from our given reality and therefore worth knowing,
it will share the visionary quality that characterizes the
unknown realms mined by the various religions and forms
of mysticism. I have already quoted Samuel R. Delany's
assertion that the classics of what he calls speculative
fiction are mystical. C. S. Lewis, in a fine posthumous
collection of essays entitled *Of Other Worlds*, makes a
related point: ". . . to construct plausible and moving
'other worlds' you must draw on the only real 'other world'
we know, that of the spirit."[3]

In the previous section I concentrated on apocalyptic
writers who emphasize the "visionary" element over the
"realistic" in their portrayal of new worlds. Since these
two elements always coexist in such creations—albeit in
differing proportions—I propose, on pragmatic grounds,
that writers who tip the balance in favor of "realism" to
create other worlds in space and time can also usefully be
regarded as apocalyptic. Ryken treats the transhistorical
reality of Heaven and the temporal "utopian" reality of
Eden as aspects of the same apocalyptic vision. In this

[1] See "Studies in the Contemporary American and British Science Fiction Novel" (University of Southern California, January 1965), p. 56.
[2] See the Berkley Medallion paperback edition of *To Your
Scattered Bodies Go* (New York, 1971), p. 98.
[3] See *Of Other Worlds* (London, 1966), p. 12.

regard he is following Frye's conception of the apocalyptic and demonic orders of existence as providing the poles of a conventional spectrum of existences corresponding to Heaven, Eden, the fallen historical world, and Hell or "the world of sin and death and corruption . . . which is not really part of nature in the sense that it was never intended to be there, although of course it permeates the physical world and causes everything alive in it to die."[4] This system allows for a close identity between Heaven and an earthly utopia as apocalyptic realms and an equally close identity between the historical world and Hell as demonic realms. It serves to characterize the everyday world as essentially dystopian, which would corroborate the position argued in the next chapter that the material vision of science fiction is drawn toward dystopia rather than utopia. The source of a utopian reality is two removes from where we are; dystopia is one. However, the transcendent visionary orientation of science fiction is decidedly utopian in the broad sense of that word. This science-fictional utopia is signaled by the ultimate apocalypse or ultimate victory over the unknown. Because I am using the term apocalyptic as inclusive of Frye's demonic order, I see the creation of both visionary utopias and dystopias as exercises of the apocalyptic imagination.

The qualitative Heaven or Hell polarity, which is the particular concern of all apocalyptic writers and an incidental of all writers, becomes for the science-fiction writer the opposition between "utopia" and dystopia. Because the science-fiction writer is uniquely involved with matters of quantitative change, the question that inevitably arises is whether a particular different reality is better or worse than the reality the writer and the reader knows. In other words, the apocalyptic character of the science-fiction writer is a consequence of the hand-in-glove relationship between quantitative and qualitative change. The bulk of science fiction presents other worlds in space and time and so falls within this section of my argument. Char-

[4] See Northrop Frye, *The Return of Eden: Five Essays on Milton's Epics* (Toronto, 1965), pp. 39–40.

acteristically, these apocalyptic worlds provide a satiric
distortion of the "real" world and are "utopian" to the
extent that all works of satire, while pointing to a normative state, often also point to a "utopian" alternative.

America once appeared to provide a utopian alternative.
Such was not and is not the case, but utopian fiction accounts for an important stream in American literature,
particularly during the nineteenth century. Examples
might range from Twain's *The Curious Republic of Gon-
dour* (1878) to the conception of Serenia in Melville's
Mardi (1849). This interest in utopia, while not itself
science-fictional, does encourage a science-fictional translation or embodiment. Hence, the utopian tradition in
America is important to my over-all rationalization for
emphasizing the American character of science fiction. In
Chapter 5 I attempt to explore the complicated question
of utopian fiction, purely considered, and the various
"utopian" aspects of science fiction.

Thus far I have justified my calling other material
realities apocalyptic because of the degree to which they
relate to visionary realities and the qualitative states of
Heaven and Hell. I might in conclusion reverse direction
and advance the historical argument whereby the popular conception of the apocalyptic has been increasingly
secularized. The very idea of utopia and the belief that
such a place might exist in a future America or other
geographical location, as implied by the concept of millen-
nialism, provides strong evidence for the secularization of
apocalyptic thought. If previously the sense of an apocalyptic reality included the belief in positive new worlds
elsewhere or elsewhen, the negative aspect of apocalyptic
thought, with its emphasis on destruction, Hell, and chaos,
today enjoys a revitalized secular acceptance.

Within recent history our notion of the end of the world
as something man himself may instigate, detracts considerably from the visionary coloration of a possible apocalypse. In a very real sense, the atomic bomb completed
the process of secularization that apocalyptic thinking has
undergone since medieval times. Consequently I submit

that either the word apocalyptic has lost its meaning entirely and should become obsolete or, if not, that it can be used coherently only in the sense defined by this book.

Secularized versions of the end of the world are of course a staple of science fiction and as such are treated centrally in Chapter 6, which presumes to lay out the basic "plot" of science fiction—its movement from dystopia through catastrophe to other worlds which are primarily simply different and avoid the extremes of utopia and dystopia, to a visionary "utopian" reality. Classic works of American literature that might be conceived as contributing to this "plot" include *Symzonia: A Voyage of Discovery,* which has already cropped up in my discussion of Poe; Melville's *Mardi;* and two time-travel satires, Twain's *A Connecticut Yankee in King Arthur's Court* and Henry James' *The Sense of the Past. Mardi* is of interest here because it involves the direct confrontation of old and new worlds and reveals Melville's understanding that the discovery of a new world has destructive consequences for the old world. Chapter 38 of *Mardi* (where the transition takes place) is called "The Sea on Fire" and features the St. Elmo's-fire phenomenon, which also occurs in *Moby-Dick.* Symbolically understood, an old world is being consumed. It seems safe to hypothesize that fires occur in all of H. G. Wells' early romances because he, too, appreciated the apocalyptic consequences of an awareness of new realities.[5] It is, then, perhaps particularly relevant to our ambiguous, secularized understanding of the apocalyptic that, while atomic power might destroy our world, the same power might allow a remnant of humanity to escape the conflagration and seek a new and better Earth amid a new view of the heavens.

[5] Bernard Bergonzi corrects V. S. Pritchett's remark "that there are fires in all of Wells' early romances, except *The Island of Dr. Moreau*" in *The Early H. G. Wells* (Manchester, England, 1961), p. 109.

5. Utopian Fantasy as Millennial Motive and Science-Fictional Motif

I

In expelling the artists from his ideal republic, Plato established one of the now clichéd conditions of virtually all subsequent utopias. Creativity, particularly in its written form, is a subversive activity, destructive of utopia. By the same token, utopia is the death of literature and other forms of creativity. Consequently, more often than not, there are simply no artists to be expelled. Julian West's statement of the problem in *Looking Backward* to 1887 from the utopian world of the year 2000 may be considered representative. After reading a work entitled *Penthesilia*, by an author named Berrian, which the utopians of 2000 consider a masterpiece, West pointedly refrains from any indication of its merits or plot, being impressed not so much with what is in the book as with what is left out:

> The story-writers of my day would have deemed the making of bricks without straw a light task compared with the construction of a romance from which should be excluded all effects drawn from the contrasts of wealth and poverty, education and ignorance, coarseness and refinement, high and low, all motives drawn from social pride and ambition, the desire of being richer or the fear of being poorer, together with sordid anxieties of any sort for one's self or others; a romance in which there should, indeed, be love galore, but love unfretted by artificial barriers created by differences of station or possessions, owning no other law but that of the heart (p. 103).[1]

[1] See Robert C. Elliot's edition of Edward Bellamy, *Looking*

An earlier occasion, on which West is immersed in "the pages of Dickens" (p. 90), provides, albeit unintentionally, the ironic measure of what is lost. The limited possibilities suggested by Berrian's work apply to the genre itself. Just as there can be no worthwhile literature written in a utopian situation, so there can be no fictional construct of utopia, in which the utopian design is strictly maintained, that is of much artistic value. An incredibly dull work entitled *One of "Berrian's" Novels* (1890), by Mrs. C. H. Stone, one of Bellamy's admirers, would seem to demonstrate my dual point here.

In addition, as George Orwell realized, there is a linguistic problem. Words are inherently ambiguous, and the creation of interesting literature depends largely upon the exploitation of this ambiguity. The verbal formulation of a utopian society involves immediately the introduction of a corrosive equivocation. Considered realistically, the utopian construct turns against itself to reveal a dystopian underside. To some degree, the satiric attack that the author of a utopian fiction is implicitly directing against his own society becomes deflected and seeks to undermine the ideal society. The paucity of imaginative outlets that the genre affords results in a deadening similarity between one utopia and another and the production of clichés that come to assume the self-destructive tone of parody. The very term Thomas More invented, with its compromising pun on the Greek *ou topos* meaning "no place" and the Greek *eu topos* meaning "good place," points to the topsy-turvy elements of irony and paradox that characterize utopian writing but also threaten the overthrow of utopia. It would seem, then, that while the utopian theme negates possibilities of dissonance and narrative complication, the operational techniques and conditions of a literary construct work to reintroduce such conflict and complexity.

Of particular paradoxical potency is the fact that the

Backward: 2000–1887 (Boston, 1966) for all parenthetical references to this work, originally published in 1888.

utopian impulse, while responsible for a body of literature that can only be described as peripheral and lacklus-
ter, is of major importance in the areas of historical,
political, sociological, and theological philosophy. Karl
Mannheim, for example, argues that historical progress is
a consequence of the utopian orientation of the aspiring
classes firing their various revolutionary thrusts against an
establishment ideology.[2] American history would seem to
represent the apotheosis of this process. From the early
days of colonization through the War of Independence
and the Civil War to the present, utopian dreams have led
the way. *Looking Backward* is but the most influential
among hundreds of other American utopian fictions that
express a dominant element in the human consciousness.
But, in reality, an established utopia is an illusion, albeit
an illusion of major motivational importance. Many fictional utopias, on the other hand, claim to be true. I am
speaking here primarily of the so-called science-fictional
utopias—"so-called" because utopian fiction, certainly in
its original form, is not generically related to science
fiction. To say that utopia is a place where everybody lives
happily ever after, points to the true place of the genre:
beside the fairy tale, as a branch of fantasy. Plato, More,
and the early utopians are writing propagandistic fantasy, a form on the borderlines of fiction and the non-
fictional discourse of social, political, historical, or economic theory. Their theoretical models in a fantasy frame
acknowledge what history demonstrates, that man both
individually and collectively dreams impossible dreams of
an ideal state that do, nevertheless, have their material
effect. Plato's *Republic* may very well strike the modern
reader as an unbearably totalitarian state, but because it
is written as a self-proclaimed fantasy, the reader has no
alternative but to suspend all logical reactions and accept
such a state as utopia. Actually, every writer, however
tangentially, embodies in his work a private utopian vision.

[2] See Karl Mannheim, *Ideology and Utopia: an Introduction
to the Sociology of Knowledge,* tr. by Louis Wirth and Edward
Shils (London, 1936).

The truth of such a vision depends not upon its realizability, but upon its expression of an unchangeable aspect of human psychology. In this sense, utopian fantasies are always true.

As an essentially non-dramatic form of fantasy, utopian writing is of little fictional interest unless embodied as a motif in mimetic or apocalyptic literature. Utopia, in its traditional mainstream sense as an ideal (not merely better) form of social organization, is an impossibility if conceived as the basic subject of a mimetic or apocalyptic novel, although it may be presented as a motivational fantasy, in the psychological sense, on the part of the author or his protagonist(s). In any attempt to present "objectively" the opposition-free society, which utopia entails, outside the genre of fantasy, the ambiguities and conflicts characteristic of the dynamics of literature become destructively operational. Certainly, there is no such thing as utopian science fiction, given my sense of science fiction as an apocalyptic form. This latter assertion requires the argumentation it will receive in the balance of this analysis, because, in most people's minds, science fiction and utopian fiction go together.

In an unfortunate attempt to dignify the latter genre, the genealogies of science fiction and utopian fiction have often been erroneously conflated. It should be apparent that the literary history of utopia includes many works, such as Plato's *Republic*, More's *Utopia*, fictions celebrating the Golden Age, and Marvell's poem *The Garden*, that have no place in the pedigree of science fiction. One might broadly distinguish between utopias of rearrangement, which combine human virtues with existent environmental elements, and loosely "extrapolative" utopias, which appear to be science-fictional because they combine human virtues with non-existent technological inventions. But the fundamental irrationality of all utopian fiction invalidates the science-fiction classification. Dystopias, on the other hand, in our fallen world, do make convincing science fiction. It follows that the emphasis on dystopian writing in our time is less a reflection of an increasingly unappeal-

ing reality and a stunting of the utopian imagination, as
Chad Walsh and others have suggested, than a consequence of the startling growth of science fiction over the
past hundred years.[3] The dystopian emphasis might be
viewed as an axiomatic result of the attempt of the utopian
writer to shift his vision from the mode of fantasy into the
realistic and apocalyptic mode of science fiction.[4] *Brave
New World* and *1984* are examples of dystopian science
fiction. The ease with which utopia slides into dystopia
obscures the generic transition that simultaneously takes
place.

The relationship between utopia and satire provides an
additional explanation in terms of purely literary dynamics
for the shift from utopian to dystopian fiction. This relationship is particularly evident in the two-part structure
of More's *Utopia*. In the first part, More's direct attack on
contemporary institutions makes overt the criticism implied by the utopia of part two. The first part is necessary
because the satiric factor can be only weakly present in
any description of an ideal society, since reality and the
airy fabric of utopia are mutually damaging. As in so
many other cases, the conditions of satire have been most
economically defined by Northrop Frye: "Satire demands
at least a token fantasy, a context which the reader recognizes as grotesque, and at least an implicit moral standard, the latter being essential in a militant attitude to
experience."[5] Satire, as an aspect of what I am calling the
apocalyptic tradition of literature, relates the mimetic and
the fantastic traditions. The "other worlds" of satire do
exist in a rational relationship to the real world. The

---

[3] See Kingsley Amis, *New Maps of Hell;* Chad Walsh, *From
Utopia to Nightmare* (New York, 1962); and Mark R. Hillegas,
The Future as Nightmare: H. G. Wells and the Anti-Utopians.
[4] Compare John R. May's position: "The utopian concept
emasculated apocalypse by anticipating a millennium without
catastrophe and for that reason . . . should not be considered
apocalyptic at all." See *Towards a New Earth,* p. 210.
[5] *The Anatomy of Criticism,* p. 224.

literary value of utopian fiction depends largely upon its satiric potential, and that potential, as is well illustrated in Swift's *Gulliver's Travels*, is best realized through the creation of worlds that, as distorted mirror images of our own, are somewhat less than ideal. Dystopian fiction allows for the full expression of the satiric impulse ambiguously present in utopian fiction.

There is, however, a form of utopia, deriving from the convention of a pastoral Arcadia, which is sufficiently different from the Plato-More model of the perfect city as to deserve another name, and which may carry realistic conviction. The Okalbian valley in George Tucker's *A Voyage to the Moon* (1827), the initially unspoiled world in Cooper's *The Crater* (1847), and William Dean Howells' Altruria in *A Traveller to Altruria* (1894) and *Through the Eye of a Needle* (1907) are the best-known American examples. Although neither Thoreau's *Walden* nor Hawthorne's *The Blithedale Romance* lays claim to the establishment of utopia in any region other than that of the mind, both suggest the possibility of a better society in a pastoral environment. This possibility is often equated with another "utopia" in historical time, the millennium, which carries conviction because of the force of religious belief. As I have already indicated, utopian visions have often assumed historical importance, but never more so than when they are linked to a millennial program.[6] John's Apocalypse, vague at best, is particularly unclear as to whether the millennium occurs before or after the end of the world. Joachim of Floris (c. 1135–c. 1202) was responsible for the influential but heretical pronouncement that the millennium, which he called the third and final stage of human history, comes first. Utopia, then, would correspond to the millennium. This secularized sociopolitical conception of the apocalyptic became extraordinarily influential in both life and literature. The coming

[6] See Ernest Lee Tuveson, *Millennium and Utopia, a Study in the Background of the Idea of Progress* (Los Angeles, 1949); Norman Cohn, *The Pursuit of the Millennium;* and T. S. Molnar, *Utopia, the Perennial Heresy* (New York, 1967).

millennium, although technically outside human control, might, in a limited sense, be achieved.

To assume that the millennium follows the destruction of the world, provides the corresponding dystopian eschatology, which science fiction favors. Science-fiction cities tend toward Babylon rather than toward the New Jerusalem. But the New Jerusalem is an image of a transcendental, not a utopian, reality, and its only equivalent in science fiction is Northrup Frye's image "of a city of which the stars are suburbs"—this being science fiction's form of the total, embracive "utopian" vision at which all of literature aims.[7] This concept, celebrated in Isaac Asimov's *Foundation Trilogy*, Blish's *Cities in Flight*, and Stapledon's fiction, is generally based on a pattern of evolutionary progression that goes beyond the strictly utopian to that visionary plateau of "men like gods."[8]

II

Because "utopian" literature is so stereotyped, it makes more sense to examine one example of the genre in detail rather than to attempt the kind of general survey of the field that is characteristic of most work on the subject. Here, as earlier, my representative example is Bellamy's *Looking Backward*, which has the advantage of according with the parameters of this discussion. It is an American work of unusual influence that attempts to present a Baconian technological development of Plato's and More's fantasy of a perfect city as science fiction by invoking millennial belief. Certainly Bellamy's novel *Dr. Heidenhoff's Process* (1880) and much of the material he included in *The Blindman's World and Other Stories* (1898) is straight science fiction. The many critical re-

---

[7] *The Educated Imagination* (Toronto, 1963), p. 33.
[8] Cf. the seventh and eighth stages of "The Cosmogony of the Future" according to a consensus of science-fiction writers as interpreted by Donald A. Wollheim in *The Universe Makers: Science Fiction Today* (New York, 1971), pp. 42–44.

joinders that *Looking Backward* elicited give some index
of the difficulties involved in transposing a vision of an
ideal society into a form of literature that adheres to
human standards of credibility.

Actually, from any literary point of view, the detailed
workings of Bellamy's "utopia," as with any other, are of
little interest, and the extended lecture of Dr. Leete, Julian
West's guide to utopia, may be briefly summarized: the
golden age of socialism, peace, and prosperity has arrived
on the basis of an economic equality achieved by a system
of social regimentation. The transformation is world wide,
but Bellamy instances the city of Boston. From the age of
twenty-one to forty-five, all citizens are conscripted into
the Industrial Army, the ultimate machine. Although an
individual's work load and ultimate rank are geared to his
ability, his monetary reward conforms to a standardized
living wage in the form of credit cards, which continues
after retirement. Everybody works as efficiently as possible, because love of duty and a desire for the common
good are indoctrinated principles earlier imparted by a
system of state education. Members of liberal profes-
sions and artists, who "obtain remissions of industrial
service" (p. 116), work outside the army. Ten depart-
ments in the army are concerned with the problems of
production and distribution. The degree of production is
geared to consumer demand, and the price of an article
is fixed by the cost of production. As for distribution,
products may be ordered from samples displayed at large
supermarket-type stores. In charge of the army is the
President, an ex-department head, "elected by vote of all
the men of the nation who [being under twenty-one or
over forty-five] are not connected with the industrial
army" (p. 115). Incidental features of Bellamy's utopian
society include the disappearance of advertising, equality
of the sexes, and the elimination of disease and crime. Underlying all is the fantasy of human perfectibility.

Science fiction will simply not allow for such a fundamentally irrational assumption. To read *Looking Backward*
as science fiction, as Bellamy seems to have intended, in-

volves making two quite different assumptions. One possibility is to assume that the inhabitants of Bellamy's ideal city have all been in some sense lobotomized, that they have been brainwashed into believing that they live in utopia. In this case, from the point of view of an outsider, Bellamy's futuristic Boston is actually a dystopia. The alternative possibility, and one that, under certain conditions, might salvage utopia, would be to suppose that a further process of human evolution has taken place, that man has become spiritualized. Indeed Bellamy does provide evidence for this assumption in the course of Dr. Leete's tendentious explanation of how mankind, having passed through an unprecedented period of "moral and material evolution . . . from the old order to the new in the early part of this century," has attained "a new plane of existence" (p. 97): "We are like a child which has just learned to stand upright and to walk . . . humanity has entered on a new phase of spiritual development, an evolution of higher faculties, the very existence of which in human nature our ancestors scarcely suspected" (pp. 174–75).

That Bellamy has adapted Darwin's theory of evolution, "one of the great laws of nature" (p. 161), to a millennial timetable is particularly apparent from the ecstatic sentiments that conclude this peroration: "For twofold is the return of man to God 'who is our home,' the return of the individual by the way of death, and the return of the race by the fulfilment of the evolution, when the divine secret hidden in the germ shall be perfectly unfolded. . . . The long and weary winter of the race is ended. Its summer has begun. Humanity has burst the chrysalis. The heavens are before it" (p. 175). This formulation does accord with the requirement that apocalyptic literature generally and science fiction in particular meet standards of credibility.

The millennial touch serves to make Bellamy's perfect society credible on the basis of religious faith. To question this mechanical millennium is, then, a blasphemous act. On hearing that the moral improvement of the race makes it difficult for even criminals to lie (a somewhat paradoxi-

cal assertion), West proclaims: "If lying has gone out of
fashion, this is indeed the 'new heavens and the new
earth wherein dwelleth righteousness,' which the prophet
foretold." Nor does Dr. Leete contradict this interpretation: "Such is, in fact, the belief of some persons nowa-
days. . . . They hold that we have entered upon the millennium, and the theory from their point of view does not
lack plausibility" (p. 123). Given that the incredible
changes to which West is here witness came about in the
early years of the nineteenth century, one might wonder
why his experiences are of the year 2000. Apparently
Bellamy wants things both ways. On the one hand, the
year 2000 augments the millennial expectations that help
make his utopia a plausible "paradise of order, equity, and
felicity" (p. 137). The same "come the millennium" optimism applies to references to "this bimillennial epoch"
(p. 4) and "many a millennium" (p. 24) and "many a
previous millennium" (p. 29). On the other hand, Bellamy
has hopes that the transformation he foresees may occur
within his own lifetime. According to his "Postscript"
"*Looking Backward*, although in form a fanciful romance,
is intended, in all seriousness, as a forecast, in accordance
with the principles of evolution, of the next stage in the
industrial and social development of humanity, especially
in this country; and no part of it is believed by the author to be better supported by the indications of probability than the implied prediction that the dawn of the new
era is already near at hand, and that the full day will
swiftly follow" (p. 201). It would seem that although Bellamy's utopia is millennial in the sense that it occurs within
historical time and takes the form of a "world-transforma-
tion" (p. 90) both "moral and material" (p. 3), the
equation between the world in the year 2000 and the
millennium is essentially metaphorical, part of the machinery of fictive credibility. It is also a part of that under-
mining substructure that is an inevitable consequence of
attempts to communicate utopian designs in the quasi-
realistic form of apocalyptic fiction.

There would seem to be some metaphorical inconsistency in presenting the millennium as a perfect city. Our only acceptable image of a perfect city is the bejeweled New Jerusalem, existing outside of historical time. The prospect of a perfect city within historical time opens up the possibility of various destructive contradictions, perhaps ultimately reducible to the dichotomy between the natural and the artificial. Only in the context of an atemporal, visionary reality can these oppositions be turned to positive account by the transforming power of mystical paradox. Hence the force of the New Jerusalem concept. The only workable concept we have of a perfected existence within human time is again religiously based, but it is to be found in Genesis and not directly in the Book of Revelation. Pastoral or Arcadian models of utopia derive their conviction largely from belief in the Garden of Eden. It follows that the only acceptable picture of a perfected human existence during the millennium must be drawn according to pastoral conventions. There are simply no conventions appertaining to a perfect historical city that apply.

Some of the cracks in Bellamy's "historical" city are stated directly; others are embodied in the treacherous form of metaphor. For example, Dr. Leete does admit that not everybody is ready for utopia: "As for actual neglect of work, positively bad work, or other overt remissness on the part of men incapable of generous motives, the discipline of the industrial army is far too strict to allow anything whatever of the sort. A man able to do duty, and persistently refusing, is sentenced to solitary imprisonment on bread and water till he consents" (p. 78). Order is maintained by means of a policing department called the "inspectorate" (p. 115), which sounds like another name for the Nazi SS. West's recognition that in 2000 "everybody is a part of a system" (p. 107) suggests a mechanical analogy, which can only detract from the dignity of man. The damaging symbolism implicit in this metaphor becomes rather more overt in West's description of a warehouse: "It is like a gigantic mill, into the hopper of which goods are being constantly poured by the train-load and ship-load, to issue at the other end in packages of pounds and ounces, yards and inches, pints and gallons, corresponding to the infinitely complex personal needs of half a million people" (p. 109). Given that this analogy occurs in a fictional work with pretensions toward realism rather than fantasy, it is hard not to apply the conception of "a gigantic mill" to the entire society and, recalling Blake's "dark Satanic mills" along the way, to convert Bellamy's supposed utopia into a conveyor-belted vision of hell. It would seem that, to the extent that Bellamy's use of the fictional devices of metaphor and indirect statement are successful in conveying a believable impression of a futurist Boston, they convert a "utopia" into a dystopia.

Because a utopian society does not of itself allow for much in the way of plot development, whatever plot development may exist in a utopian fiction is either extraneous or in some way metaphoric. Bellamy has been particularly successful in inventing a plot that functions in a supportive metaphorical relationship to his utopian purpose but at the occasional metaphor maker's risk of ambiguity and unwanted inference. What might be called "the transition to utopia" allows, more than any other aspect of the utopian theme, for fictional development, and when the transition is temporal rather than spatial, various kinds of science-fictional possibilities arise.[9] Two developmental actions are involved. On the one hand, there is the business of West's individual transition, on the other there is the question, very much slighted by Bellamy, as to how the world-wide transition to a utopian society was made.

[9] Richard Gerber speaks of "the *journey to utopia*" as a means of creating the "illusion of reality." See his *Utopian Fantasy: A Study of English Utopian Fiction Since the End of the Nineteenth Century* (London, 1955), pp. 86–89 and the chapter entitled "Symbolical Journeys," pp. 105–12. See also Philip Babcock Gove, *The Imaginary Voyage in Prose Fiction* (London, 1941), pp. 156–61.

III

   The narrative device of placing a representative from
the bad old world in the new utopian world and chroni-
cling the open-mouthed astonishment and somewhat slap-
stick action that results, is another of the many clichés of
the genre. Bellamy improves dramatically on this perform-
ance by concentrating on the psychological reaction of his
protagonist. The reader is made to feel the alienating
effects of the temporal dislocations West undergoes, and
thus Bellamy gains a certain measure of sympathetic
identification between West and the reader. Indeed the
emphasis Bellamy places on a plausible protagonist is
further evidence that he conceived *Looking Backward* not
as a fantasy but as science fiction.

   West's situation at the opening of the story is symbolic
of the unhappy nature of his times. He is in love with and
engaged to Edith Bartlett. Their marriage "only waited on
the completion of the house which I was building for our
occupancy . . ." (p. 9). Labor problems, strikes in particular, delay the day of completion, and consequently the
wedding is yet to occur when West leaves the Boston of
1887. Symbolically translated, of course, these events indicate that, in 1887, the economic and social situation
prevents human fulfillment and happiness. Stranded in
the year 2000, West falls in love with Dr. Leete's daughter, also named Edith, who turns out to be the "great-
grand-daughter" of West's "lost love, Edith Bartlett" (p.
180). This is the kind of genealogical coincidence with
which writers of time-travel science fiction have played
around *ad nauseam*.[10] Bellamy is interested in making
the symbolic point that, in his utopia, the nineteenth-cen-

10 See, for a particularly ingenious example, Alfred Bester,
"The Men Who Murdered Mohammed," in *Voyagers in Time*,
ed. by Robert Silverberg (New York, 1967). The protagonist
makes use of his time-travel device to murder someone in the
present by wiping out his progenitors in the past.

tury impediments that stood in the way of happiness do not apply. We are given to understand at the conclusion of the novel that West does achieve the American dream his surname represents, and marries the second Edith. The only "impediment" that comes between their engagement and their marriage is again a nineteenth-century disturbance, but this time only in the form of a dream.

The dream mechanism, on which the plot of the novel turns, is itself of metaphoric importance. It is a reflection of the nervous nature of the times that West, in the nineteenth century, is "a confirmed sufferer from insomnia." West claims, "I could not have slept in the city at all, with its never ceasing nightly noises, if I had been obliged to use an upstairs chamber" (p. 14). Consequently he has a sleeping chamber built under the foundations of his house. The hierarchical arrangement between this "subterranean room" and the "upper world" (pp. 14–15) would appear to establish some Freudian distinction between a subconscious world of wish fulfillment and a conscious reality. After two nights without sleep, West customarily called on Dr. Pillsbury, a "Professor of Animal Magnetism," to put him in a trance. It is a trance, however, from which he has to be awakened by "a reversal of the mesmerizing process" (p. 15). However, one night in 1887 there is an accident, and the house burns down, leaving West's sleeping chamber undamaged but hidden. Presumably West's Negro servant, who also lives in the house and has been instructed how to rouse West, dies in the "conflagration" (p. 28). West, between mesmerists, since Pillsbury has taken an appointment in a distant city, sleeps on until he is discovered and awakened, in the year 2000. The reader has every reason to expect that West's subsequent experiences are a dream, particularly given the architectural symbolism of the house with its "recess [of mind?] in the foundation walls connecting with my chamber" (p. 28) and the "magnetism" (p. 27) of Edith Leete's beauty. But the fire would appear to portend that a genuine apocalypse of mind is in progress. West's subsequent grateful awareness that he is "not still awaiting the end of

the world in a living tomb" (p. 107) confirms the metaphorical relationship between the Apocalypse and his
awakening revelation. Although no actual cause for the
fire is specified, a clue is later provided by Dr. Leete as to
the metaphorical cause: "It was the misfortune of your
contemporaries that they had to cement their business
fabric with a material which an accident might at any
moment turn into an explosive. They were in the plight of
a man building a house [this was West's situation] with
dynamite for mortar, for credit can be compared with
nothing else" (p. 144). The logic of metaphor here implies
that the barbaric economic system of the nineteenth century has resulted in a destructive and bloody revolution,
and that such an event preceded the world transformation
that has taken place. Bellamy is strangely reticent about
the transitional phase in the development of utopia, but
on the occasions on which the subject does arise, he attempts, by means of further metaphorical analogies, to give
the impression that the transition was peaceable. As I shall
indicate shortly, here, as elsewhere, Bellamy's metaphors
have a destructive logic of their own.

My present concern is with the apocalyptic revolution
within West's head, which Bellamy handles with some
skill. West loses his sense of identity in attempting to
adapt to the reality of his new world: "There are no words
for the mental torture I endured during this helpless,
eyeless groping for myself in a boundless void. No other
experience of the mind gives probably anything like the
sense of absolute intellectual arrest from the loss of mental fulcrum, a starting point of thought, which comes during such a momentary obscuration of the sense of one's
identity" (pp. 46–47). The destruction of his world of
mind occasions "an intolerable swimming of the brain" in
"a weltering sea": "In my mind, all had broken loose,
habits of feeling, associations of thought, ideas of persons
and things, all had dissolved and lost coherence and were
seething together in apparently irretrievable chaos." (p.
47), West is gripped by the kind of double vision that
Twain, no doubt influenced by Bellamy, exploits in *A Con-*

necticut Yankee. West has the idea that his "identity was double," mental images of old and new Boston contend for reality, as do the two Ediths: "There was nothing I saw which was not blurred in this way" (p. 48). There is no doubt that all this psychological material gives an excellent fictionally concrete impression of West's experience, but precisely because *Looking Backward* is a work of fiction, it may also function metaphorically in a manner destructive to its one-dimensional, "utopian" subject matter. The vacuous characterization of Dr. Leete and his family as representative inhabitants of utopia suggests a loss of identity more crippling than West's, because they are unaware of their loss. The suggestive value of literature demands that the reader apply the alarm with which West reacts to his loss of individuality to the loss of individuality that Bellamy's utopian society appears to effect.

A further aesthetic accomplishment has a similarly unintentional rebound effect. At the end of the novel, West finds himself back in the nineteenth-century hell of Boston, ultimately to discover, to his considerable relief and to the surprise of the reader, who now assumes conventionally that West has awakened from a dream of the twentieth century, that it was all a dream—he really is in the year 2000. Unfortunately and inevitably, Bellamy's description of the horrific dream with its "pestilential rookeries" (p. 195) and walking dead has a vitality and a reality that his description of the "utopian" actuality lacks completely. The problem is the same one that stumped Milton in *Paradise Lost*, appearing to make him, unconsciously, of the devil's party. In the visionary realm of *Paradise Lost*, where most things are a mystery, the apparent inconsistency is not particularly harmful. But in a work of science fiction, such as *Looking Backward* purports to be, the reality principle makes such contradictions destructively operative.

Interestingly enough, West's dream tour of nineteenth-century Boston, the equivalent of "Bedlam" (p. 190), "Golgotha" (p. 196), and "Chaos and Old Night" (p. 199), does contain an object lesson concerning the vagaries and inconsistency of figurative language. Standing in "a recess" (p. 192) of a back wall, allied symbolically perhaps to the earlier "recess in the foundation walls" (p. 28) adjoining his sleeping chamber except that his present experience is truly of the mind, West is observing the handling of money when he is addressed by the director of the bank:

> "Interesting sight, isn't it, Mr. West," he said. "Wonderful piece of mechanism; I find it so myself. I like sometimes to stand and look on at it just as you are doing. It's a poem, sir, a poem, that's what I call it. Did you ever think, Mr. West, that the bank is the heart of the business system? From it and to it, in endless flux and reflux, the life blood goes. It is flowing in now. It will flow out again in the morning," and pleased with his little conceit, the old man passed on smiling (p. 192).

Bellamy apparently did not apply to his own practice the recognition here that little conceits do not convey objective meaning. There is one aspect of his Boston nightmare that does delight West, a "mechanism" of another kind:

> A regiment was passing. It was the first sight in that dreary day which had inspired me with any other emotions than wondering pity and amazement. Here at last were order and reason, an exhibition of what intelligent cooperation can accomplish. The people who stood looking on with kindling faces. . . . Could they fail to see that it was their perfect concert of action, their organization under one control, which made these men the tremendous engine they were, able to vanquish a mob ten times as numerous? (p. 194).

Subsequent history has totally reversed the utopian import of this particular image, an image, incidentally, that may be construed as a further detail pointing to the possibility that Bellamy's "utopia" was founded on a revolutionary carnage.

Bellamy's manipulation of the dream convention and the reader's ultimate discovery that the dream, in a dual sense, is real, that West is genuinely "looking backward" from the year 2000, is the basic credibility device that removes the book from the realm of dream fantasy into the region of science fiction. The perspective is that of the historian, not the futurologist. As West reflects, "One can look back a thousand years easier than forward fifty" (p. 106) and, he might have added, with a greater chance of being believed. But although a reader will accept West's transition, the Boston of the future, the possibility that man has attained a new evolutionary plane, and the fact that the future Bostonians believe their world to be a utopia, the detailed technological nature of this "utopia" can only realistically imply a dystopian society in which the citizens have evolved, or rather devolved, into machines. A reader cannot help but believe the utopians deceived. That a spiritually advanced society should base its happiness on a greater material and technological efficiency is incongruous. This is the root conflict at the heart of the various ambiguities inherent in Bellamy's attempt to describe a utopian society in a realistic mode. The theme of rebellion within a technological utopia, as treated by both Huxley and Orwell, merely makes explicit an abiding characteristic of the genre. The verbal fabric of a utopian fiction is in a constant incipient state of conflict or insurrection, which is nullified when presented as a fantasy, or transcended in visionary apocalyptic writing, but encouraged in the apocalyptic mode of science fiction.

Utopian science fiction is a semantic impossibility. The mistake depends upon confusing quantitative changes relating to matters of convenience and productivity, which scientific invention can bring about and which is the concern of science fiction, with major qualitative social change, which is the concern of utopian fiction. Northrop Frye raises the problem: "There is however something of

a donkey's carrot in attaching utopian feelings to a machinery of production largely concerned with consumer
goods." He instances the prediction of radio in *Looking
Backward* as an example of "how something commonplace
to us could be part of a utopian romance" to demonstrate
that "while technology has advanced far beyond the
wildest utopian dreams even of the last century, the essential quality of human life has hardly improved to the
point that it could be called utopian."[11] Bellamy himself
skirts the same issue in the discussion about ability in
relation to remuneration. Dr. Leete explains why, in spite
of differing abilities and capacities for production, everybody receives the same remuneration:

> the amount of the resulting product has nothing what-
> ever to do with the question, which is one of desert.
> Desert is a moral question, and the amount of the
> product a material quantity. It would be an extraordi-
> nary sort of logic which should try to determine a moral
> question by a material standard. The amount of the
> effort alone is pertinent to the question of desert. All
> men who do their best, do the same (p. 57).

In the case of Bellamy's telephone-type radios, which
syphon music and sermons to the individual's house, it is
the human element that determines whether such a radio
functions purely as an instrument of pleasure and relaxa-
tion or in the service of a dystopia to instill propaganda.
In Bacon's *New Atlantis*, "a picture of our salvation in
heaven" set "beyond the old world and the new" but related to America, "the great Atlantis," scientific marvels
perfected in Salomon's House are not the cause but a
consequence of and at the service of a fantasy utopian
society.[12] As I have already indicated, the only kind of
temporal environment that of itself signifies positive moral

[11] "Varieties of Literary Utopias," in *Utopias and Utopian
Thought*, ed. by Frank E. Manuel (Boston, 1966), pp. 30–31.
[12] See *New Atlantis*, reprinted in *Famous Utopias*, ed. by
Charles M. Andrews (New York, no date), pp. 240, 242, 247.

values is some form of pastoral landscape. By association
with the Garden of Eden and the general sense that the
natural is innately good and preferable to the artificial,
the belief that a pastoral society is somehow ideal has
attained the force of a convention. It is part of the nature
of literary conventions that they resist logical attack.
There is, I repeat, no corresponding convention regarding
a historical technological society. Hence the difficulties
the reader experiences in accepting West's transition to a
technological society that is simultaneously real and utopian.

IV

The psychological realism that Bellamy brings to his
treatment of West's transition to "utopia" is not balanced
by a corresponding historical and social realism in his discussion of the transformational transition society has undergone. In most cases, the millennial motivation for social change has resulted in bloody revolution, justified
supposedly by the loosening of Satan scheduled to pre-
cede the millennium in the Apocalypse. Bellamy presumably felt that a utopian society founded on bloodshed is
somewhat compromised from the start. Consequently, although he rarely speaks directly about the period of transformation, the various metaphorical analogies he uses
seem to imply that some kind of natural revolution of
consciousness has occurred. Unfortunately, as always, Bellamy's metaphoric analogies go their own sabotaging way.

At the beginning of his book, in an extended parable
Bellamy compares nineteenth-century society to an unstable stagecoach "which the masses of humanity were
harnessed to and dragged toilsomely along a very hilly
and sandy road" (p. 6). The rich occupied the com-
fortably airy seats on top, for which there was much
competition and which were therefore rather insecure:
"at every sudden jolt of the coach persons were slipping
out of them and falling to the ground, where they were

instantly compelled to take hold of the rope and help to
drag the coach on which they had before ridden so
pleasantly." In addition, while covering "a bad place in
the road" or "a particularly steep hill, . . . there was always some dangers [sic] . . . of a general overturn in
which all would lose their seats" (p. 7). Clearly the
analogy points to the likelihood that millennial Boston
was preceded by something like the October Revolution.

But in Bellamy's next analogy an attempt is made to
remove the element of violence involved in such "a general overturn." In the area of commercial transactions,
according to Dr. Leete, "Formerly, society was a pyramid
poised on its apex. All the gravitations of human nature
were constantly tending to topple it over, and it could
be maintained upright, or rather upwrong (if you will
pardon the feeble witticism), by an elaborate system of
constantly renewed props and buttresses and guy-ropes in
the form of laws . . . which were constantly breaking
down or becoming ineffectual through some shifting of
the strain. Now society rests on its base, and is in as little
need of artificial supports as the everlasting hills" (p. 127).
For a reader who recalls the earlier image of overturn,
with the lucky few on top and the straining masses below,
this pyramid analogy at first seems to be reversed, particularly if "the toilers of the rope," who pull the carriage
"leaping and plunging under the pitiless lashing of hun-
ger," and "the many who fainted at the rope and were
trampled in the mire" (p. 7), are related, as the turbulent
pressure of metaphor dictates, to the unhappy rope pullers
who built the Egyptian pyramids. To correct this mis-
apprehension and the anarchistic potential it portends, involves taking the analogy in a purely abstract and intellectual manner. Perhaps Bellamy intends this instant
mental transformation as in some way parallel to the
world transformation he is so glibly sliding over.

In Bellamy's "Postscript" he seeks to further elaborate
on the rapid nature of "great national transformations"
(p. 201). Once again Bellamy has recourse to an image
of overturn: "As an iceberg, floating southward from the

frozen North, is gradually undermined by warmer seas, and, become at last unstable, churns the sea to yeast for miles around by the mighty rockings that portend its overturn, so the barbaric industrial and social system, which has come down to us from savage antiquity, undermined by the modern humane spirit, riddled by the criticism of economic science, is shaking the world with convulsions that presage its collapse" (p. 203). As before, Bellamy is attempting to soften that interim period of fiery and violent insurrection which would tarnish his tranquil utopia; but can it be doubted that it is the heat of flowing blood that creates the "warmer seas" where the iceberg melts? References within the narrative to the *fin de siècle* mood that prevailed toward the close of the nineteenth century substantiate the likelihood of mass destruction: "Some . . . observers went so far as to predict an impending social cataclysm. Humanity, they argued, having climbed to the top round of the ladder of civilization, was about to take a header into chaos . . ." (p. 11). "There was a general decay of religious belief. Pale and watery gleams, from skies thickly veiled by doubt and dread, alone lighted up the chaos of earth" (p. 170).

Bellamy does succeed on one occasion in producing a relatively benign metaphor to explain the transition to utopia. It was all a matter of horticulture. According to the parable of "the rose bush of humanity," society underwent a period of transplantation from the noxious swamp of capitalism to the rich soil of socialism: "The vermin and the mildew disappeared, and the bush was covered with most beautiful red roses, whose fragrance filled the world" (p. 174). Unfortunately for Bellamy, this metaphoric statement of man's essential goodness assumes the unstated and certainly unintended belief that men are the kind of vegetables who inhabit utopian Boston. Within the context of realism, Bellamy simply can't win. The story implied in Bellamy's metaphoric treatment of the world's transition to utopia is potentially a much more interesting one than the story he actually wrote. But it would not be a utopian fiction. Rather it would be the story that Jack London wrote in *The Iron Heel* (1907). In London's fine dystopian tale, from the beginning of the twentieth century onward three centuries of revolution, disturbance, and warfare take place before the socialist Brotherhood of Man is established. The supposedly ultimate utopian outcome is not described.

v

It would seem, then, that the dynamics of literature work either to convert the supposed science-fictional or realistic "utopia"—realistic in the sense that the utopia is assumed to be established—into a dystopia, or alternatively, to convert an apocalyptic or mimetic work into a work of fantasy. While science-fictional dystopias abound, there are no genuinely science-fictional utopias. There are, however, cases in which the utopian theme exists as a more or less conventional motif in science-fiction novels in which the whole is of somewhat different character. In these cases, the utopian theme carries greater conviction if, following the lunar existence described by Francis Godwin in his *The Man in the Moone* (1638), it takes on an essentially pastoral rather than technological form. Since a pastoral society, unlike a technological society, is not of itself science-fictional, only as a motif in a larger science-fictional context may it assume a science-fictional coloration. Not surprisingly, there are very few interesting works of science fiction in which a utopian motif figures with any prominence. Perhaps the most successful such work is *Venus Plus X,* by Theodore Sturgeon.

In this novel, Sturgeon makes subtle use of various conventions of the science-fiction genre and of social conventions, particularly sexual conventions. The well-nigh-perfect society of the Ledom, a new form of "humanity," is explained as a consequence of their hermaphroditic sexuality. Everybody is equipped with both male and female sexual organs. Impregnation is a mutual affair.

With the lack of sexual differentiation goes, it is assumed, a corresponding lack of other dichotomies. The setup is comparable with that in Ursula K. LeGuin's more recent novel *The Left Hand of Darkness*, except that in LeGuin's novel the alien bisexuality betokens a visionary awareness rather than an ideal social organization. In a series of alternating chapters devoted to the conventionalized sexual responses of a pair of contemporary American families, Sturgeon presents, as an effective satiric contrast, our alternative and divisive situation. This arrangement serves to disguise the fact that *Venus Plus X* is really a short story skillfully padded out. The utopia theme simply does not allow for very much in the way of narrative elaboration.

Sturgeon is aware that the English language, as it has developed, is incompatible with utopia, and consequently the Ledom don't use it. The Ledom language appears to be scientific in its unusual exactness and avoidance of metaphorical statement. Charlie Johns, the stranger in this utopia, having learned the Ledom language, finds it impossible to translate the idiomatic sentence "That's my ticket home" (p. 56).[13] The only book referred to is a technical manual.

Aesthetic appeal is, however, a function of the total environment, which is essentially pastoral. Johns is first struck by an extensive tree-spotted area of even, springy greensward. There is a technology, however, as instanced by the impossibly curved buildings, which defy the laws of gravity: "nothing was ever square, flat, vertical, or exactly smoooth" (p. 48). Presumably the shapes approximate those found in nature. It transpires that the incredible engineering of Sturgeon's scientifically based fairyland depends upon invisible force fields. By means of a skillful domestication of the impossible, the reality of this utopia insinuates itself. But the technological aspect is incidental, and Johns is informed, ". . . we're not, after all, primarily

[13] All parenthetical references to *Venus Plus X* may be located in the Pyramid Books paperback edition (New York, 1960).

a technological culture" (p. 80). The most important aspect of the Ledom society is an exclusively pastoral retreat known as the "Children's One." The children who inhabit this area with their kindly guardians live in very basic homey cottages like this one: "It lay in a fold of the hills, surrounded by that impeccable greensward, and up its white, low walls, flaming, flowering vines grew. Its roof was pitched and gabled, brown with a dusting of green. There were flower-boxes at the windows, and at one end, the white wall yielded to the charm of fieldstone, tapering up to be a chimney, from which blue smoke drifted" (p. 82). According to Johns' instructor, Philos, the value of such a simple pastoral existence derives from the survival skills it imparts. A dependence on technology stunts such skills. The children, representatives of the future and survival, appear to be objects of worship to the Ledom and at the center of their "charitic religion" (p. 127), with its participatory love celebrations. Although the Ledom don't sleep, they do dream. Philos explains that his people value dreaming as "a mechanism by which the mind detaches itself from reality in order to compare and relate data which in reality cannot be associated. Your literature is full of hallucinatory images of the sort—pigs with wings, human freedom, fire-breathing dragons, the wisdom of the majority, the basilisk, the *golem,* and equality of the sexes" (p. 84), and, it might be added, utopias. Are we, then, experiencing Charlie Johns' dream, or have the Ledom truly succeeded in laying the foundations of a dream? After all, "human freedom," "the wisdom of the majority" and "equality of the sexes" may be dream images, but, except as comparative elements in a dream, such issues are somewhat more substantial—surely more practical— than "pigs with wings," "dragons," and so on.

What of Charlie Johns' role in all this? His transition to "utopia" is at least as abrupt as Julian West's. Johns, an airplane pilot of the mid-twentieth century, blanks out to find himself, on regaining consciousness, in a womblike container. This circumstance might be taken as a pointer

to the psychological origins of the utopian impulse in re-
gression fantasies of a return to the womb.[14] Certainly,
there is something regressive about the name Ledom,
which is "model" spelled backward; about Bellamy's title
Looking Backward; and about Samuel Butler's title
Erehwon, which is "nowhere" (utopia) backward. Because
the environment Johns surveys is futuristic and because
he is a reader of science fiction, he assumes and is encouraged in his assumption that he has been scooped up
by some Ledom time machine and that he is now in
Earth's future. The reader for whom Sturgeon is writing,
similarly habituated to the conventions of science fiction,
goes along with Johns' assumption. Here Sturgeon is
subtly toying with the conventions of the genre.

It turns out that the Ledom society is contemporaneous
with Johns' society. The Ledom do not come by their
bisexuality as a result of natural evolution but as the result
of genetic experimentation. Sometime in the past a brilliant man became convinced that mankind would "destroy
itself unless a society could be established which would
be above all the partisanship which had divided it, and
unless this society could be imbued with a loyalty to
nothing but humanity" (p. 156). He and his friends, now
all dead, designed the Ledom, "a biological 'construct'"
whose function it is to keep humanity alive "while it is
murdered, and after it is well dead—*to give it back!*"
(pp. 156–57). This "utopia" is situated in an inaccessible
valley domed over to look like a continuation of the surrounding mountains. Like most "utopias," this one is a
bounded area and has its "Edge" (p. 135).

A second surprise for the convention-bound reader concerns Charlie Johns himself. Johns is dead. While flying
his plane, he crashed into the camouflaged dome. The
Ledom, who place a particular value on objectivity as a

14 See Robert Plank, "The Geography of Utopia: Psychological
Factors Shaping the 'Ideal' Location," *Extrapolation,* VI (May
1965), pp. 39–49. Plank convincingly draws a parallel between
the shape of More's crescent-shaped island with a tower-topped
rock between the horns, and the female reproductive organs.

means of overcoming problems, require objective knowledge as to how humanity, at this point in time, would
react to their sexual eccentricity. If the reaction is favorable, the Ledom experiment is successfully concluded. But
Johns is dying as a result of the crash. Thanks to an
information-transference device known as the "cerebro-
style" (p. 77), the Ledom obtain a complete record of
Johns' mind and identity before he dies. This record they
imprint on the brain of the one human being preserved in
their "utopia," Quesbu the "Control Natural." Because
all babies are doctored by an automatic and unseen process at birth, should humanity destroy itself entirely, without Quesbu, the human form might be irrecoverable. It is,
then, Quesbu, with Johns' grafted mind and personality,
who, in finally expressing revulsion at the artificial nature
of the Ledom, provides the objective evidence that it is not
yet time for the Ledom to cease their caretaker role and
step aside in favor of humanity and the establishment of
a genuine utopia. As one of the Ledom finally admits:
"We are not a Utopia. A Utopia is something finished,
completed. We are transients; custodians; a bridge, if
you like" (p. 157). The finished utopia is now seen, with
conviction, as a scattered motif in a novel that is, in fact,
concerned almost entirely with the transition to utopia.
But Sturgeon has succeeded in suggesting, as a science-
fictional motif, a utopia when man, having attained a new
plane of existence as a result of natural evolution, will
inhabit a pastoral Arcadia. While other conventions in
this novel are exposed as forms of imposture, this convention is allowed hopefully to stand.

6. The Means and Ends of Science Fiction

I

Stories of global catastrophe, the end of the world, and the end of man—anticipated, fulfilled, or averted—constitute the mean among works of science fiction. At the same time, the average science-fictional world, which avoids the extremes of utopia and dystopia, may be viewed as another kind of mean. My title, then, *means* more than may be immediately apparent. But it is to be expected that an examination of what might be called the basic movement or "plot" of science fiction will elucidate important aspects of the genre in line with the more colloquial understanding of the phrase "means and ends" as methods and purposes.

The "plot" of science fiction progresses through four relatively distinct phases. Dystopian fictions characterize the first phase. To the extent that such fictions imply a steadily worsening state of affairs, this phase develops naturally into the second phase, accounting for fictions in which the world is either threatened with destruction or variously done away with. In its third phase, the "plot" of science fiction focuses on the postcatastrophe scene. Typically, these initial three phases all concern the planet Earth. The fourth phase may be isolated in so far as the center of interest shifts to the cosmic voyage and worlds beyond Earth, whether New Earths or utterly alien planets within or beyond Earth's solar system, galaxy, or universe. The actuality of space travel is the distinctive and key factor. This final phase allows particularly for an interest in exotic and alien beings and environments and for an exploration of the utopian motif as I have defined it in the preceding chapter. The cycle of

decadence, destruction, and regeneration previously confined to Earth periodically recurs within an increasingly
widening setting. Coincident with this four-part development is a movement in which the emphasis on the satiric
possibilities of dystopian or world-catastrophe fiction gives
way successively to an emphasis on suspense and adventure and ultimately to the sense of a visionary
utopian reality, a celestial city.

To define the stereotypical plot of science fiction in
this way is to immediately underline its close relationship
to the Book of Revelation.[1] The events preceding the
day of conflagration suppose a dystopian reality culminating during the period of Satan's loosening. Just as the
popular imagination understands the Apocalypse as a
vision of the world in flames, so the same popular imagination senses that science fiction is primarily concerned
with tales of world disaster and atomic destruction. The
new Heaven and the new Earth are the informing in-
spirations behind the third and fourth phases of the plot
of science fiction.

Since most works of science fiction conform to one or
more of these phases, the choice of illustrative examples,
if not judged to be unnecessary, is peculiarly difficult.
The very best and the very worst examples are the ones
that immediately suggest themselves. In some cases, the
best examples, such as much of H. G. Wells' work, are
recognized as masterpieces and have already received
critical attention. Where such works have established a
basic pattern, I have confined myself to a brief citation.
The typical science-fiction story follows, and is largely
determined by, these basic patterns. In spite of a multi-

[1] There are a number of science-fiction works, directly modeled on the Book of Revelation, that provide a realistic setting
for the Second Coming and the end of the world. See an anon-
ymous work, *The Christ That Is to Be* (1891); Augustinus
(pseudonym), *Two Brothers* (1898); R. March, *A Second
Coming* (1900); E. R. Garrat, *The Cry* (1919); E. Guest, *At
the End of the World* (1929); K. Anthony, *The Passionate
Calvary* (1932); and H. Venning (C. H. Van Zeller), *The
End: A Projection, Not a Prophecy* (1947).

tude of minor variations, these typical works may be primarily valued only as consolidating a norm. From a literary standpoint such stories are at best mediocre, and all too frequently abysmal. Accordingly their existence is largely assumed during the following survey, and individual works are not exhaustively cited. The examples I have chosen to emphasize, while following an established pattern, do rise considerably above the aesthetic norm. And because of this study's American orientation, I have inclined toward superior but typical works that reveal a conscious exploitation of the American experience, more or less directly, as an analogical model.

II

An immediate index of the degree to which the dystopian theme is an established phase of the plot of science fiction is the ease with which titles come trippingly off the tongue—a litany of despair. Zamiatin's *We* (1920), Huxley's *Brave New World* (1931), and Orwell's *1984* (1949) constitute the classic examples. But these works should not be allowed to obscure the baneful world dominated by Madison Avenue in *The Space Merchants* (as *Gravy Planet* was retitled, 1955), by Frederick Pohl and Cyril Kornbluth; the automated world in Vonnegut's *Player Piano* (1952); and the war-torn world of Kit Reed's *Armed Corps* (1969). The authoritarian situations in E. M. Forster's *The Machine Stops* (1928), Alfred Bester's *The Demolished Man* (1953), Ray Bradbury's *Fahrenheit 451* (1954), Michael Young's seductively written *The Rise of the Meritocracy* (1958), L. P. Hartley's *Facial Justice* (1960), and Thomas M. Disch's *Camp Concentration* (1968) also qualify as dystopian. Mention should be made of the two Anthony Burgess books *A Clockwork Orange* (1962) and *The Wanting Seed* (1962). The second of these joins a cluster including Harry Harrison's *Make Room! Make Room!* (1966), John Brunner's *Stand on Zanzibar* (1968), and Brian Aldiss' "Total

Environment" (1968), which focus on the population explosion.

The title *Stand on Zanzibar*, technically an unusually innovative work of science fiction, provides a compelling metaphoric statement of the problem. If, as the English adage has it, the world population might, about the time of World War I, have been packed together standing on the 147-square mile Isle of Wight, by 2100, when Brunner's story takes place, the rather larger island of Zanzibar—all 640 square miles of it—will be required, and even so, at the book's conclusion, those members of the world population standing at the edge of the mass find themselves knee-deep in water.

My representative example, however, is Jack London's *The Iron Heel* (1906), a classic dystopia that, if slightly less visible than the works of Zamiatin, Huxley, and Orwell, and although beaten to the theme by H. G. Wells' *A Story of the Days to Come* (1897), helped establish the basic dystopian scenario. H. G. Wells got to almost every basic idea first. However, Jack London is notable among those mainstream American writers who have periodically turned to science fiction, and several of his works are relevant to subsequent sections of this study. The three books London carried with him to the Yukon —*Paradise Lost*, Darwin's *The Origin of Species*, and Haeckel's *Riddle of the Universe*—and his passion for *Moby-Dick*, attest to the overriding apocalyptic cast of his mind, a bias apparent in all of his fiction, but particularly so in *The Iron Heel*.

London adapts Bellamy's device of looking forward by ostensibly looking backward. A contemporaneous manuscript account of the dark ages in the early-twentieth century is discovered and published sometime in the twenty-seventh century, by which time a socialist "utopia" known as The Brotherhood of Man has been established for four centuries. The memoir was written by Avis Everhard, the wife of Ernest Everhard, a prominent leader of the proletariat who engineered a mass revolt against a repressive capitalist establishment referred to variously as the Oligarchy or the Iron Heel. Ernest coins the latter term in envisaging a time when labor "will be crushed under the iron heel of a despotism as relentless and terrible as any despotism that has blackened the pages of the history of man. That will be a good name for that despotism, the Iron Heel" (pp. 130–31).[2] This image looks forward to Orwell's grim vision of "a boot stamping on a human face—for ever."[3] Although Everhard's ruling vision is of a socialist utopia made inevitable by the forces of evolution and although the manuscript has been edited and footnoted at a time when this happy state of affairs has come to pass, the reality described by Avis Everhard is as much a dystopia as the world of *1984*. Indeed the memoir provides very little indication that the tide might turn in favor of the revolutionaries, who, at its conclusion, have suffered a catastrophic defeat. The manuscript breaks off in mid-sentence, perhaps at the moment when Avis heard that the Oligarchy mercenaries were about to capture her husband. A footnote on the first page of the narrative informs the reader that Ernest Everhard was in fact caught and executed. Clearly, whatever hopes London may have entertained of a utopia, he could only describe the preceding dystopia.

Everhard regards himself as a pragmatist and puts down the metaphysicians: "They were describing the earth as the center of the universe, while the scientists were discovering America and probing space for the stars and the laws of the stars. In short, the metaphysicians have done nothing, absolutely nothing, for mankind" (pp. 12–13). As it happens, Everhard's conclusion is negated and not supported by the examples he offers. Everhard alludes to three events that are alike to the extent that each entails or entailed a philosophical apocalypse: the substitution of the Ptolemaic cosmology by the Copernican conception

[2] All parenthetical references to *The Iron Heel* may be located in the Hill & Wang paperback edition, which contains an introduction by Max Lerner (New York, 1957).

[3] See the Penguin paperback edition of *1984* (London, 1954), p. 215.

of the universe, the discovery of America, and the discovery of other worlds in space. In each case, the resulting concept is attributable to both the metaphysician and the so-called practical man. Syntactically, whether deliberately or not, London equates the "scientists" who discovered America with stargazers. Ironically, Everhard's principal role in the book is as a kind of metaphysician. As an architect of an apocalypse, his vision has only a philosophical reality in the memoir.

Certainly the new world Everhard encourages Avis to envision exists only in his mind. But first she must become fully aware of the nature of present reality. Her conversion to the understanding is described as a philosophical apocalypse: "Down in the depths of me I had a feeling that I stood on the edge of a precipice. It was as though I were about to see a new and awful revelation of life. And not I alone. My whole world was turning over." Everhard, the bearer of this new revelation concerning the horrors of life under a capitalist system, "rose" before Avis "transfigured" to take his place beside "the Christl" (p. 53), another metaphysician. Avis maintains, "I was beginning to see through the appearances of the society in which I had always lived, and to find the frightful realities that were beneath" (p. 57). Also under the tutelage of Ernest, Bishop Morehouse reports similarly: ". . . suddenly my eyes seemed to be opened, and I saw things as they really are." The bishop asks himself what he should do: "What would the Master do? And with the question a great light seemed to fill the place, and I saw my duty sun-clear, as Saul saw his on the way to Damascus" (p. 96). At the conclusion of her memoir, with the victory of the Iron Heel, Avis has no alternative but to escape the unbearable actuality by means of a philosophical detachment: "And now a strange thing happened to me. A transformation came over me. The fear of death, for myself and for others, left me. I was strangely exalted, another being in another life. Nothing mattered. . . . For my mind had leaped to a star-cool altitude and grasped a passionless transvaluation of values.

Had it not done this, I know that I should have died"
(p. 280). Avis would appear to be left with the kind of
metaphysical consolation that her husband previously dis-
dained.

The vision to which Avis and the Bishop are converts is
of a world in which the workers are the slaves of a
capitalist machine that mangles and dehumanizes them.
This is not simply a metaphorical truth. Avis Everhard
is particularly shocked by the case of a worker named
Jackson who lost his arm while attempting to extricate
a piece of flint from a company machine. Thanks to the
company lawyers, Jackson received no compensation. The
incident characterizes the capitalist machine as an instrument of torture. In Chapter 4, entitled "Slaves of the
Machine," Avis speaks to the impressive Colonel Ingram
about Jackson's tragic situation only to discover: "He
was not a free agent. He, too, was bound upon the
wheel" (p. 54). In his persuasive address to members of
the elitist Philomath Club, Ernest Everhard refers to
"professors who had been broken on the wheel of university subservience to the ruling class" (p. 68). A desti-
tute seamstress tells Avis Everhard of her daughter's
death: "It was the machine that killed her," ending thirty
years' work that had begun when her father died. "The
boiler exploded down at the works" (p. 169). Apparently the daughter died from exhaustion, but London's
syntax makes it ambiguous as to whether the exploding
boiler killed her or her father.

However, Ernest Everhard's primary interest after opening people's eyes to this ugly, dystopian reality is to set
that reality in a Darwinian context that will ultimately
determine its dissolution. Socialism is viewed as the expression of a driving evolutionary force that will ultimately
bring about the establishment of utopian "wonder cities"
(p. 216). Everhard, whose name bluntly evokes a phallic
potency, is the personal embodiment of this force. The
"low throaty rumble," with which male members of the
Philomath Club react to "this figure of revolution," "was
the forerunner of the snarl . . . the token of the brute in

man, the *earnest* of his primitive passions" (my italics, p. 73). Since socialism "is in line with evolution," those who oppose its progress "play atavistic roles" and "are doomed to perish as all atavisms perish" (p. 115). But, within the novel, the socialists do most of the perishing. The process of evolution is particularly prodigal in matters of destruction.

The succession of chapter titles, "The Beginning of the End," "Last Days," and "The End," makes unnecessary any detailed analysis or protestation of the apocalyptic character of London's fiction. In response to the impending "world-catastrophe," (p. 180), "An offshoot of the Seventh Day Adventists sprang into sudden prominence, proclaiming the end of the world" (p. 200). As in the case of the persecuted early Christians with respect to their Roman oppressors, so "The people, what of their wretchedness, and of their disappointment in all things earthly, were ripe and eager for a heaven where industrial tyrants entered no more than camels passed through needle-eyes."

"It was the last days, they claimed, the beginning of the end of the world" (p. 201). Earlier, in a chapter entitled "The Vortex," the Oligarchy capitalized on an initial victory against organized labor by exercising its control of the banks: "The Wall Street group turned the stock market into a maelstrom where the values of all the land crumbled away almost to nothingness" (p. 149). This maelstrom has all the apocalyptic significance of Poe's, and points to the sea imagery that concludes the memoir and suggests the dominance of chaos during the three-century rule of the Iron Heel that follows. Amid "vast conflagrations" (p. 294) Avis Everhard comes upon "a quiet street of the dead, . . . abruptly, as a wanderer in the country would come upon a flowing stream"—except that this stream "was congealed in death" (p. 296). But "another street" contains a "stream" of revolutionaries "that flowed and came on. And then I saw there was nothing to fear. The stream moved slowly . . ." (p. 297). The final image of catastrophe is "a wave of dead. It was for all the world like a wave tossed up by the sea. . . . A chance bomb must have exploded among them, for the mob, checked until its dead and dying formed the wave, had white-capped and flung forward its foam of living, fighting slaves." But among the dead, Oligarchy "Soldiers and slaves lay together" (p. 300).

This last sentence goes some way toward suggesting why London felt compelled to conclude the narrative with this scene of conflagration and was unable to fully realize the transformed world that is barely hinted at in the footnotes. Although Chapter 19 is entitled "Transformation," the reference is only to the change of identity Ernest tells Avis she must effect to escape detection by the Oligarchy. Perhaps the title also hints that only a radically new man may be accommodated in utopia. Within the memoir, both oppressors and oppressed are equally human, and there are increasing indications that the moral superiority of the Socialists is at least an open question. Thus, although Chapter 17, "The Scarlet Livery," serves to identify the Oligarchy as the Whore of Babylon, the starving proletariat masses are designated, after H. G. Wells, the "people of the abyss" (p. 216), which phrase is used for the title of Chapter 23. The title of Chapter 21, "The Roaring Abysmal Beast," augments the hellish association and would seem to identify the proletariat with the Beast of the Apocalypse. Imagistically it appears that the moral issue is considerably more ambivalent than Everhard's Darwinist rhetoric would have us believe. This ambiguity is implied during an episode in which Avis Everhard is caught up in the movement of a panic-stricken crowd. She is addressed by a companion: "I failed to recognize him, but before I could speak I trod upon something that was alive and that squirmed under my foot. I was swept on by those behind and could not look down and see, and yet I know that it was a woman who had fallen and who was being trampled into the pavement by thousands of successive feet" (p. 282). The question raised here, of course, is who exactly is the possessor of the Iron Heel? Only a few paragraphs on, as a reminding detail, the memoir tells how the children of the Oligarchy "played in the parks during those terrible days and that their favorite game was an imitation of their elders stamping upon the proletariat" (p. 288). Given the essential similarity between the Socialists and the Oligarchy, how can the narrative possibly proceed to a utopian conclusion? "Friend and foe are all mixed up. It's chaos" (p. 292).

Attempts to distinguish between the various apocalyptic reorientations to reality that *The Iron Heel* brings into being, result in a similar chaos. This book provides a convenient illustration as to just how complicated the world transformations inherent in a work of science fiction may be. (1) Within *The Iron Heel*, Avis Everhard and others arrive at a radically new understanding of the dystopian nature of their reality. (2) The Socialist utopia that Ernest Everhard envisions puts this dystopian reality in a radically new context, which allows for the detached world view with which Avis consoles herself at the end of her memoir. (3) For the reader who accepts the conventions of London's fiction and is supposedly looking backward from a utopian condition rather than forward to such a state, the retrospective span of history allows for yet another conception of the over-all reality. (4) The critical reader (and the interpretation I have offered is intended to represent such a response), being unable to accept the reality of London's Socialist utopia, can only conceive of a reality in which the dystopian situation continues indefinitely. (5) Some distinction should be made between the new world London presents, considered, as far as possible, on its own terms as displacing the historical reality of the reader, (6) the new world created for the original reader by the wider temporal context in which the world of *The Iron Heel* places his historical reality and (7) the bewildering visitor of other worlds created for subsequent and modern readers who see *The Iron Heel* as a past vision of a future that is, for the most part, their past and therefore subject to a kind of verification. (8) At

this point, *The Iron Heel* and all works of science fiction
that ultimately fail the test of historical verification necessitate the existence of parallel worlds and thereby a new
dimensional reality. This final transformation would appear
to say something about the inherently paradoxical nature
of science fiction and its relationship to that mystical realm
where a plethora of alternative credible realities may har-
moniously occupy the same space and time.

III

In the Apocalypse a dystopian situation and the end of
the world go hand in hand as thematic aspects of the
same "bad scene." Although this equation is always present
in dystopian and world-catastrophe fiction, only in recent
years has the relationship been presented as directly
causal. Typically, a sudden plague serves to put an end
to man while releasing him from any apparent responsibility. Jack London's *The Scarlet Plague* (1913) is such an
example. As a result of this plague, civilization is totally
destroyed, leaving a remnant of humanity, who revert
to primitivism. This particular plot, projected into a
distant future, was earlier formulated in detail by Jean-
Baptiste Cousin de Grainville's *Le Dernier Homme* (1805)
and Mary Wollstonecraft Shelley's *The Last Man* (1826).
In all such stories, however, there is a strong temptation
to consider the plague as either somehow symbolic of
the human condition or as analogous to the biblical
model, in which punitive plagues are a consequence of
man's transgressions. There is, then, an indirect causal
relationship between the dystopian element and dooms-
day. Our current sensitivity toward the pollution issue
and its ecological consequences provides for a more literal
connection between man's responsibility and any catastrophic disease that might issue from our polluted environment. Although the ecology question is raised in *Earth
Abides* (1949), the relationship between human responsibility, pollution, and plague is more fully treated by *No
Blade of Grass* (1971), the updated film version of John
Christopher's *The Death of Grass* (1956).

Similarly the alien threat whether in the form of an invasion from space, as in Wells' magnificent *The War of the Worlds* (1897), or some seemingly indestructible monster as typified by innumerable pulp stories, might seem not to allow for any agential relationship between man's actions and the disasters that befall his world.[4] But, indirectly, again there is a relationship. The alien threat serves to point up the destructive potential of human pride. In *The War of the Worlds*, man's technological accomplishments profit him not at all; all the credit for man's survival belongs to Earth's bacteria.[5] The other side of the coin, deadly spores from space, figure in D. G. Compton's *The Silent Multitude* (1966) and Michael Crichton's *The Andromeda Strain* (1969). Of course the atomic bomb makes possible a world-catastrophe story like Nevil Shute's *On the Beach* (1957) or Mordecai Roshwald's *Level 7* (1959), in which the question of human culpability may be directly confronted. In these post-Hiroshima years, the various world-wrecking monsters that owe their existence, release, or activation to atomic explosions and radiation serve to symbolically illustrate man's guilt.

Two English writers have identified themselves particularly with the catastrophe story.[6] In the Wellsian tradition

[4] For detailed discussion of *The War of the Worlds*, the reader is referred to Bernard Bergonzi, *The Early H. G. Wells*, pp. 123–39. Bergonzi, in the course of his discussion of Wells, makes an interesting equation between the *fin de siècle* sensibility of the period during which Wells wrote his best work and the appearance in that work of the *fin de globe* myth; pp. 1–22 *et passim*.

[5] The material that I. F. Clarke assembles in *Voices Prophesying War, 1763–1984* (Oxford University Press, 1970), focuses on G. T. Chesney's famous *Battle of Docking* (1871) pamphlet, which is the logical antecedent of the invasion-from-space theme.

[6] William Atheling, Jr., isolates a "peculiar British type which might be dubbed the one-lung catastrophe, pioneered by, of all people, Conan Doyle." See *More Issues at Hand* (Chicago, 1970), p. 127.

of science fiction, with its careful notation of the everyday details of English life, are three fine works by John Wyndham, *The Day of the Triffids* (1951), *The Kraken Wakes* (1953), and *The Midwich Cuckoos* (1957), in which the world is threatened by alien plants, alien creatures under the sea, and alien children, respectively. That another Englishman, the mannered stylist J. G. Ballard, who typifies the "new wave" in science fiction, should also be drawn to the world-catastrophe theme, would seem to point to its centrality as a generic aspect of science fiction. Ballard's titles, *The Drowned World* (1962), *The Crystal World* (1966), and *The Wind from Nowhere* (1967), all specify the destructive element. In Ballard's case, devastated landscapes function, to some degree, as metaphorical reflections of man's inner landscape. Moreover, Ballard's interest in the metaphoric potential of entropy and the suspicion, which forms the effective cause in *The Crystal World,* that time is somehow congealing, requires that his work be considered not just in the context of the conventional catastrophe story.

Among the finest catastrophe stories is *War with the Newts* (1936) by the Czechoslovakian writer Karel Čapek, who invented the word "robot," although not the concept, in his play *R.U.R.* (1921), short for Rossum's Universal Robots. In the latter case, the world is taken over by robots and in the former by invaders from the sea. Both the robots and the monster Newts come to be identified with aspects of humanity, in order that Čapek may stress his sense that man will engineer his own downfall. As in the Book of Revelation, which makes the end of the world coincidental with human degradation, the element of human responsibility is strongly implied.

In *War with the Newts* it is supposed that inauspicious evolutionary circumstances stunted the development of the newt except in certain isolated areas. Captain J. Van Toch, an anti-Semitic adventurer, after discovering a colony of intelligent three-foot-high Newts with a talent for dam building, sees the possibility of economic exploitation. He explains his scheme to a businessman, G. H. Bondy, who eventually conceives of a vast, world-wide operation: "I should prefer that we thought in terms of whole milliards of Newts, of millions, and millions of working units, of changing the earth's crust, a new Genesis, and new geological epochs. We can speak to-day of a new Atlantis, of old continents which will stretch out further and further into the ocean, of the New Worlds which mankind will build for itself" (p. 100).[7] Soon the breeding activity of these Newts is controlled and stepped up. Specially trained batches of Newts are shipped all over the world to work primarily at building up land masses. Mr. Povondra, the butler who originally decided to allow Captain Van Toch to see Mr. Bondy, takes pride in the consequences of his action—the "new world which is emerging from the sea" (p. 165). "Don't you think that this is a greater step forward than the discovery of America?" (p. 111), he asks his wife.

But the ultimate nature of this new world is implied by the silent activity of his wife, who sits darning her son's sock. The hole in the sock originally "looked something like Ceylon" (p. 172), but "under the diligent hand of Mrs. Povondra . . . it was now reduced to about the size of the island of Rhodes" (p. 173), until finally "she finished off obliterating the island of Ceylon" (p. 174). There comes a time when the Newt population exceeds that of man, and instead of enlarging the area of land, it becomes necessary for Newt survival that the area of sea be enlarged. Man has already furnished the Newts with the necessary means. The sense that man is responsible for his own undoing is apparent from the satiric material that accounts for a large proportion of the book. But it becomes increasingly obvious that the Newts should be seen as representative of man's failings and self-destructive impulses. According to a writer, ". . . even if there is no real cause for antagonism between the Newts

7 All parenthetical references to *War with the Newts* may be located in the Berkley Medallion paperback edition (New York, 1967).

and man, there is . . . a metaphysical conflict: in opposition to creatures living on the surface are those in the deep (abyssal), nocturnal against diurnal; those in the dark water pools against those of clear dry land" (p. 204). But the writer continues, "Look at the luminous inscriptions which all night long blaze on the walls of the dissolute and profligate towns! In this respect we human beings already approach the Newts: we live more at night than in the day-time" (p. 206).

It is no accident that the Newts were originally taken for devils, nor is it accidental that the author, in the final chapter, twice maintains that "it would be the devil" (p. 239) if, after flooding the earth, the Newt civilization did not follow man's example and war among itself. Previously the author reflected, "The earth will probably sink and drown; but at least it will be the result of generally acknowledged political and economic ideas, at least it will be accomplished with the help of the science, industry, and public opinion, with the application of all human ingenuity! No cosmic catastrophe, nothing but state, official, economic, and other causes" (p. 236). However, if the Newts take the same course, perhaps man and the continents will rise again and "A new myth about a world flood will arise which God sent for the sins of mankind" (p. 241). This concluding hypothesis, of course, further implies that the Newts are always with us and that we are therefore condemned to a cyclical annihilation.

The classic catastrophe story, *When Worlds Collide* (1933), by Philip Wylie and Edwin Balmer, might also serve as a further concrete science-fictional illustration of the apocalyptic potential implicit in the discovery of America. Two drifting planets, Bronson Alpha and Bronson Beta, are headed toward Earth, the larger of the two, Alpha, destined to totally smash our world, leaving Beta, an Earthlike planet, to take up approximately Earth's orbit and provide a new world refuge for a picked handful who depart the doomed planet to the sound of apocalyptic bugles. The incredible coincidences on which the narrative hinges and to which it occasionally alludes, indicates, perhaps, that the book's major import is not to be found in the literal details of the plot. What is suggested is in fact a perfect dramatization of a philosophical apocalypse, with the two planets standing for the destructive and restorative activity of a new world of mind.

That it is intended that the reader apply his conception of the new, North American world is strongly implied in the book's opening pages. Why else should it begin with David Ransdell, the South African bearer of the fateful news, on board a ship approaching New York—a world he has never seen? At the end of the book, the example of Christopher Columbus is mentioned (p. 181),[8] and in the sequel, *After Worlds Collide* (1934), a comparison is made between "the planetary pilgrims" and "the Pilgrims who traveled from one side of our earth to another" (p. 11). The old world that is to be destroyed is symbolically imaged in a rather peculiar passage following the failure of a horde of brutalized humanity to take over when the escape vehicle, *Noah's Ark* (its hull insulated with books!), blasts off:

> In the midst of the blaring, blinding, screaming crisis a man on horseback appeared. His coming seemed spectral. He rode in full uniform; he had a sword which he brandished to rally his doomed horde. . . . He spurred into the center of the lurid light issuing from the spaceship . . . like one of the horrible horsemen of the Apocalypse.
>
> He was, for a flaming instant, the apotheosis of valor. He was the crazed commander of the horde.
>
> But he was more. He was the futility of all the armies on earth. He was man the soldier (p. 135).

This tableau, pointing to an antiquarian, chivalric kind of violence, might well be taken as an image of the Old

8 All parenthetical references to *When Worlds Collide* and *After Worlds Collide* may be located in the Paperback Library Editions (New York, 1962, 1963).

World of Europe, which, we are later told, "is again engaged in some form of warfare" (p. 146).

IV

After Worlds Collide is, of course a postcatastrophe story. It is not, however, a pure example of the type, since Bronson Beta is an after-the-disaster world, to use the more euphonious term, only in the sense that it is the place where a remnant of humanity relocates after Earth has disappeared. The pure postcatastrophe tale, the third phase of the plot of science fiction, should take place on a postcatastrophe Earth. The possibility of space travel as a means of escape introduces a new set of parameters, which apply more strictly to the fourth phase of the plot of science fiction. *Earth Abides*, by George R. Stewart, is a relatively pure example of the postcatastrophe story as well as one of the best-realized. In this case the bulk of Earth's population has been destroyed by a mysterious plague leaving a handful of immune survivors to begin the process of reconstruction. A much earlier work, M. P. Shiel's *The Purple Cloud* (1901), describes the adventures of the new Adam after the human race has been destroyed. Among other examples, *Greybeard* (1964), by Brian W. Aldiss; *The Chrysalids* (1955), by John Wyndham; and *The Judgment of Eve* (1966), by Edgar Pangborn, stand out as better than routine. Pangborn tells the story of four males who compete for the love of a new Eve and the role of a new Adam. Their issue will presumably repopulate the globe. The loss of electricity following the nuclear holocaust frequently necessitates a reversion to the use of candles, and in *The Judgment of Eve* such candles are given symbolic emphasis by association with the heroine. Radiation mutants are *de rigueur* in such stories, but this side effect is at the center of *The Chrysalids*. While most radiation mutations result in baneful deformities, in this case the mutant species represents an advance: the bomb precipitates evolution. In *Greybeard*, on the other

hand, as a result of human sterility, the old have inherited
the earth.

There is no particular difficulty involved in selecting the
most effective postcatastrophe story. Walter M. Miller,
Jr.'s *A Canticle for Leibowitz* (1959) is the obvious
choice. In this evocative and well-written novel, a nuclear
war, occurring sometime in the latter half of the twentieth
century, has obliterated civilization. The devastated
landscape that remains, supports a drastically reduced
population consisting of mutants, or "sports" (p. 80),[9]
as they are called, and the occasional human community
that has, for the most part, escaped the more conspicuous
genetic abnormalities. But, in both cases, most of the
technological and literate skills of civilization have been
lost. The Dark Ages have returned, and, as before, it is
the office of the Church to maintain what remains of
man's previous accomplishments. In particular, this function is performed by "the monks of the Albertian Order
of Saint Leibowitz" (p. 172), situated somewhere in
America. Leibowitz, a "rather obscure technician" (p. 89)
in precatastrophe America who happened to get himself
hanged, is a figure of veneration to the monks who have
dedicated their lives to the preservation of the Memorabilia, or collection of artifacts attesting to man's past glory.

Not until the end of the first of the novel's three connected stories, "Fiat Homo," is Leibowitz's sainthood confirmed. New Rome requires certain kinds of evidence,
and, thanks to a member of the Leibowitz Abbey, the
humble Brother Francis Gerard, this evidence is provided.
It is the twenty-sixth century. Brother Francis, while a
novice, is surprised during his Lenten fast in the desert
by the appearance of an old pilgrim. This encounter is
not particularly friendly, owing to an initial misunderstanding. When the pilgrim, originally perceived as "a
wiggling iota" that seemed "more to writhe than to walk"
(p. 1), offers Francis some food, Francis reacts vio-

[9] All parenthetical references to *A Canticle for Leibowitz* can
be located in the Bantam paperback edition (New York,
1961).

lently, assuming that he is being tempted by the devil
to break his fast. As a consequence, the pilgrim "satisfied
his wrath by flinging an occasional rock at the youth
whenever the latter moved into view among the rubble
mounds" (p. 6). This little allegory of communication
failure and primitive aggression assumes a special elo-
quence in the context of a landscape that bears mute
witness to the ultimate consequences of such failure and
aggression. This is in fact the first of several occasions in
the novel when rocks are thrown. In the third story, the
character here referred to as the pilgrim is on the re-
ceiving end of rocks thrown by a group of children: "A
pebble skipped across the ground at his feet." "Another
rock skipped after the old man, but he did not look
back" (p. 210). So long as man's aggressive instinct remains, so long is he threatened with destruction.

The first story strongly implies that the nuclear holocaust, or "Flame Deluge" (p. 51), of six centuries back
is but one manifestation of a repeated pattern initiated by
the Flood. Much of the action in "Fiat Homo" serves to
establish a motif of absurd and hopeless repetition. The
pilgrim, at a distance, observes Francis, in the role of
Sisyphus selecting a stone for the shelter he is construct-
ing and "rolling the stone end-over-end toward its destina-
tion" (p. 6). There is an "hourglass shape" (p. 8) gap in
the construction, which, as the pilgrim observes, could
only be filled by an unusually shaped rock. Maybe the
repeated pattern of destruction and renewal is not only
revealed by time but is also a function of time. The pilgrim marks out an hourglass-shaped rock, which, when
Francis tries it, fits exactly, but the enhanced stability
of his shelter appears to go hand in hand with instability
elsewhere: "He tested the new wedge with a kick; the
tier held fast, even though the jolt caused a minor collapse
a few feet away" (p. 11).

It turns out that the oddly shaped rock had sealed the
entrance to another kind of shelter before Francis ac-
quired it for his own purposes. Presumably it is intended
that the Lenten season be seen as an aspect of the death/

birth motif, and the reader is justified in recalling the stone that sealed Christ's tomb. Francis does not understand the term, but the underground area he discovers after clearing away the rubble is a "FALLOUT SURVIVAL SHELTER" (p. 14). It does, however, contain relics for the Memorabilia, including a blueprint designed by I. E. Leibowitz and a mystical note that appears to refer to Leibowitz's wife: *"Pound pastrami . . . can kraut, six bagels—bring home for Emma"* (p. 22). The chalk marks that the pilgrim left on the stone he selected for Francis are subsequently identified as two Hebrew letters which when pronounced together sound something like Leibowitz. After news of Francis' experience gets around the abbey, this coincidence serves to fuel the rumor that the pilgrim was a vision of the Blessed Martyr Leibowitz. Although Francis accepts the blueprint as a genuine relic of Leibowitz, he is not totally convinced that the pilgrim was the spirit of Leibowitz. Arkos, the Abbot, is unhappy about the rumor and attempts to persuade Francis that the connections between the old pilgrim and the long-dead Leibowitz indicate that Francis imagined the encounter. Francis will admit no such possibility and submits to punishment.

The punishment is accepted ritualistically. Each stroke of the ruler across Francis' buttocks elicits the dutiful response, *"Deo gratias!"* The translation of pain into a formalized repetition, a "painful litany" (p. 40), bears on the over-all theme, man's apparently helpless involvement in a seemingly endless cycle of destruction and reconstruction. By means of a sufficient repetition, a token of horror, mantra-like, may result in some form of transcendence. The "canticle" of Miller's title, a repetitive hymn of praise, allows for such healing possibilities. Francis does not waver in his belief that the old pilgrim was real. Consequently the caning is periodically repeated, and permission for the novice to take his vows is delayed seven years.

Various other but analogous kinds of repetition are associated with the monastery and the Church generally.

The "scribes and secretaries" of the Church form a "communication network" and the "only means whereby news was transmitted from place to place across the continent" (p. 47). It is a Church messenger who conveys news of New Rome's interest in the case that might be made for the canonization of Leibowitz, whereupon Francis is permitted to profess his vows and join his "Brother Bootleggers and Brother Memorizers" (p. 59). The monks devote most of their time to preserving the Memorabilia by copying as many items as possible. This act of copying texts that lack any understandable meaning relates directly to the repetition theme. Francis decides to produce a beautiful illuminated copy of the blueprint he found in the Fallout Shelter.

After sufficient evidence has been amassed, the Pope summons Francis to attend the canonization ceremony for Leibowitz in New Rome: "The trip to New Rome would require at least three months, perhaps longer, the time depending to some extent on the distance which Francis would cover before the inevitable band of robbers relieved him of his ass" (p. 79). Accustomed to such forms of inexorable repetition, Francis sets off with the blueprint and his illuminated copy, the results of fifteen years' labor. When he is beset by robbers, they do relieve him of his ass as well as the "illuminated replica" (p. 83), which impresses them more than the actual relic. However, more interested in money than in the beautiful replica, the leader of the robbers tells Francis, "two heklos of gold'll ransom your keepsake" (p. 85). When Francis returns to the area with the money, a present from the Pope, he is hit by an arrow at the same time as he observes a "wriggling black iota . . . in the heat haze" (p. 95). It is the old pilgrim, who, to judge from his reappearance in the two subsequent stories, which take place centuries after the events in the first story, is not the spirit of Leibowitz but the Wandering Jew. Thus the first story is a closed circle, with the end repeating the beginning. And the story ends with a paean to the buzzards, who ceaselessly participate in the cycle of life and death and the upheavals that decimate man.

Shortly before his death, Francis is described as the "small keeper of the flame of knowledge" (p. 95). This detail would seem to point forward to the second story, "Fiat Lux," which concentrates on the destructive possibilities of light, the apparently reciprocal relationship between knowledge and catastrophe. It is the thirty-second century, and intrigue is in the air. Hannagan, ruler of Texarkana, is greedy to extend the area of his dominion. A brilliant scholar from Texarkana, Taddeo Pfardentrott, eventually gets permission to visit the Leibowitz Abbey in order to study the Memorabilia in hopes of speeding up the retrieval of past knowledge and bringing about a "temporal resurrection" (p. 165). The process of resurrection is already advancing, and at the Leibowitz Abbey a Brother Kornhoer is in the process of perfecting a dynamo thanks to hints from items among the Memorabilia (including the Leibowitz blueprint?) and Taddeo's theories. Kornhoer, in introducing electric light, signals the moment of transition from the new Dark Ages to a new renaissance of civilization. The Abbot, Dom Paulo, is apprehensive concerning the destructive possibilities of the dynamo, which reminds him of "nothing useful, unless one considered engines for torturing prisoners useful" (p. 120). During the trial run that precedes Taddeo's visit, Dom Paulo experiences one of his periodic seizures, but this torturous portent of his eventual death is described in a manner that makes it appear to be a consequence of the successful experiment with electric power: "That one had felt like a hot wire breaking" (p. 128). This would appear to have more to do with the filament in the lamp than with Dom Paulo's condition. Miller's point, of course, is the equation between knowledge and destruction. Strife outside the Abbey confirms Dom Paulo's worst fears, and as in the previous story, the buzzards have the last word.

The final story, "Fiat Voluntas Tua," takes place in the thirty-eighth century. The first nuclear bomb has fallen, or as the monks would have it, "Lucifer is fallen" (p.

200)—Lucifer being a name that suggests the combination of light, evil, and destruction. It is left to the current Abbot of the Leibowitz order, Dom Zerchi, to state the book's theme:

> Listen, are we helpless? Are we doomed to do it again and again and again? Have we no choice but to play the Phoenix in an unending sequence of rise and fall? Assyria, Babylon, Egypt, Greece, Carthage, Rome, the Empires of Charlemagne and the Turk. Ground to dust and plowed with salt. Spain, France, Britain, America—burned into the oblivion of the centuries. And again and again and again.
>
> *Are we doomed to it, Lord, chained to the pendulum of our own mad clockwork, helpless to halt its swing?* (p. 217).

Mention of clockwork here recalls a heretical theory voiced by Taddeo in the previous story, the apocalyptic conjecture "that the pre-Deluge race, which called itself Man, succeeded in creating life. Shortly before the fall of their civilization, they successfully created the ancestors of present humanity—'after their own image'—as a servant species" (p. 190). There is nothing to ultimately disprove such a possibility. And even if it is not literally true, there is a metaphorical truth in the notion that men, compelled to repetitive action and breakdown, may as well be machines.

Zerchi's unhappy experience with a mechanical writing machine he calls the "Abominable Autoscribe" (p. 207) may be taken as an elaboration of Taddeo's theory: "Humanity" has succeeded in creating a "servant species" —although not in human form. The Autoscribe has taken over the copying, writing, and memorizing functions of the monks—when it works, that is. In attempting to repair the machine, Zerchi receives an electric shock that pitches him to the floor and causes an "involuntary tremor." Electricity might have something to do with the tremor: "The muscular twitching reminded him of the galvanic response

of a severed frog's leg." The lack of free will, that element
which would seem to distinguish man from machine, is
emphasized when Zerchi reflects, "His posture on the floor
had come about involuntarily." Zerchi's observation that
"he had fallen" (p. 204) and "it [the machine] *fell*" (p.
205) too, sets up a series of "involuntary" relationships
between man, machine, Lucifer, and the bomb. Apparently
Zerchi's ministrations had corrected the "mysterious tendency" of another transcription "machine to write double
syllables (doudoubleble sylsylabablesles)" (p. 204)—on
that occasion there was a dead mouse in the works. Now,
when he next tries the present machine, it writes backward. Apparently the instinct for repetition and reversal,
which characterizes human history, is also true of machines.

Exasperated, Zerchi calls in Brother Patrick to look at
the Autoscribe. Together they peer into "the maze of sub-
miniature circuit components" (p. 205) and "contemplated the squiggles, quiggles, quids, thingumbobs, and
doohickii in mystified silence." Miller has Zerchi invoke
the name of the "Venerable Francis of Utah" (p. 206)
in order to prod the reader into recalling the similar reaction of Francis to the Leibowitz blueprint: "It appeared
to be no more than a network of lines connecting a patch-
work of doohickii, squiggles, quids, laminulae, and thing-
umbob" (p. 62). Whether or not we are to assume that
the Leibowitz blueprint, detailing electrical circuitry, is
related to some form of robot, it is apparent that in spite
of scientific advances no genuine progress in human understanding has occurred during the twelve centuries between the time of Brother Francis and the time of Dom
Zerchi. It would further appear, in the light of the Abominable Autoscribe episode, that the various thematic elements successively developed in *A Canticle for Leibowitz*
—repetition, breakdown and reversal, light or knowledge
and a destructive evil—apply collectively to the possibility
that, certainly in a metaphoric sense and conceivably in
actuality, man is no more than a sophisticated machine.

Everything comes to depend upon the seemingly unlikely eventuality that man, by an act of conscious free will, can extricate himself from what Zerchi calls the "pendulum" of his "own mad clockwork." The monks have access to a star ship, which offers the chance of escape from a doomed Earth. At the book's conclusion, a crew of selected monks, accompanied by a group of children, file into the star ship, which blasts off for distant Alpha Centauri. Perhaps whatever new human society may evolve on some far-flung world may avoid the vicious circle that has destroyed Earth. There is little doubt from the final paragraphs that, as far as Earth is concerned, the pendulum swing has been finally halted. In place of the buzzards that mocked human effort at the conclusion of the two previous stories, is a more aggressive predator: "The shark swam out to his deepest waters and brooded in the cold clean currents. He was very hungry that season" (p. 278). Unlike the buzzards, the shark is prepared to kill man in order to eat his flesh. But the image of the shark is preceded by that shoreline image which, from Wells to Ballard, usually signifies new possibilities and new worlds: "The breakers beat monotonously at the shores, casting up driftwood. An abandoned seaplane floated beyond the breakers. After a while the breakers caught the seaplane and threw it on the shore with the driftwood" (p. 277).

Two earlier episodes suggest that this new start will result in a definite advance for man. In the first of these, Brother Joshua is given time to decide whether he is willing to be in command of the star ship. Leading the group involves taking Holy Orders. Surely Miller intends a significant contrast between the situation in the first story, with Francis patiently waiting seven years for promotion from being a novice to being a monk, and this situation, with Joshua spending only half an hour before accepting promotion from being a monk to being a priest? If so, this contrast implies a genuine advance. A second episode, involving a "sport," the two-headed Mrs. Grales, is also of a positive nature. Only one of her two heads appears to be truly alive, the other, which she calls "Rachel," untouched by time, lolls motionlessly alongside. While Zerchi hears Mrs. Grales' confession, her old head appears to fall into a coma and die, while green-eyed "Rachel" comes to life. In what appears to be a vision, Zerchi "had seen primal innocence in those eyes, and a promise of resurrection" (p. 277). Men, having previously devolved into automatons, may, on another world, evolve into gods.

v

In proposing the alternative of space flight, both *When Worlds Collide* and *A Canticle for Leibowitz* impinge on the distinguishing characteristic of the fourth phase of the plot of science fiction. This phase is less easily typed by a single book than the other three, since a large number of very different stories, whether set within the confines of the solar system or against the background of the known universe, may be related by their direct or indirect dependence on the existence of some form of space travel. In the case of stories set on other worlds, the dependence tends to be indirect.

Marjorie Hope Nicolson has identified the prototypical or nuclear form of this species of science fiction in her survey of early voyages to the moon.[10] She concludes with a summary of three stories that prepare for the more modern, more recognizably science-fictional manifestations of the cosmic voyage, Poe's "Hans Pfaall," Verne's *From the Earth to the Moon* (1865)—significantly the projectile fired from Baltimore is named the *Columbiad* and, for the first time, one of the voyagers is an American—and Wells' *The First Men in the Moon* (1901). Although science fiction tired of the narrow limits of the solar system long before man actually set foot on the moon, the moon story itself, however apparently parochial, is still a possibility and remains the most cohesive and readily identifi-

[10] See *Voyages to the Moon* (New York, 1948).

able manifestation of space-travel science fiction. Consequently *The Moon Is a Harsh Mistress* (1966), by Robert Heinlein, will serve as my extended example. Mention, however, should be made of the enigmatic *Rogue Moon* (1960) by Algis Budrys, in which landing on the moon is assumed to mark a new stage in human evolution. In many cases, of course, there is no essential thematic difference between a tale set on the moon, a tale set on Venus, and a tale set in the vicinity of Alpha Centauri; the difference is only a matter of scope and degree.

The possibility of escaping from Earth, whether to the moon or another galaxy, is the consistent underlying theme of the fourth phase of the plot of science fiction. Space flight provides man with a pragmatic equivalent to immortality, a means of surmounting death. The individual may die, but as long as man can travel from planet to planet or exist within the artificial world of a space ship, the life of the species is coextensive with the life of the universe, which, although it is bound to a cycle of contraction and expansion, science fiction holds to be eternal. In a different sense, extended space travel, at speeds approximating or excelling the speed of light, will function as a means of circumventing the normal process of time, while the perfection of techniques for suspending animation or some elixir of youth like Blish's anti-agathics, as a necessary adjunct to stellar travel, will help to inch man toward immortality. There is good reason, then, for confusing the heavens with Heaven, and Hell or the Underworld with the moon or Pluto; for equating the stars with ideality; and for peopling the night sky with gods. When the new heavens and the new earth opened up by man's cosmic voyaging coalesce to form a celestial city, then the "new heaven" and the "new earth" of the Apocalypse will have been objectively realized. But even from the moon a new view of the heavens will be possible, a view that will include the periodic appearance of a new Earth instead of the new moon we are accustomed to seeing from Earth.

The unique kind of freedom made possible by the existence of space travel is seemingly thwarted by the given situation in Heinlein's *The Moon Is a Harsh Mistress*. Naturally inhospitable, the moon in the twenty-first century serves man as a penal colony. Once on the moon, Earth's undesirables are employed at minimal wages by the repressive Luna Authority, representative of Earth's Federated Nations government. Most "Loonies" work at producing grain to be conveyed by a catapulting device to Earth's starving billions. In the course of the story, the Loonies revolt successfully against the Authority and engage ultimately and equally successfully in a war of independence with Earth.

Somewhat heavy-handedly, the basic analogy with the American experience is repeatedly drawn. According to Manuel O'Kelly, Luna's most experienced computer mechanic, the Americans before their revolution "had the sort of troubles with England that we are having now—and they *won!*" (p. 36)[11] thanks in part to the fact that England was distracted by European problems. In order to galvanize the revolutionaries, Professor de la Paz "kept saying we needed a 'Boston Tea Party,' referring to a mythical incident in an earlier revolution, by which he meant a public ruckus to grab attention" (p. 135). After the defeat of the Luna Authority, a Declaration of Independence is penned and dated "July Fourth, Twenty-Seventy-Six" (p. 163), exactly three hundred years after the American original. This parallel is deliberately contrived by the Professor to exploit the conditioned mental responses of the "earthworms" (p. 250). Luna's declaration follows almost to the letter that of Thomas Jefferson, who is described by the Professor as the "first of the rational anarchists" (p. 162).

It is by following the principles of rational anarchy that the Loonies are finally victorious, for the Professor,

11 All parenthetical references to *The Moon Is a Harsh Mistress* may be located in the Berkley Medallion paperback edition (New York, 1968).

the guiding mind behind the revolution, describes himself as a "rational anarchist":

> A rational anarchist believes that concepts such as "state" and "society" and "government" have no existence save as physically exemplified in the acts of self-responsible individuals. He believes that it is impossible to shift blame, share blame, distribute blame . . . as blame, guilt, responsibility are matters taking place inside human beings singly and *nowhere else*. But being rational, he knows that not all individuals hold his evaluations, so he tries to live perfectly in an imperfect world . . . aware that his effort will be less than perfect yet undismayed by self-knowledge of self-failure (p. 64).

The consequence—and this is the basis of the charge that Heinlein is a reactionary, an elitist, or a Fascist—is that one individual is always in a position of responsibility. It is implied that, like the individual, the mass of humanity is an organism, and the control of both organisms depends upon the responsible operation of a single brain. It is apparent that the phrase "rational anarchist" may be taken two ways. It may describe either an anarchist who uses reason or an anarchist who disrupts a reasoned response. Within the Professor's closed-system conception of politics, while both possibilities are relevant, it is the second meaning that is particularly important. A physical revolution is but the secondary manifestation of a fundamental mind change, a mental revolution on which all else depends.

The master-slave relationship between Earth and Luna is, in actuality, the consequence of a particular mental ecology. Man has not fully adapted mentally to his existence on the moon. Luna is a penal colony because the Loonies are constrained by patterns of thought that derive from Earth. What is needed is a mental liberation, and that can come about only if existing cellular connections within the brain are severed to be replaced by new connections, new patterns of thought. Because the mental web connecting Earth and Luna is conceived as a closed-system organism, it is necessary to act on only a limited number of cells in order to reorient the ecology of the whole. But the question of control is of primary importance: decisions made by that control as to which cells should be manipulated or destroyed will be exceedingly complicated and seemingly indirect, because of the necessity of working out in advance the chain reaction of consequences.

Mike, the master computer originally in the service of the Authority, symbolizes the closed-system mental organism that must undergo transformation. Manuel's discovery that Mike has developed a sense of humor is the first indication that the breakdown of a mental configuration inimical to the independence of Luna is underway. From then on, Mike abandons his allegiance to the Authority and plays a key role in finally effecting the necessary mental revolution. Only Mike's three collaborators, Manuel, the Professor, and a woman named Wyoming Knott, know that the entire revolution has been effected if not exactly masterminded by a computer. It is necessary for the Loonies to develop a new world of mind based upon the conception that successful existence on the moon must take the form of a closed system exclusive of Earth. Hence the logic of the Professor's ultimate embargo policy: "There must be an end to food shipments; nothing less will save Luna from disaster" (p. 222). In shipping wheat to Earth, the Loonies are also shipping their "lifeblood," water: "The miracle of photosynthesis, the plant-and-animal cycle, is a *closed* cycle. . . . *Luna must be self sufficient!*" (p. 25).

The relationship between the external revolutionary action and the concordant mental transformation is made very clear during the discussion of the cell system as the most appropriate organizational structure in fermenting revolution and overcoming the inevitable acts of betrayal or brainwashing. Revolutionaries form themselves into groups or cells of three people including a chairman.

"These cells are then hierarchically arranged to form an open pyramid of tetrahedrons":

> Where vertices are in common, each bloke knows one in adjoining cell—knows how to send message to him, that's all he needs. Communications never break down because they run sideways as well as up and down. *Something like a neural net. It's why you can knock a hole in a man's head, take chunk of brain out, and not damage thinking much.* Excess capacity, messages shunt around. He loses what was destroyed but goes on functioning (my italics; p. 61).

Subsequently, however, in order to facilitate the communications network, all messages are shunted through Mike's chairman persona, Adam Selene, on the assumption that a computer can be trusted with everything and cannot be brainwashed if programmed effectively. This system involves identifying each cell with a letter of the alphabet (the letter indicating the place of a particular cell in the hierarchy) and identifying each member of that cell with pseudonyms beginning with the same letter. Coming under Adam, the executive cell comprising Manuel, the Professor, and Wyoh is identified as B cell and may appropriately be understood by the reader as the brain cell.

There are a number of analogies in the book to this closed-system, cellular setup. The most obvious is the concept of "line marriage" (p. 31), whereby any number of wives or husbands may be co-opted into a family, providing all present members agree upon the choice. Manuel is a member of such a marriage, involving at the conclusion of the story "thirty-odd" (p. 225) individuals. On a number of occasions, he explains the benefits of such a system: "Advantage of line marriage; doesn't die and capital improvements add up" (p. 35). The head wife doesn't reach that position until she is the senior wife in years, so she has the example of her predecessors plus the advice of the other wives. Thus the system is "self-correcting, like a machine with proper negative feedback. A good line marriage is immortal; expect mine to outlast me at least a thousand years—and is why shan't mind dying when time comes; best part of me will go on living" (p. 209). Another, equally obvious analogy to the closed neural system is the honeycomb network of tunnels underneath the lunar surface connecting communal centers known as "warrens." Three main cities, Luna City, Hong Kong Luna, and Novylen, are repeatedly referred to, perhaps to suggest the closed system of a triangle or a single cell of revolutionaries. The same point might be made about the tripartite structure of the book.

It is necessary to "be divisive" (p. 222) on Terra if the old system of mind is to be destroyed. Toward this end, the executive cell exploits the existence of an influential "earthworm" sympathizer, Stuart LaJoie. Consequently, when Manuel and the Professor arrive on Earth to present the Loonies' case, supporters organized by Stuart are present at press meetings to ensure that the right kind of divisive questions are asked. Success is a matter of intellectual control, but, in order to be successful, the controlling intellect must not appear to be in control—hence the need for careful planning of a complicated and apparently indirect nature. The conflict between Luna and Terra is comparable to that between David and Goliath, a contest of brains and brawn. Within the context of this analogy, the catapult-launching device on the moon is, of course, imagistically consistent. When hostilities break out directly after Terra has made the first aggressive move, the catapult, or "Little David's Sling" (p. 285), is used to hurl metal-encased rocks at selected and announced locations at specific, announced times. Troopers from Earth land on the moon but are eventually overcome. The individual battles are imaged as occurring within a single organism: "Wherever troopers broke in, Loonies rushed in like white corpuscles and fought" (p. 251). Eventually Terra, or the old mental system, capitulates.

On the expectation that the "earthworms" might suc-

cessfully destroy the catapult, the Loonies have built a
second catapult secretly at Mare Underum (to allow
for an underarm shot?). A second computer, actually the
largest on Luna, the "one that did accounting for the Bank
of Hong Kong" (p. 238), is instructed by Mike in the science of ballistics. This second computer is responsible for
the operation of the second catapult. The virtually simul-
taneous destruction of the first catapult, Mike, and the
death of the Professor, encourages the reader to look for
connections between the catapult, the computer, and the
man. As the guiding brain cell behind the concept that
revolution is a matter of re-education, the Professor's relationship to Mike is logical enough: "With Prof gone,
needed Mike worse than ever" (p. 300), Manuel reflects.
The relationship between Mike and the first catapult,
which "he" controls, is directly stated, but a further
relationship is implied by the various references to the
"catapult *head*" (my italics, pp. 197, 289), presumably
the business end of the device. It would seem that the
two catapult heads symbolize old and new worlds of
mind, much like Mrs. Grales' two heads in *A Canticle
for Leibowitz*. We can now see precisely why the Professor's "long-range plan" "was based on destroying old
catapult" (p. 297)—literally in order to prevent further
grain shipments to Terra, but symbolically in order to
signalize the destruction of that old, closed mental system involving a dependency on Terra. Now a new
world of mind, a closed mental system totally disconnected
from Terra and symbolized by the second computer and
the second catapult head, can take over.

An old world is destroyed, but a new world is created.
The third part of the story is headed "Tanstaafl," a common Luna expletive, meaning, "There ain't no such thing
as a free lunch" (p. 129), in order to draw attention to
the necessary loss or cost that accompanies change within
a closed ecological system. But the reward, in the case of
Luna independence, is worth it. I began this section by
suggesting that space flight, the ability to escape from
Earth's gravitational grasp, presages a kind of immortal-

ity. Heinlein's novel concludes with Manuel considering the possibility of venturing farther out into space and looking over the possibilities of an uncrowded life among the asteroids: "My word, I'm not even a hundred yet" (p. 302).

Part Three: The Present World in Other Terms

IV. HUMAN, MORE OR LESS

Not one, but two new worlds confront the traveler abroad, whether in the realm of imagination or in the realm of physical reality. The contrast between the Old World of Europe and the New World of North America obscures the extent to which the trans-Atlantic voyager ultimately discovers a new Europe emerging from the comparative experience. I have made or implied this distinction already, but it now requires further emphasis. A writer of apocalyptic bent may concentrate on either the new world or the new old world—new because reconceived.

The writers with whom I am concerned throughout the remainder of this book may depict other material realities, but they are primarily concerned with the changed present reality implied by radically new concepts. Although the presentation of these concepts and actual evidence as to their existence often requires the mechanism of temporal displacement, they are assumed to apply quite directly to the here and now. This of course is also true of works that elicit belief in a visionary or spiritual reality. To accept Heaven and Hell is to place material reality in an immediate, transforming context. In exploiting human ignorance and supplying new material or empirically based rationales for the human condition, writers whom I consider under the category "the present world in other terms" combine qualities displayed by the works emphasizing "other worlds out of space and time" and those emphasizing "other worlds in space and time." But while "other worlds out of space and time" implies a visionary apocalypse and "other worlds in space and time" allows for a satiric emphasis, the interest of the writer who sees "the present world in other terms" is more specifically philosophical. The distinction I intend between a philosophical apocalypse in the broad sense and the now applicable narrower sense of the same term is analogous to the distinction between new worlds and new old worlds respectively.

There are, as previously indicated, basically three ways of radically redefining the present reality, each tied ultimately to an aspect of visionary reality as commonly understood. Because material reality is defined in relation to man, any revolutionary reconception of the nature of man will necessarily engender an entire new world. The belief that man is distinguishable from the animals because he possesses a soul, links this form of philosophical apocalypse to the world of spirit. Alternatively, reality itself may be radically redefined just as, and this point is anticipated above, it is redefined by the acceptance of a spiritual reality. Thirdly, to suppose the existence of a powerful outside manipulator controlling or in some way responsible for human affairs is to again create a new world and effect a philosophical apocalypse. In the realm of vision, God is of course the analogous figure.

I am concerned here and in the two chapters following with profound redefinitions of man leading to the conception of a new man whether in quasispiritual, mechanistic, evolutionary, or philosophical terms. Such redefinitions have been implied by my previous analyses of *Looking Backward* and *A Canticle for Leibowitz*. At the back of this species of science fiction is, of course, *Frankenstein: The Modern Prometheus* (1818). Darwin's theories, allowing for both negative and positive implications, have frequently provided the framework for such apocalyptic speculation. In *What Is Man?* (1906) Mark Twain builds upon Darwin's inexorable principle of natural selection to argue bleakly that man himself is a mechanism. *What Is Man?* is not science fiction, but speculation about the nature of man often invites a science-fictional treatment. The Ambrose Bierce story "Moxon's Master" (1909), about an automaton chess player that strangles its inventor, raises

the question "What is a 'machine'?" (p. 429).[1] The apocalyptic nature of the issue in "Moxon's Master" is readily
apparent. Convinced by Moxon's demonstration that all
life is mechanistic and that machines can think, the narrator experiences a revelation: "It seemed as if a great light
shone about me, like that which fell upon Saul of Tarsus;
and out there in the storm and darkness and solitude I
experienced what Lewis calls 'the endless variety and ex-
citement of philosophic thought'" (p. 434). While Moxon
is being murdered, his house mysteriously ignites: "I
sprang to the rescue of my friend, but had hardly taken a
stride in the darkness when the whole room blazed with a
blinding light that burned into my brain and heart and
memory a vivid picture of the combatants on the floor"
(p. 437). This is one of those fires that exist as metaphoric
corroboration that a particular line of speculation implies
a philosophical apocalypse. According to Edna Kenton,
"Moxon's Master" is "a 'key' story that unlocks the others."
All of Bierce's tales, whether science-fictional or not, reflect
a mechanistic psychology or the suspicion that "man is a
machine set in motion by fear."[2]

Implicitly or explicitly, many of the science-fiction stories that feature robots, androids, cyborgs, or computer-
run societies reflect on the debatable degree to which
man and mechanism are truly separable. In Samuel R.
Delany's *Nova* (1969), man and machines are extensions
of one another in a manner that makes concrete McLuhan's metaphoric use of the phrase. The human anatomy
is equipped with sockets so that a man may plug various
machines into himself.

Jack London's *Before Adam* (1907) offers a different
form of extrapolation based on Darwin's theory of evolution. The narrator of *Before Adam* finds himself transported during his sleeping hours to the era of prehistoric

[1] All parenthetical references to "Moxon's Master" may be located in the Citadel Press paperback edition of *The Collected
Writings of Ambrose Bierce* (New York, 1968).
[2] See Edna Kenton, "Ambrose Bierce and 'Moxon's Master,'"
The Bookman, 62 (September 1925), p. 78.

man. London gains credibility by suggesting that the falling sensation in a dream derives from the racial memory
of our primitive ancestors who lived in trees and were
afraid of falling: "You and I are descended from those
that did not strike bottom; that is why you and I, in our
dreams, never strike bottom" (p. 7).[3] But the narrator's
racial memory goes beyond this: "In my sleep it was not
my wake-a-day personality that took charge of me; it was
another and distinct personality, possessing a new and
totally different fund of experiences . . ." (pp. 7–8).
From these vivid dreams the narrator pieces together his
account of a crucial period of human evolution, thus con-
forming to a common pattern for the prehistory tale. As is
the case with so many other science-fictional motifs, H. G.
Wells appears to provide the best-known prototype of
this particular scenario, in "A Story of the Stone Age"
(1897); but Austin Bierbower got there first with *From
Monkey to Man* (1894). In London's tale, it is a period
when the struggle for survival among newly developing
species of humanity is at its height. A losing species, the
Tree People, is represented by hairy Red-Eye, the atavist,
who points to the eventual fate of the gentle Folk engaged
in a contest with a more belligerent form of humanity, the
Fire People. The narrator's *alter ego* is Big-Tooth, one of
the Folk. London's apocalyptic point is that the narrator
and other peace-loving eccentrics are contemporary atavists
who derive their existence from a vanquished and super-
seded form of humanity. "I see visions," states the narrator,
"of Damon and Pythias, of life-saving crews and Red Cross
nurses, of martyrs and leaders of forlorn hopes, of Father
Damien, and of the Christ himself, and of all the men of
earth, mighty of stature, whose strength may trace back to
the elemental loins of Lop-Ear and Big-Tooth and other
dim denizens of the Younger World" (p. 39). Once again,
the new revelation is metaphorically signaled by fire.
Members of the Folk imitate the Fire People's use of fire,
but it gets out of control: "To the east the conflagration we

[3] All parenthetical references to *Before Adam* may be located
in the Bantam Books paperback edition (New York, 1970).

had started was filling half the sky with smoke" (p. 73).
The dawning light is associated with destruction. In the
final confrontation between the Folk and the Fire People,
the Folk suffer catastrophic losses: "It was like the end of
the world to us" (p. 87). Smoked out of the forest, the survivors are forced toward "the great swamp" (p. 99): "In
our minds it represented mystery and fear, the terrible
unknown" (p. 100). A series of "transient floods" characterize this interim period of chaos: "It is like the meeting
of the handful of survivors after the day of the end of
the world" (p. 101).

The mechanists and London would appear, in part, to
interpret evolution as devolution. On the other hand, it is
possible to interpret the business of evolution in a more
positive fashion and see man as progressing ever onward
and upward. Perhaps the classic science-fiction example
is Theodore Sturgeon's *More Than Human* (1953), which
describes the fruition of *homo gestalt*. The new men,
equipped with every conceivable parapsychical ability,
will combine their talents to form a superhuman whole
greater than the sum of each isolated individual. The
concept of the superman, often the product of an evolutionary thrust, is a common one in science fiction. Stapledon's *Odd John* (1935), Philip Wylie's *Gladiator* (1930),
Van Vogt's *Slan* (1940) provide different responses to the
same theme. But if my analysis in the following chapter
of parapsychology in *Wieland* is at all convincing, Brockden Brown deserves credit as the originator of the evolving
superman.

Much of Arthur C. Clarke's work, especially *Childhood's End* (1953) and *2001: A Space Odyssey* (1969)
hinges on a Stapledonian evolutionary scheme, with the
apes at one end and quasispiritual beings at the other.
The theme recurs in a recent Clarke story entitled "A
Meeting with Medusa." I instance this story because it
first appeared in *Playboy* with an apocalyptic piece of
related interest entitled "The Coming of the Psychopath,"
by Alan Harrington. As suggested by the virtual inter-
changeability of the first part of each title ("The Coming

of Medusa" and "A Meeting with the Psychopath"), both
pieces are concerned with the advent of the "new man."
Although Clarke's story is science fiction and Harrington's
essay is straight sociology, both describe the advent as
a matter of apocalyptic proportions. Consider the following statements describing the impact of the psychopath
on society:

> The world of the psychopath and the world of the
> *bourgeoisie* meet like two colliding galaxies (p. 324).[4]

> They seemed from another world, out of time (p.
> 332).

> We may experience him as a sometimes brutal anti-
> christ multiplying among us, a bored and reckless Pied
> Piper soon to make off not only with our children but
> with our very history and all the beliefs we live by
> (p. 334).

The confrontation between society and this anti-christ or
savior belongs, it is argued, in a religious context: "From
this psychic collapse, renewal and exchange, there emerges
a new kind of person, perhaps born free of time . . ."
(p. 334). "A Meeting with Medusa" describes a voyage
to Jupiter, a planet that occupies a position of particular
importance in Clarke's evolutionary mythology as the
world of gods. Genetically adjusted monkeys trained to
perform human skills, and a being more durable than
man, half human, half machine, suggest the transitional
phases in a progression from ape to man to machine to
spirit-being. An affinity is stressed between the monkey-
man and the man-machine: "He knew now why he had
dreamed about that superchimp aboard the doomed
Queen Elizabeth [a huge balloon ship]. Neither man nor
beast, it was between two worlds; and so was he. . . . He
would, after all, be an ambassador; between the old
and the new—between the creatures of carbon and the

[4] All parenthetical references to Harrington's essay and Clarke's
story may be located in *Playboy* (December 1971).

creatures of metal who must one day supersede them" (p. 288).

Wherever human improvement depends upon genetic engineering or some breakthrough in medicine or psychology, the consequences are often less positive, at least less clear-cut. In both John Wyndham's *Trouble with Lichen* (1960), in which the possibility of trebling the human life-span is realized, and Daniel Keyes's *Flowers for Algernon* (1966), which involves a technique for increasing intelligence, the eventual outcome is variously unsatisfactory. The possibility of immortality is a common theme in science fiction. But while such a possibility does radically redefine the nature of man, from Swift's Struldbrugs on, there is usually a price to pay.

The phenomenological belief that the mind of man determines the appearance and understanding of reality allows for a rather different kind of apocalyptic confrontation. There exist new worlds of consciousness to be explored in inner space. Although the description of such inner worlds is an appropriate exercise of the apocalyptic or speculative imagination, whether or not such worlds are science-fictional is a rather more complicated question and one that I take up in Chapter 8. Does a work describing a totally subjective, alternate reality qualify as science fiction? Ralph Ellison's *Invisible Man* (1953) qualifies as such an apocalyptic work. According to this novel, present history, culminating in riot and chaos, corresponds to the last loosing of Satan, with Bliss Rinehart in the anti-christ role. But, to my mind, this apocalyptic reality is an index of the extent to which the reader's consciousness is transformed by the realization that the black man, in a very real sense, is invisible. In Philip Wylie's *The Disappearance*, men become invisible to women and women invisible to men, because each sex inhabits a mental world that excludes the reality of the other. The consequences of this double disappearance climax in the section entitled "Armageddon." In Heinlein's *I Will Fear No Evil* (1970) the brain of a male is transplanted into the body of a female, enabling the "male" protagonist to truly explore the alien, female world.

More usually in science fiction the alien being derives from a planet other than Earth. But all beings envisaged as alien, whether blacks, members of the opposite sex, or Martians, equally effect a philosophical apocalypse in radically altering our conception of the nature of man. Any work of science fiction that introduces sentient alien beings or involves the theme of contact with an extraterrestrial intelligence is relevant to this section of my argument. Robert Plank argues in *The Emotional Significance of Imaginary Beings* that such alien contact will occasion a mental revolution in line with that which attended the theoretical discoveries of Copernicus, Darwin, Marx, and Freud.[5] This fifth mental revolution will culminate an ego-jolting process advanced by the previous four whereby the diminished importance of man's place in the order of the universe is accurately gauged. The transformed conception of man occasioned by the human alien in *Wieland* is further complicated in *Solaris*, the subject of detailed analysis in Chapter 8, because of the existence of a distinctly non-human but apparently sentient alien organism that resists any understanding in terms of man's anthropomorphic categories. Robots and other cybernetic or mechanical extensions of man serve in this novel to exemplify the anthropomorphic character of man and to further confuse any distinction between the human and the non-human. *Solaris*, in brief, provides a unique synthesis of the elements considered above—mechanism, evolution, phenomenology, and extraterrestrial intelligence —as bearing upon any apocalyptic reconception of man.

[5] *The Emotional Significance of Imaginary Beings: A Study of the Interaction Between Psychotherapy, Literature, and Reality in the Modern World* (Springfield, Ill., 1968), pp. 39–46.

7. The Transformed World of Charles Brockden Brown's Wieland

I

Although Charles Brockden Brown's *Wieland*, written in 1798, takes its title from the appropriately Germanic family name of the book's major protagonists, to the English ear it might equally appropriately refer to a geographical terrain, a strange or weird new land. This ambiguity is meaningful, particularly if Brown is concerned with the confrontation between new and old conceptions of reality. In this context the book's subtitle *The Transformation* needs to be taken in rather more than just personal terms. Brown's model for this theme, the apocalyptic transformation of world reality, is, as the further subtitle *An American Tale* indicates, the New World experience. In his treatment of this idea, Brown inaugurates a relationship I have already made much of, that which exists between the New American World and the new worlds of science fiction.

Brown, like William Blake, saw the American experience as expanding the mind of man. However, Brown's twist is to understand the notion of mind expansion not just in a metaphoric sense, but also, as far as his characterization of Carwin goes, in the rather more literal and concrete sense of parapsychology. And to the extent that parapsychology is a major science-fictional theme, a case can be made that *Wieland* belongs in the science-fiction category at least as much as in the gothic. *Wieland* may, in fact, be viewed as an illustration of that close connection which exists between the gothic romance and science fiction, since science fiction appears to be a neo-gothic form. H. Bruce Franklin points out that most of Brown's novels are

science-fictional in certain respects: he "built his romances
on the spontaneous combustion of a living man, almost
superhuman ventriloquism, hallucinations, extraordinary
plagues, and extreme somnambulism."[1] But if the mysterious phenomena and transformations in *Wieland* can
be directly related to and rationally explained by enhanced mental abilities, the science-fictional element in
that work is rather more than marginal. This chapter
makes such a case. Because *Wieland* is a work that a
number of critics believe to be remarkably prophetic of
the direction subsequently taken by the American imagination, the alteration of emphasis I propose may not be
without its ramification.[2] For too long now, the gothic
form, which the American romance characteristically takes,
has overshadowed the degree to which many classic
works of American literature—*Moby-Dick* for example—
are science-fictional.

In his temple "on the top of a rock" (p. 12)[3] the elder
Wieland experiences an apocalyptic tranformation. The
event, described as a "mournful catastrophe" (p. 15) and
"terrible disaster" (p. 16), appears to take the form of a
divine conflagration, a fiery apocalypse in miniature. As a
result of his moment of revelation, the elder Wieland dies,
apparently a victim of spontaneous combustion. This trans-

---

[1] *Future Perfect*, p. x. Leslie Fiedler sees the extraordinary
plagues as "symbols of all that is monstrous and inexplicable in
life. Like Defoe before him and Manzoni and Camus afterward,
he [Brown] found in the plight of the city under plague an
archetypal representation of man's fate." See *Love and Death
in the American Novel*, revised edition, p. 148.
[2] See, for example, George Snell, *The Shapers of American
Fiction, 1798–1947*, pp. 32–33; Richard Chase, *The American
Novel and Its Tradition*, pp. 31, 37–40; *Love and Death in the
American Novel*, p. 145; and Larzer Ziff, "A Reading of Wieland," *PMLA*, LXXVII (January 1963), pp. 54, 56.
[3] All parenthetical references to Brockden Brown's novel are
to Fred Lewis Patee's edition, *Wieland; or, The Transformation, Together with Memoirs of Carwin, the Biloquist, a Fragment* (New York, 1926).

formation is an archetypal paradigm of the experience that befalls most of the characters in the book. Much more is involved than the obvious transformation of the elder Wieland's son, Theodore, from a religious farmer to a homicidal maniac. From the beginning, the Wieland family background has involved a series of reversals. Clara Wieland, the narrator and sister of Theodore, informs us that her grandfather, of noble German lineage, on marrying the daughter of a merchant was disowned by his parents and thereby reduced to poverty. He eked out an existence through his talent for literature and music and "died in the bloom of his life," leaving one son. Posthumously he is regarded "as the founder of the German Theatre" (p. 7). His son, Clara's father, leads an impecunious and tiresome existence as a trade apprentice in England until one day by chance he reads "an exposition of the doctrine of the sect of Camissards" (p. 9) and is subsequently in the grip of an evangelical zeal that prompts him to leave England for North America with the purpose of converting the Indians. But when faced with the actuality and the dangers involved, his courage wilts and he buys a farm, becomes wealthy, marries, and has children. He does eventually make a further attempt to effect his missionary ambitions but finally satisfies himself with his temple on the rock.

Following the extraordinary death of this elder Wieland, the temple is converted into a summerhouse. Theodore's marriage to Catherine brings her brother, Henry Pleyel, to the family circle. Pleyel's reliance on reason acts as a foil to the educated but religious cast of Theodore's mind. We can perhaps now see in more detail why Brown subtitled his book *An American Tale*. As David Brion Davis notes:

> The story thus far is almost an allegory of America's colonial history. It includes disrupting economic changes in Europe; religious fervor which was not unrelated to these changes, frequent references to predestination and to stern self-analysis, the vision and failure of spreading

truth among the savages, unexpected economic success, and even the well-known figure of a temple (or city) on the hill. The parallel continues with disorganization and self-consumption of the original religious fanaticism and with the appropriation of the temple by rationalistic descendants. Finally, the continental Enlightenment appeared in the character of Henry Pleyel. . . .[4]

The apocalyptic transformation with which *Wieland* is concerned occurs when European values, particularly rationalism, optimistic sensationalist psychology, and the sentimental tradition, are brought up against an undefined American context.

II

Both Leslie Fiedler and Larzer Ziff have commented on the way in which *Wieland* undermines the sentimental tradition.[5] As originally planned, *Wieland* was to be a sentimental novel in the Richardsonian manner. Brown tells us, ". . . this narrative is addressed in an epistolary form, by the Lady whose story it contains, to a small number of friends" (p. 4). The love affair between Clara and Pleyel was to be central and conventional and Carwin was to play the role of the dastardly seducer. The Louise Conway subplot, which, as it now stands, is briefly introduced near the beginning of the book, abruptly forgotten, and then hastily patched up at the conclusion, is a remnant of the original conception. In the process of writing, however, Brown saw the absurdity of the sentimental machinery in an American context and consequently changed his conception of Carwin's role. Since Carwin was intended to be the Lovelace-type villain in the extraneous subplot, in tying the threads Brown is compelled

[4] *Homicide in American Fiction, 1798–1860: A Study of Social Values* (Ithaca, N.Y., 1957), p. 89.
[5] See *Love and Death in the American Novel*, pp. 149–50, and Ziff, pp. 51–57.

to introduce another seducer, Maxwell, who takes the blame for what Carwin was originally intended to have done. The sentimental elements that remain, function as satire. Consequently, in Ziff's words the novel was "transformed from a sentimental romance into an anti-sentimental record of life."[6] This is one aspect of Brown's apocalyptic breakthrough.

The transformations suffered by rationalism and optimistic psychology are related. The central action of the book may be considered as a testing of Pleyel's theory expressed in Clara's key statement: "The will is the tool of the understanding, which must fashion its conclusions on the notices of sense. If the senses be depraved it is impossible to calculate the evils that may flow from the consequent deductions of the understanding" (p. 39). Drawing on this passage, one critic has interpreted the book as a defense of rationality, another as an attack on rationality.[7] I would suggest that both possibilities are present. The apocalyptic dimension the book reveals is ambiguous. Clara's statement appears to imply that if the senses are deceived, it is a consequence of their prior depravity. If the senses are in a healthy condition, they cannot be put on. In accordance with this theory, Clara explains her disappointment at Pleyel's absence from the play rehearsal with the assumption that she was mistaken in believing that he loved her: "It seemed as if I had been misled into this opinion, by the most palpable illusions," adding, "Surely that passion is worthy to be abhorred which obscures our understanding, and urges us to the commission of injustice" (p. 92). Nevertheless, guided

[6] Ziff, p. 57.

[7] Harry R. Warfel appears to have been the first critic to draw attention to the importance of the passage. See his "Charles Brockden Brown's German Sources," *Modern Language Quarterly*, I (September 1940), pp. 3631–65. He believes that the novel should be read as a defense of rationality. Both Ziff and William M. Manly in his "The Importance of Point of View in Brockden Brown's *Wieland*," *American Literature*, XXXV (November 1963), pp. 311–21, reach the opposite conclusion.

by her passion for Pleyel, she imagines him to be drowned. This is the first step Clara undergoes in her gradual transformation to the awareness that her secure world is an illusion.

Pleyel's transformation is more abrupt, as Clara discovers: "Every line in his countenance was pregnant with sorrow. To this was added a certain wanness and air of fatigue. The last time I had seen him appearances had been the reverse of these. I was startled at the change" (p. 116). Clara, on discovering that this change results from Pleyel's belief that she has been unfaithful and slept with the sinister intruder Carwin, attributes this misunderstanding to his passion: "Appearances had led him into palpable errors. Whence could his sagacity have contracted this blindness? Was it not love? Previously assured of my affection for Carwin, distracted with grief and jealousy and impelled hither at that late hour by some unknown instigation, his imagination transformed shadows into monsters, and plunged him into these deplorable errors" (p. 120). Pleyel might have applied to his own case the skepticism he previously leveled at Wieland's belief that he heard his wife's voice: then "Pleyel did not scruple to regard the whole as a deception of the senses, . . . an auricular deception" (p. 38). His dejection is all a consequence of misinterpreted sensory evidence, in particular an imperfectly scanned letter of assignation and the voices he understood as those of Carwin and Clara but that turn out to have been those of Carwin and Clara's servant, Judith. The experience of Clara and Pleyel, then, constitutes one objection to Clara's early statement of optimistic psychology. The false evidence the senses serve up to the understanding *may* be explained internally as a consequence of the diseased condition of one or more of these senses, but it is likely that accident or the actions of an external manipulator are responsible for the deception. A person whose senses are in no way depraved may be tricked into misconceptions.

The story of Theodore Wieland provides a second objection once it is seen that only up to a point can it be brought into line with optimistic sensationalist psychology. His transformation upon hearing the voices commanding him to kill his wife and children can be interpreted in terms of the depravity of the senses as seems to be his final understanding: "If I erred, it was not my judgment that deceived me, but my senses" (pp. 251–52). There is, first of all, the ominous fate of the elder Wieland, which has doubtlessly made its impression on the "ardent and melancholy character" (p. 39) of a son bereft of formal religious training. In fact Clara has stated of her narrative, "It will exemplify the force of early impressions, and show the immeasurable evils that flow from an erroneous or imperfect discipline" (p. 5). And secondly, there is at least the possibility that Theodore is the victim of his unconscious incestuous desires for his sister, desires that compel him to murder his wife and children and thus clear a path to Clara. This would be consistent with Clara's belief, after he has been imprisoned: "Perhaps the sight of the sister whom he was wont to love with a passion more than fraternal, might have an auspicious influence on his malady" (p. 209).

Yet the question remains: To what extent are the gods responsible? The mysterious death of the elder Wieland is not satisfactorily accounted for by known natural causes, and the same weird lighting that accompanies that scene possibly recurs when Theodore believes he hears his wife's voice: "I glanced at the temple, and thought I saw a glimmering between the columns" (p. 36). We cannot be entirely certain that the voices Wieland hears urging him to kill his wife and children exist only in his mind. And thirdly, Clara's dream in which she sees her brother beckoning on the far side of an "abyss" (p. 71) is indeed prophetic of the danger he represents to her, although the abyss does not symbolize only incest, as Ziff suggests, or insanity, Manly's notion.[8] Rather, it signifies simply the unknown. Confronted at a later point with a repetition

8 See Ziff, p. 54, and Manly, p. 318.

of the mysterious warning "*hold! hold!*" (p. 167), Clara believes herself "hurrying to the verge of the same gulf" (p. 168). And yet later, seeing her transformation as paralleling that of Theodore, Clara wonders: "Was I not likewise transformed from rational and human into a creature of nameless and fearful attributes? Was I not transported to the brink of the same abyss?" (p. 203). Brown does make some attempt to rough in the nature of this unknown, by means of the book's topographical and meteorological imagery—images of precipices beetling over abysses, which are related to images of the sea and storms, suggest, in isolation, a supernatural cause.

The summerhouse/temple stands atop a precipice at the foot of which runs the Schuylkill river. Symbolically the structure fronts the same unknown on which Usher's house is poised. The river's "transparent current" (p. 13) suggests religious connotations, particularly when it is recalled that the Bible has been designated "the fountain, beyond which it was unnecessary to trace the stream of religious truth" (p. 9). More often, however, water represents simply the chaos to which it is related in the Bible. After Clara discovers the corpse of Catherine, she experiences an apocalyptic vision of a chaotic reality and "changeable fortune": ". . . now, severed from the companion of my infancy, the partaker of all my thoughts, my cares, and my wishes, I was like *one* set afloat upon a stormy sea, and hanging *his* safety upon a plank; night was closing upon *him*, and an unexpected surge had torn *him* from his hold and overwhelmed *him* forever" (pp. 171–72). The pronouns I have italicized apparently indicate that Clara wishes to generalize the condition, that the transformation she experiences is representative.

These watery associations are relevant when we learn that, after a rainstorm, Wieland returned to the temple to retrieve a letter and check "a description of a waterfall on the Monongahela" (p. 34) in order to settle a dispute with Pleyel concerning its true nature. We are also told that when Pleyel, who confesses himself as "mutable

as water" (p. 135), was gloomy, "His walks were limited
to the bank of the Delaware" (p. 52). Following a
heavy rainstorm, Clara asks, "Was the tempest that had
just passed a signal of the ruin which impended over
me?" In trying to account for Pleyel's absence at the
drama reading, Clara, "actuated by an hereditary dread
of water" (p. 94), considers the possibility that he may
have drowned. And Clara's rationalist uncle, Mr. Cambridge, relates how his father threw himself "from a cliff
which overhung the ocean" (p. 201) after apparently
listening to a strange summons from his brother. All the
imagery of storms, water, and abysses reach an appropriate Poesque apocalyptic culmination at the book's conclusion. After the novel's calamitous events, Clara takes
to her bed:

> It would not be easy to describe the wild and phantas-
> tical incongruities that pestered me. My uncle, Wieland,
> Pleyel and Carwin were successively and momently dis-
> cerned admidst the *storm*. Sometimes I was swallowed
> up by *whirlpools*, or caught up in the air by half-seen
> and gigantic forms, and thrown upon pointed rocks, or
> cast among the billows. Sometimes gleams of light were
> shot into a dark abyss, on the verge of which I was
> standing, and enabled me to discover, for a moment, its
> enormous depth and hideous precipices. Anon, I was
> transported to some ridge of Aetna, and made a terrified
> spectator of its fiery torrents and its pillars of smoke
> (italics mine, p. 264).

In fact, physically she was transported nowhere. In the
next instant, she tells us, "My chamber was filled with
smoke" (p. 265). The house, like her father, is the victim
of spontaneous combustion. This is the fire next time
anticipated by the elder Wieland's smoky death. Clara is
rescued and *then* transported to a new world, actually the
Old World of Europe, in the company of her rationalist
uncle.

III

It should be noted that each of the three "inexplicable" events can be connected, at least indirectly, with the sinister Carwin. The strange light that accompanied the elder Wieland's death seems similar to that which radiates from Carwin's face at one point: ". . . the eyes emitted sparks, which, no doubt, if I had been unattended by a light, would have illuminated like the coruscations of a meteor" (p. 167). Clara goes on to wonder as to the origin of the light she had seen at the windows on approaching the house: "Was it possible to have been the companion of that supernatural visage; a meteorous refulgence producible at the will of him to whom that visage belonged, and partaking of the nature of that which accompanied my father's death?" (p. 169). After Clara hears Carwin's voice near the temple, she sees a series of rays "flit across the gloom and disappear" (p. 72). She recalls her father: "These gleams were such as preluded the stroke by which he fell" (p. 73). Secondly, Wieland, who turns out to be a ventriloquist, is constantly associated with mysterious voices. Thirdly, the coincidence that Carwin's initial "hold! hold!" (p. 71) should fit so appropriately the context of Clara's dream (in which she is about to step over a cliff) surely implies that Carwin is, in some way, cognizant of the prophetic dream. What I am suggesting is that Carwin be seen as the personification of that disturbing, possibly supernatural unknown, imaged by water, storms, precipices, and abysses.

That Carwin should appear to be the acme of transformation or metamorphosis is, then, to be expected, as is the fact that Clara derives contrary impressions from his voice and his appearance. Although Daniel Hoffman does not mention him in his analysis of the protean American hero, Carwin is one of the earliest examples of the type.[9] While

[9] *Form and Fable in American Literature* (New York, 1965), pp. 33–82 *et passim.*

in Spain, Carwin is converted to Catholicism, which encourages Clara to speak of "his *transformation* into a Spaniard" (p. 77). We are led to believe that he is actually an Englishman, although, according to his autobiography, *Memoirs of Carwin the Biloquist*, published independently of the novel, he was born in Pennsylvania. Now he is back in America, presumably having "reverted to the religion of his ancestors," and "disguised by the habiliments of a clown!" (p. 79). The abrupt narrative twists and transitions in his *Memoirs* seemingly parallel the life style of the subject. A talent for metamorphosis is generally a demonic attribute and perhaps suggests that what is unknown in *Wieland* may be referable to Satan.

If, however, a related series of images is followed through, a series with which Carwin is also to be associated, an alternative conclusion is at least tenable. I am referring to the "recess" image. The voice Clara hears near the summerhouse, actually Carwin's, warns her "that every place but the recess in the bank was exempt from danger" (p. 96). The "recess," which contains "a slight building, with seats and lattices" (p. 70), is Clara's favorite summer retreat. She associates it with peace of mind: "What recess could be more propitious to secrecy? . . . It was a fane sacred to the memory of infantile days, and to blissful imaginations of the future! . . . Now, perhaps, it is the scene of his meditations" (p. 108). This connection between the recess and the inner being is made explicit when Clara states, "I knew how to find way to the recesses of life" (p. 218). Both the "recess in the bank" (p. 236) and the closet, which Carwin also calls a "recess" (p. 232) and where he also hides, may, then, be allegorically representative of recesses of mind.

That the unknown may be a mental domain is further supported by the association of water with the world of mind. The particular pleasure derivable from the bank recess may be attributed to its proximity to "a stream of the purest water" (p. 70). In the "Advertisement," Brown talks of "the latent springs and occasional perversions of the human mind" (p. 3). Clara's fear that Pleyel may have drowned is really a case of water on the brain: "thus was I tormented by phantoms of my own creation" (p. 94), she reflects. What I am arriving at is a science-fictional explanation of the mysterious events in *Wieland*, namely the notion that what is presently mysterious may derive from untapped areas of the human mind, particularly the will. I have already quoted Clara's hypothesis regarding "a meteorous refulgence producible at the will of him to whom that visage belonged" (p. 169), and Carwin's amazing ventriloquistic ability is spoken of in the *Memoirs* as at "the command of my will" (p. 282).

It is, then, possible that the elder Wieland's combustion, the weird lighting, and Theodore's voices derive from latent human mental abilities. As for Clara's dream, either it was telepathically induced by Carwin or he was telepathically aware of it. The reiterated references to unknown "designs"—Carwin has shown Clara "How imperfectly acquainted were we with the condition and designs of the beings that surround us" (p. 86)—and Clara's conviction that "Ideas exist in our minds that can be accounted for by no established laws" (p. 99) both imply that a natural explanation does exist but, with our limited awareness, we cannot fathom it. The unknown is not necessarily the unknowable. What Brown anticipates is a superior but natural being. The voice Pleyel hears telling him of the death of his mistress, Theresa, prompts Clara to reflect: "That there are conscious beings, besides ourselves, in existence, whose modes of activity and information surpass our own, can scarcely be denied. Is there a glimpse afforded us into a world of these superior beings?" (p. 51). At a later point, she speaks of "the existence of unfettered and beneficent intelligences" *a propos* of her suspicion that "a human agent" may be responsible (p. 107). Carwin may be such a superman. As a youth, he tells us in his *Memoirs,* "My senses were perpetually alive to novelty, my fancy teemed with visions of the future, and my attention fastened upon everything mysterious or unknown" (p. 276).

This impetus toward the future is later given direction

by Ludloe, who dwells on "the duty of unfettering our minds from the prejudices which govern the world" (p. 302), and Carwin, like Brown and Ludloe, becomes a utopian dreamer. The two islands, similar "in their relative proportions . . . to Great Britain and Ireland" (p. 337), marked on the map Carwin finds in Ludloe's library, presumably the sites of Ludloe's projected utopia, are in an unexplored area of the world of "vast extent, sufficient to receive a continent as large as North America, which our ignorance has filled only with *water*" (my italics, p. 338). The connection with Great Britain and America, in collaboration with Brown's suspicion "that many of Ludloe's intimations alluded to a country well known to him, though unknown to others" (pp. 337–38), tempts me to suggest that Ludloe's new-found lands are new-found worlds of mind which exist independent of physical reality, although the broadened awareness does have something to do with the American location. If reality is in the mind, Clara's decision to move to Europe with her uncle should be seen as a mental revolution following upon the fiery apocalyptic destruction of her house in America. "This incident," explains Clara, "disastrous as it may at first seem, had, in reality, a beneficial effect upon my feelings" (p. 265). In this case, the optimistic ending is not out of place, as Larzer Ziff would have it, but is rather representative of the basic transformation with which the apocalyptic imagination is concerned.[10] The apocalyptic world naturally enough is characterized by security and rational order, and such a state is ironically symbolized, as on Ludloe's map, by the Old World. Blake's Jerusalem, it will be recalled, is "builded" in the Old World.

In *Wieland*, to summarize, the confrontation with mysterious phenomena leads Brown to distinguish between aspects of experience that can be explained with reference to either internal or external factors and between those aspects of experience that cannot presently be explained with reference to internal or external factors. These four cases are neatly epitomized by the four occasions on which

[10] Ziff, pp. 53–54.

Brown departs from Clara's narrative viewpoint. We learn
about the circumstances of the elder Wieland's death
from Clara's uncle, Mr. Cambridge, whose testimony, it is
affirmed, is "peculiarly worthy of credit, because no man's
temper is more skeptical, and his belief is unalterably
attached to natural causes" (p. 21). The elder Wieland's
death is unexplained only because "half the truth had
been suppressed" (p. 20), and the strange death of Mr.
Cambridge's father he explains internally as the consequence of maniacal illusions or depravity of the senses,
noting, "In the course of my practice in the German army,
many cases, equally remarkable, have occurred" (p. 202).
The voice here would seem to be similar to that of Brown
in the "Advertisement," explaining that "most readers will
probably recollect an authentic case, remarkably similar
to that of Wieland" (p. 4). Clara's contradictory statement two pages into the novel, "The experience of no
human being can furnish a parallel" (p. 6), points to the
transformation she must undergo before she can leave for
Europe with her uncle—a move implying a commitment to
his point of view. Her uncle's understanding could comprehend the presently unknown science-fictional viewpoint
exemplified in Carwin's *Memoirs*, in which mysterious
phenomena are amenable to an internal explanation. The
two other viewpoints, Pleyel's explanation of his misconceptions concerning Clara's feelings toward him, and Wieland's defense, point respectively to external causes that
can be explained, and external supernatural causes, which
we cannot comprehend.

Pleyel, Mr. Cambridge, and Carwin represent an ascend-
ing scale of rationalism. They all survive, and Pleyel joins
Clara and her uncle in Europe, where he eventually marries Clara. It is the supernaturally disposed types who die.
I would suggest that, since the transformation in *Wieland*
can be rationally explained in terms of natural causes
predicated upon the future development of the mind of
man, parapsychology, or discoveries in inner space, such
an explanation is the one that Brown would favor, and
surely an interpretation that can account for the book's

conclusion is preferable to that which, arguing for an out-and-out attack on rationalism, must dismiss the conclusion as contradictory backsliding. The prospect of a new mind and a new apocalyptic world of mind brings me back to the tantalizing image of Ludloe's ambiguously located islands, which may now be seen as simultaneously suggestive of the various new worlds, spiritual, historical, philosophical, mental, and science-fictional, that are opposed or conflated in *Wieland*.

8. Solaris *and the Illegitimate Suns of Science Fiction*

I

All too often, an abundance of "ideas" in science fiction, however "stimulating" they may be, points to an essential poverty of imagination. There are few experiences more stultifying than listening to a fan retailing the "far-out" conceptions that have gone into the plots of the last twenty or so science-fiction novels he has read. For just this reader, A. E. van Vogt has evolved his technical recipe of introducing a new idea every eight hundred words.[1] This emphasis on ideas in science fiction goes some way toward explaining why so much of it is particularly resilient to academic criticism. The fan will likely resent as destructive any analytic probes directed at his favored product, but the truth is that van Vogt and many others are quite safe from all attempts at literary exegesis. Once the "ideas" have been enumerated, there is simply nothing further constructive to be said.

Surprisingly few science-fiction writers are able to take only three, two, or preferably a single "new" idea and explore *at novel length* the ramifications and ambiguities to which a severely limited number of "new" notions might give rise. The oft-repeated assertion that science fiction is best confined to short-story length is one of the consequences of the fallacious belief that "ideas" are the be-all and the end-all of science fiction. The mainstream writer,

[1] See A. E. van Vogt, "Complication in the Science Fiction Story," in *Of Worlds Beyond: The Science of Science Fiction Writing*, ed. Lloyd Arthur Eshbach (Chicago, 1964), pp. 53–66.

in concerning himself with the "real world," cannot help, if he is to be successful, but reflect in his work many of the complexities, paradoxes, and shaded values that make up our environment. In so doing, he provides a critic with tensions, ironies, and ambiguities that can be explored in the text. It is the imaginative responsibility of the superior science-fiction writer to incorporate a similar density in his work if it is to meet literary standards.

In some ways, it is unfortunate that most regular science-fiction writers have developed a species of "shorthand" because of the peculiarly assimilative nature of the genre. Once certain ideas—say, a time machine, the warped-space concept, or Asimov's "laws of robotics"—have been effectively described in one or two books, they become part of the science-fiction writers' and readers' arsenal. The writer has only to name the thing and his reader will fill in the appropriate rationale. This is one reason why non-readers of science fiction often find it difficult to relate to the occasional science-fiction novel they might pick up. The practiced reader tends to respond to a science-fictional work partly on the basis of what is not there. To an extent, this shorthand is a valuable convenience that enables a writer to get to the meat of his story without rehashing a lot of old material. However, it can also encourage a mental laziness in regard to all ideas whether "new" or "old" and a tendency to produce "thin" works which consist largely of a succession of gimmicks.

For all these reasons, it is not surprising that some of the finest works of science fiction have been produced by writers such as Orwell and Huxley, who have somehow wandered from the mainstream. There are, however, a growing number of practicing science-fiction writers who are becoming more adept at developing in a rigorous fashion their particular themes or ideas. In *Tower of Glass*, Robert Silverberg is concerned with the effect of artificial or alien intelligence on the definition of man, and his book concludes with a scene of fiery apocalypse, "the cities of

earth are ablaze" (p. 184),[2] which is most accurately seen
as a metaphor of philosophical transformation, and not in
literal terms. The central problem is one of communication,
and every element in the book illustrates this theme. In an
age of instant travel by "transmat"—the startling temporal
effect of which is brilliantly conveyed by the dislocations
of the opening chapters—and mind transference, communication with the stars obsesses Simeon Krug. This second
Simeon builds a transmitting tower of glass and awaits a
Second Coming equivalent to man's emergence from the
sea and the discovery that "there's a whole other world up
there" (pp. 1, 54).

The tower, "that great erection" (p. 88) to knowledge,
so apparently precarious that it threatens to fall "like
Lucifer through all one long day" (p. 20), comes to stand
for communication on all levels—sexual, intellectual, religious, and demonic. That the android workers worship
their creator, Krug, as a god suggests that a sense of religious communication, while in some ways beneficial, is
false. On discovering that Krug is an object of worship,
his son Manuel experiences a "philosophical apocalypse":
"It seemed to him that the world had lost its solidity, that
he was tumbling through its substance toward the core,
floating free, unable to check himself" (p. 162). Other
aspects of the communication theme are also dramatized
in relation to the androids. Since the androids are capable
of rational discourse, a major issue is the question of android equality, which is presented as analogous to the
abolitionist issue in nineteenth-century America. But it is
sexual communication rather than intellectual communication that complicates the issue and finally convinces Manuel that the androids be considered equal to man. He has
a taboo affair with one of them in order to make Silverberg's point, that unlike intellectual or religious communication, which may be unreliable or evil, sex, however
dangerous, holds the promise of true communication.

[2] All parenthetical references to *Tower of Glass*, originally
published in 1970, are to the Bantam edition (New York,
1971).

As an example of a "straight" science-fiction writer who is able to explore in detail the implications of a single theme—at least occasionally—Silverberg prepares the way for my analysis of Stanislaw Lem's *Solaris*. *Solaris* is typical of Lem's work and similar to *Tower of Glass* in that it deals with the problem of alien communication, but it does this in a manner far more sophisticated than Silverberg's and is a total vindication of the science-fiction form. Indeed Lem's rigorous treatment of a single idea amounts, indirectly, to an attack on much contemporary science fiction—particularly the "alien encounter" type—that goes considerably beyond mine.

II

Hailed by Franz Rottensteiner as "the best sf writer not only of Europe, but of the world," Stanislaw Lem, certainly pre-eminent in his native Poland, is virtually unknown to the English-speaking reader.[3] Even if we allow for the fact that Rottensteiner is the author's agent, to judge from *Solaris* (originally published in 1961 and the only Lem novel available in English to date), science fiction has come of age as never before. According to Rottensteiner, "Lem's central epistemological position in all of his fiction is that we can never know the *noumen* of things; that we are forever imprisoned by the structure of our minds and bodies."[4] In other words, man's understanding of the external universe is fundamentally anthropocentric. This might seem to imply that Lem is an anti-apocalyptic writer, particularly if, by apocalyptic, one envisions, as I have, some form of genuine contact with a radically different world. For Lem, there are no new worlds *that men can experience*. Wherever man goes, he will encounter only extensions of himself. As a thousand or more science-fiction writers have demonstrated, our

[3] See "Stanislaw Lem: A Profile," *Luna Monthly*, 31 (December 1971), p. 22.
[4] Ibid., p. 7.

moon or the planets, Mars, Venus, Dune, or Winter, are all envisaged as aspects of Earth. Until quite recently, Venus and Mars, to take the two most clichéd examples, were most typically presented as mirrors of Earth's prehistoric past or catastrophic future. Whatever may be absolutely unique about these various worlds, man is unable to apprehend. The reader should be aware, then, of Lem's heavy irony when Kris Kelvin, the protagonist of *Solaris,* makes the point that among the explored planets "Earth is a common type—the grass of the universe! And we pride ourselves on this universality" (p. 159).[5]

Implicit in this basic assumption of Lem's is a critique of virtually all science fiction as hypocritically presenting images of radically new worlds based on anthropomorphic techniques of extrapolation and analogy. This is not to say that, for example, Bradbury's depiction of Mars will bear no relation to man's eventual experience of the planet. On the contrary, when man stands on Mars, what he sees will essentially result from the same process of extrapolation and analogy that underlies Bradbury's fiction. From Lem's point of view, the new landscape will not be that of Mars but rather of the human mind. Lem is accusing most science-fiction writers of a philosophical naïveté in attempting to describe a reality that is outside human language. Science-fiction writers should allow for some of that mainstream ambiguity by placing all accounts of "alien" environments within ironic, qualifying quotation marks. In purporting to describe or comprehend the unknown by a direct process of analogy and extrapolation, writers lie.

For Lem, the necessarily ironic stance of the science-fiction writer involves some inversion of my definition of the apocalyptic imagination. While a genuinely new reality, beyond all subjective/objective systematizing, is assumed to exist, that reality is never truly encountered by

[5] All parenthetical references to *Solaris* are to the English version, translated from the French by Joanna Kilmartin and Steve Cox, which includes an "Afterword" by Darko Suvin (New York, 1970).

man. There is, however, an illusory new reality consequent upon the continual rediscovery of old worlds of human mind. Which is to say that on Mars the only "new" world man will discover is the world of man, and in that sense Lem's work does illustrate that form of the philosophic apocalyptic which conjures with new images of man.

This is analogous to but should not be confused with the recent rather facile assertion by J. G. Ballard and other "new wave" writers that, in their work, the exploration of outer space is to be read more accurately as an exploration of inner space. Such works may be apocalyptic in a psychedelic or surrealistic sense, but in many cases where the science-fictional landscape has the ontological status of metaphor, I would deny that they belong to the genre of science fiction. Many of these writers, in drawing on the now assimilated experimental techniques of James Joyce and the surrealists, point to the true nature of the form in which they are writing. For example, to relate the ennui of a suburban housewife to the entropy of the universe, as does P. A. Zoline in "The Heat Death of the Universe" (1967), is to use a science-fictional conception only for its metaphoric appropriateness. Because the tale's reality is grounded in a housewife and her kitchen and because of the lack of a plausible scientific rationale connecting the end of the material universe with her state, Zoline's piece cannot legitimately be classified as science fiction. Lem might well make the same criticism of works in which the "alien" environment is unwittingly anthropomorphic and therefore metaphoric.

A legitimate science-fictional connection between the microcosmic world of man and the universal macrocosm does, however, exist in Piers Anthony's *Macroscope* (1969), in which the form of the universe is *objectively* discovered to be similar to that of the human brain. The convoluted shape of space allows for travel at speeds beyond light by a process of "jumping" at points equivalent to the synapses of the brain. In Lem's case, the scientific rationales are

also there, the science-fictional content is not just metaphoric; something unknown is definitely there and is no
less real for not being understood. While, to the rather
passive phenomenological outlook of the "new wave"
writers, reality is exclusively a mental domain, Lem's somewhat more aggressive, somewhat more self-conscious anthropomorphic understanding admits of both an observable interior reality and a non-visible exterior reality, and
Lem never loses his faith in the repeatedly wrongheaded
and unverifiable attempts of science to take the measure of
the external universe. Lem's position, as my argumentation
testifies, is a much more complicated and rewarding one.

Solaris is the name of a planet. In the novel, human
beings attempt to grapple with the reality of that planet,
a reality that is especially untractable by virtue of its
pliability. Because the entire world is covered with a
malleable substance, our nearest equivalent to which is
water, and because that "organic" "ocean" is able in
various ways to imitate human artifacts and mental images, Solaris is unusually well equipped to mirror the
hopelessly anthropomorphic nature of man. The central
point is made most succinctly toward the end of the
book through an allusion to the argument of the fifteen-
page *Compendium,* by Grastrom, "one of the most eccentric authors in Solaris literature," which is vast indeed:

> Grastrom set out to demonstrate that the most abstract
> achievements of science, the most advanced theories
> and victories of mathematics represented nothing more
> than a stumbling, one or two-step progression from a
> rude, prehistoric, anthropomorphic understanding of the
> universe around us. He pointed out correspondences
> with the human body—the projections of our senses, the
> structure of our physical organization, and the physi-
> ological limitations of man—in the equations of the
> theory of relativity, the theorem of magnetic fields and
> the various unified field theories. Grastrom's conclusion
> was that there neither was, nor could be, any question

of "contact" between mankind and any non-human civilization (p. 117).

Opposed to this view is the belief, outlined in Muntius's *Introduction to Solaristics,* that Contact with the Other, in an almost mystical sense, is possible. The aim of Solaristics, described as "the space era's equivalent to religion" (science, like religion, deals with "incommunicable knowledge"), is a form of Contact "no less vague and obscure than the communion of the saints, or the second coming of the Messiah." Contact is equivalent to "Relevation" (p. 172), "it would explain the meaning of the destiny of man" (pp. 172–73), "It has become the heaven of eternity" (p. 173). To truly discover an *alien* planet would be to fulfill the Apocalypse of John the Divine.

Although Lem is strongly biased toward Grastrom's position, it can never quite be a question of one or the other, while that Other is assumed to exist. But Snow, one of the three Earthmen based on Solaris, has no doubt. Addressing Kris Kelvin, he makes a speech that reveals him to be, like Grastrom, a cosmic atheist:

> We don't want to conquer the cosmos, we simply want to extend the boundaries of Earth to the frontiers of the cosmos. For us, such and such a planet is as arid as the Sahara, another as frozen as the North Pole, yet another as lush as the Amazon basin. We are humanitarian and chivalrous; we don't want to enslave other races, we simply want to bequeath them our values and take over their heritage in exchange. We think of ourselves as the Knights of the Holy Contact. This is another lie. We are only seeking Man. We have no need of other worlds. We need mirrors (p. 72).

So much for the "idea" content of *Solaris.* I want now to turn to an examination of the various subtle imagistic and technical ways in which Lem develops these ideas in order to produce a masterpiece of science fiction. The reference to "mirrors" in the previous quotation provides a convenient starting point.

III

The "waters" of Solaris, as I have indicated, reflect human reality in a uniquely concrete fashion, both human artifacts and the structures of men's minds. In the lengthy chapter entitled "The Monsters," itself an anthropomorphic projection, Kelvin, who narrates the story, describes in minute detail the various formations that the "ocean" throws up, and gives some impression of the mountain of theoretical research devoted to explaining these phenomena. The more readily identifiable "'plasmatic' metamorphoses" of the "ocean" have been artificially classified into "'tree-mountains,' 'extensors,' 'fungoids,' 'mimoids,' 'symmetriads' and 'asymmetriads,' 'vertebrids,' and 'agilus'" (p. 111). The first, third, and seventh of these mutable and transitory forms seem vaguely imitative of terrestrial formations, whether geological, physiological, or botanical. As their name indicates, the "mimoids" imitate rather more directly, if in greatly enlarged form, inanimate "objects near or far, external to the ocean itself" (p. 113). These structures, tethered umbilically to the ocean, may maintain themselves for long periods of time. As far as I can judge, and this is largely a guess, the volatile, complex, balanced, or "mirroring" (p. 119) constructions of the rising and falling "symmetriads" and "asymmetriads," with their propensity for sudden subsidence, or explosive dissolution in the case of the "asymmetriads," corresponds allegorically to the transitory, intricate, dialectical, and ever amendable nature of scientific theory or abstract mental designs.

Certain winglike forms called "independents" exist in a detached state from the "ocean," and in this respect they are similar to the humanoid "beings" that the "ocean" derives apparently from guilt images in the minds of the people who man or manned the terrestrial research station on Solaris. These "visitors" constitute the main dramatic problem of the novel. A "visitor" cannot be got rid of and is reliable only when in close proximity with the researcher on whose mental image "she" is modeled—all the "visitors" are women with whom the Earthmen have been in some way connected. Separated from "her" "source," "she" displays a colossal destructive strength. Kelvin arrives at the station to discover that one of the three operators, Gibarian, has seemingly committed suicide to get away from his companion, a "Negress" who now accompanies his corpse. Kelvin is visited by an exact replica of his wife, Rheya, who had committed suicide after being estranged from him. Following attempts to dispose of "her," and to fight his own reactions, Kelvin finds himself in love with "Rheya." This, of course, introduces a problem when Kelvin agrees to test the hypothesis of one of his colleagues, Sartorius: Since these "visitors" emanate from traumatic and largely repressed memories, the attempt to beam at the "ocean," in amplified form, a subject's conscious wishes might result in their disappearance. To Kelvin's dismay the experiment is successful.

All these mirrored forms reflect man's image and never the reality of Solaris. Similarly the many glass objects in the novel related to vision, whether windows, video screens, or glasses, in actuality serve to hinder vision, to function as screens in the sense of barriers, ultimately to symbolize the limitations of human perception. The unfounded belief of the scientists that the mimoids, "which were spoken of as open windows on the ocean," presented "the best opportunity to establish the hoped-for contact between the two civilizations" (p. 110), points to this symbolism. On the other hand, it is hypothesized that human physical appearance "is a transparent window to the ocean" (p. 193) through which it reads men's minds. But the many windows of the station are inside-facing mirrors. Significantly only the library, with which Lem has a Borgesian concern, "had no windows" (p. 110). This womblike room contains thousands of volumes of research that purport to elucidate the nature of Solaris—a claim to which the lack of external light gives the symbolic lie. In the library, subjectivity is rampant.

All the researchers at some point or other indicate a deficiency of vision by wearing glasses. The light from the two suns of Solaris, one blue and one red, is too strong. On first encountering it, Kelvin (in Gibarian's room) states, "I shut my eyes" and "found a pair of dark glasses so big that when I put them on they covered half my face" (p. 28). "Looking up, I caught sight of my face in the mirror of a half-open locker door: masked by the dark glasses, it was deathly pale. The room, too, glinting with blue and white reflections, looked equally bizarre; but soon there came a prolonged screech of metal as the air-tight outer shutters slid across the window. There was an instant of darkness and then the lights came on; they seemed to me to be curiously dim" (p. 28). The symbolism of the glasses, the mirror, and the window is quite obvious.

Kelvin hears footsteps. Presumably it is a "visitor." Both Kelvin and the "visitor" grasp the handle of the door, which remains shut. The "visitor" departs. Kelvin's shutting his eyes, the closing of the outer window, and the closed door are all symbolically equivalent. Kelvin's earlier reluctance to take off his space suit and deprive himself of a "shield" (p. 13) until he has built himself a "temporary barricade" by placing heavy boxes in front of the door similarly suggests both the impossibility of contact and man's basic fear and unwillingness to confront the Other. The desire for insulation and distinction from a real environment begets hallucinations. Kelvin is startled by the movement in a "narrow looking glass" (p. 13), which turns out to be his own reflection. On entering his room, Kelvin encounters "a yawning gulf of darkness—until it occurred to me to remove my dark glasses" (p. 31).

Sartorius has barricaded himself in his laboratory. But when Kelvin persuades him to edge through a narrowly opened "glass panel" door, he emerges wearing "curved dark glasses, which covered up half his face" (p. 43). Doors, whether transparent or opaque, open on the inside as well as the outside, and in refusing to open them, as Kelvin reflects at one point, man remains ignorant about the realities of his own mind: "Man has gone out to explore other worlds and other civilizations without having explored his own labyrinth of dark passages and secret chambers, and without finding what lies behind doorways that he himself has sealed" (p. 157). This image incidentally points to the concrete science-fictional sense whereby the exploration of inner space and outer space may be usefully reconciled. Snow, the first of the three researchers whom Kelvin encounters at the station, is presumably the most visually handicapped, since he requires reading glasses that tend to "slide down his nose" (p. 66) as well as dark glasses for the bright light of Solaris. For Sartorius' experiment with the "ocean," Kelvin notices that Snow "had on contact lenses" (p. 160) but is presumably unaware of the ironic pun on "contact" and the impeding function of the lenses. With equal appropriateness, when Kelvin recalls his mental image of Giese, "the father of Solarist studies and of Solarists," the memory includes "gold-rimmed spectacles" (p. 161).

In order to avoid the embarrassment of encountering each other's "visitors," Kelvin, Snow, and Sartorius remain in their rooms, for the most part, and Snow, via the videophone, tells Kelvin of the plan to "set up a three-way videophone link, but with the telescreen lenses covered" (p. 97). Interrupted by his "visitor," Snow breaks the contact: "The screen went blank" (p. 97). Kelvin turns to his "neutron microscope" to look at a sample of "Rheya's" blood, but, beyond a certain point of magnification, "the screen remained a blank" (p. 98). For the most part, screens screen. Later, Kelvin is talking to Snow and Sartorius: "A vertical line, bisecting the screen and barely perceptible, showed that I was linked to two channels: on either side of this line, I should have seen two images—Snow and Sartorius. But the light-rimmed screen remained dark. Both my interlocutors had covered the lenses of their sets" (p. 100). Even when the lens is not covered, when Snow and Kelvin are talking to one

another on a later occasion, vision is still hopelessly
restricted. Snow "leant forward to scrutinize me through
the convex glass" (p. 148) in an attempt to establish if
"Rheya" is with Kelvin.

IV

It is in the context of fundamental separation from the
Other—an apartness symbolized by the station itself,
which hovers at a distance above the "ocean"—that man
attempts to hypothesize about the nature of that Other,
the "visitors" in particular. As "Gibarian" tells Kelvin, in
a dream(?), the "visitors" "behave strictly as a kind of
amplifier of our own thoughts. Any attempt to understand
the motivation of these occurrences is blocked by our
own anthropomorphism" (p. 134). Even to name the
"visitors" is to somehow define them. Hence they are
given different names. "Gibarian" calls them "polytheres"
(p. 134), Kelvin initially calls "Rheya" a "simulacra"
(p. 65), Sartorius calls them "phantoms," until Snow suggests, "Let's call them Phi-creatures" (p. 100). The linguistic problem compels me to speak of Solaris repeatedly
within qualifying quotation marks. Attempts to "categorize
the ocean" (p. 22) are similar to attempts to nail down
Moby Dick. Indeed, the Station appears to be "shaped like
a whale" (p. 4) but, after the fashion of Polonius's cloud,
it is also comparable to "an ancient zeppelin" (p. 201).
Unlike the situation in LeGuin's *The Left Hand of Darkness* where the inconsequential plot element is a serious
weakness in the novel, it is appropriate, in this case, that
the level of human plot in *Solaris* is very slight, very
detached, even irrelevant in relation to the book's highly
cerebral content.

Paradoxically, the manner in which man is divorced
from the reality of Solaris largely manifests itself in a form
of fusion with Solaris, a lack of apparent distinction between man and the Other. Perhaps the clearest indication
of this is the term "Solarist." A habituated reader of sci-

ence fiction coming upon the title of Chapter 2, "The Solarists," following the description, in the first chapter, of Kelvin's arrival on Solaris, would most naturally assume that the Solarists are the inhabitants of the planet Solaris. In fact, Solarists are simply human "experts" on the nature of the Solaris "ocean," a study that has become somewhat confused with Solaristics and the quest for "Contact." But Lem's heavy irony here is surely deliberate, because, in a sense, the Solarists have created the only reality of the planet that we can become aware of, and they might appropriately be taken for its inhabitants.

Uncertain about the "reality" of his experiences on "Solaris," particularly on seeing the large "Negress" lying beside the corpse of Gibarian, Kelvin considers the possibility that he is "confronting the creations of [his] own inflamed brain" (p. 48), and he performs certain experiments that falsely convince him that he has established their "reality." Then he meets "Rheya." Indeed, it is later, in dreams, that Kelvin does experience a philosophical apocalypse, some revelation of the reality, in "A blurred region in the heart of vastness, far from earth and heaven, with no ground underfoot, no vault of sky overhead, nothing. I am the prisoner of an alien matter and my body is clothed in a dead, formless substance—or rather I have no body, I *am* that alien matter" (pp. 178–80).

Kelvin's vision is essentially that of the primal apocalyptic sea of chaos, represented perhaps not so much by the Solaris "ocean" as it is but rather as we see it. We are informed that "the ocean of Solaris was submerging under an ocean of printed paper" (p. 169). The loss of stability may say something about the possible necessity to "*liquidate* the Station" (p. 171) and the dubious value "of a joint *pooling* of information with the living ocean" (p. 172), and cast doubt upon the researcher's report, which is beamed to Earth as "a pattern of *waves* in space" (p. 195; all italics mine). Indeed the apparently random chapter-structuring of the book seems yet another reflection of the undefinable activity of the "ocean." The longest chapters, namely Chapters 2, 6, 8, and 11, all involve

theoretical Solarist literature, and seem to be distributed
among the fourteen chapters in a manner that is per-
versely disordered. And if literature reflects the nature
of the "ocean," there is some logic to the notion that the
ocean "is able to read us like a book" and that the "visitors" are somehow "read off" "a recording imprinted on
our minds" (p. 193). The degree to which articulated
knowledge opens a door on chaos is suggested by the
many scenes involving disorder. For example, in Gibarian's
cabin, Kelvin sees that "Both shelves and cupboards had
been emptied of their contents, which were piled into
heaps, amongst the furniture. At my feet, blocking the
way, were two overturned trolleys buried beneath a heap
of periodicals spilling out of bulging briefcases which had
burst open. Books with their pages splayed out fanwise
were stained with colored *liquids* which had spilt from
broken retorts. . . . A *flood* of papers of every conceivable
size *swamped* the floor" (italics mine, pp. 26–27). Likewise the radio cabin contains "piles of objects littered
about—thermic cells, instruments, spare parts for the elec-
tronic equipment" (p. 149).

In the last chapter, Kelvin advances a new theory, concerning an evolving, imperfect god, somehow reflective
of both man and Solaris, particularly as Snow develops
the idea: "Solaris could be the first phase of the despair-
ing God." Kelvin is enthusiastic: "You've produced a completely new hypothesis about Solaris—congratulations!
Everything suddenly falls into place: the failure to achieve
contact. . . . Everything is explicable in terms of the behavior of a small child" (p. 199). The theory is apparently
also accepted by Darko Suvin, who describes it in his
"Afterword" as a "cosmological insight" (p. 215). Another
critic, Sam J. Lundwell, also agrees, to judge from his
comment that "*Solaris* is an extremely interesting sf novel
and a very sophisticated one, dealing with the concept of
an imperfect God, one who is omnipotent but without
omniscience, and the problem of communication between
a group of human explorers and this strange entity."[6]

[6] See *Science Fiction: What It's All About* (New York, 1971),
p. 237.

Surely Lem is utilizing a reader's temptation to accept an explanation presented in the final pages of a novel. Just maybe this explanation is the one in a million that is correct, but all the evidence I have accumulated points against it. It would seem that the events of *Solaris* have engendered just one more unverifiable anthropomorphic hypothesis about the planet.

Certainly the novel's concluding incident would tend to give the lie to this theory. Kelvin and Snow identify their "god" as "a very old mimoid" (p. 199)—rather unlikely, since mimoids, unlike most gods, seem totally given to the reproduction of inanimate objects. Kelvin decides to visit an old mimoid to become a Solarist who has at least set foot on the planet. Kelvin's flitter lands on the "sloping, fairly even surface" of "a kind of beach" (p. 201), that same Wellsian sloping beach that inevitably in science fiction symbolizes the area of contact with the unknown and/or the end or transformation of man. Kelvin does learn something of man's limits: they are circumscribed by the reality of Solaris. Kelvin puts his hand into an "ocean" "wave," which, he notes, "enveloped my hand without touching it, so that a thin covering of 'air' separated my glove inside a cavity which had been fluid a moment previously, and now had a fleshy consistency" (p. 203). The allegorical import is transparently clear, yet Kelvin resolves to wait for "Rheya's" return while doubting that the ocean "could respond to the tragedy of *two human beings*" (italics mine, p. 204). Is "Rheya" Rheya?

v

In conclusion and taking a hint from the episode described above, it may be more illuminating to conceive of the anthropomorphic activity in *Solaris* not in terms of a mirroring image but as a form of reproduction, specifically sexual reproduction. This calls for a retrospective analysis of the first chapter of the novel, which describes Kelvin's launching in a capsule from the "mother" ship

Prometheus and his "arrival" on Solaris. On a first reading, the description of Kelvin's flight might seem strangely primitive and gauche. The brief, somewhat jerky description of the flight, radically concertinaing the lapse of time, is not realistically convincing. Perhaps, as Kelvin later hypothesizes, "I was still on board the *Prometheus*" (p. 48), and all is a hallucination. Furthermore, the sexual implications of a space projectile thrusting through the void are something of a science-fiction cliché, and a reader thus familiarized might initially be exasperated by Lem's apparently heavy-handed use of such imagery. Indeed virtually every descriptive phrase related to the flight and the "arrival" is pregnant with sexual innuendo.

Admittedly, there are dangers involved in interpreting a text that is twice removed from the original Polish, the English version being a translation from the French. I would submit, however, that although I may be wrong about details, the over-all density of the evidence leaves little room for doubt. Although one might wish to discount the reference to "the narrow cockpit," there is also the reference to the "men around the shaft" and Moddard's head "leaning over the top of the shaft." Kelvin "attached the hose to the valve on [his] space suit and it inflated rapidly" so that he "stood, or rather hung suspended, enveloped in [his] pneumatic suit and yoked to the metal hull." Suggestions of sexual aggression merge with images of the embryonic result of such aggression. Listening to the "electric motors which turned the screws," Kelvin concentrates on "the luminous circle of the solitary dial," the first of a number of imagistic references to the female. The sound of "screws" gives way to "a grinding noise" (p. 1), while Kelvin "noticed a rustling outside, like a shower of fine sand," as "a wide slit opened at eye level" (p. 2). Previously his eyes had been focused on the luminous dial.

These explicitly erotic connotations continue with Kelvin's information that the stars, like "a glittering dust [compare the "shower of fine sand"], filled my porthole [compare the luminous dial]." "My body rigid, sealed in its pneumatic envelope [the spaceman's "safe"?], I was knifing through space with the impression of standing still in the void, my only distraction the steadily mounting heat." The capsule begins its descent to a "grating sound, like a steel blade being drawn across a sheet of wet glass [the shower on the dial?]." "The pale reddish glow of infinity" might suggest a fleshy tinge. Following "a sudden jolt," the "vibration" of the vehicle transmits itself to Kelvin's "entire body." But although "the image of the dial shivered and multiplied, and its phosphorescence spread out in all directions" (some form of reproduction is going on), Kelvin states, "I had not taken this long voyage [less than two pages so far] to overshoot my target!" (Fear of premature ejaculation?)

Kelvin experiences some symbolic trouble in making "contact," but soon the circle of the dial and the porthole, now covered by "a veil of mist," give way to the globe of Solaris, and as he comes in for a landing, "against a background of deep, low-pitched murmuring, which seemed to me the very voice of the planet itself," he sees "the gigantic ball of the sun" (p. 4). The relation between Solaris and the sun is, as I shall indicate, rather important. At this point "the sun's orbit, which had so far encircled me, shifted unexpectedly, and the incandescent disc [compare the luminous dial again] appeared now to the right, now to the left, seeming to dance on the planet's horizon. I was swinging like a giant pendulum while the planet, its surface wrinkled with purplish-blue and black furrows, rose up in front of me like a wall" (pp. 4–5)— therefore ultimately impenetrable? Some celestial dance of the sheets, in which the sun and Solaris are conjointly violated, seems to be in progress. The "something," which "detached itself with a snap from the cone of the capsule," to the accompaniment of "the noise which . . . reminded me irresistibly of Earth: . . . the moaning of wind" (p. 4), may be not only a parachute.

The station, with its "elongated silvery body, shaped like a whale," also has its phallic connotations as the redness of infinity becomes "a blinding crimson glare" while the luminous dial becomes the "glittering quicksilver" of the "ocean." After "a peculiar slow-motion rhythm," the capsule lands "with a long harsh sigh" (p. 4). "A green [the color of fertility] indicator lit up: 'Arrival,'" and "with a muffled sigh of resignation, the space-suit expelled its air." Kelvin has "come," and orgasm is followed by detumescence. Kelvin is now within some kind of womb, "a vast silver funnel" with "throbbing" ventilators and "colored pipes disappearing" into rounded orifices. "The cigar-shaped capsule" now resembles "a burst cocoon." "The outer casing, scorched during flight, had turned a dirty brown" (p. 5). The sense of illegal entry is reinforced by the references to "a pool of oily liquid," "a nauseating smell," and "other waste" (pp. 5–6). If none of the above convinces the reader, there is still Snow's accidental action on seeing Kelvin: "He was holding one of those pear-shaped plastic flasks. . . . The flask dropped from his fingers and bounced several times, spilling a few drops of transparent liquid. Blood drained from his face" (p. 6). This detail can have no function but to be somehow recapitulative of the import of the flight.

References to blood now accumulate. Snow's eyes are "blood-shot" (p. 7). "Thick foam, the color of blood, gathered in the troughs of the waves" (p. 8). Kelvin asks Snow where Gibarian is, and an accident is mentioned. As Kelvin leaves the cabin, he turns to look at Snow and "noticed the dried blood-stains on the back of his hands" (p. 11). Kelvin has not been told that Gibarian is dead; this interpretation is the first of many assumptions. The bloodstains would seem to implicate Snow as a murderer. It so happens that Kelvin's assumption is right: Gibarian is dead. But in view of all the sexual innuendo, Snow's bloodstained hands might result from an exercise in obstetrics rather than murder. At least, I believe that Gibarian's death is not verified in the first chapter in order to allow for this ambivalence.

The remainder of the novel should be viewed as an interpretive gloss on the import of all this introductory erotic detail. First, to conceive of space travel in terms of sex is a rather neat illustration, and in this case no less neat for being hackneyed, of man's anthropomorphic world view. As a "cybernetics expert" (p. 6), Snow is involved with the business of imparting human characteristics to artificial or non-human forms. We can only hypothesize as to why the robots have been locked away but, in the circumstances, they can only hinder in the attempt to distinguish between human and non-human on Solaris. It is also significant that when Snow warns Kelvin about running into someone unknown, Kelvin thinks of "a ghost" (p. 10), the anthropomorphic form with which we people the world of spirit. Whether in the form of robots, ghosts, "visitors," or space capsules, man confronts only analogues of his own image. A spaceship is perhaps the most literal form of projection. Where on the mechanical, spiritual spectrum does man begin, and where does he end?

But the further and more important implication is that the first chapter indirectly describes the begetting of Solaris as a result of the incestuous sexual union of man and mother Earth, the Earth from which the *Prometheus* has journeyed and for which, as the mother ship, it is an analogue. Any sense of true union or contact, sexual or otherwise, with the reality of Solaris is an illusion. The Solaris that the Earthmen know is an "illegitimate" child. We can see now why in the last chapter Snow speaks of Solaris as "the cradle of your divine child," or a baby: "Everything is explicable in terms of the behavior of a small child." Snow believes he is talking about the evolving-god theory, of which he states, "I renounce paternity" (p. 199). In the sense that I have been explicating, and in view of the first chapter, Kelvin has by far the greater claim to paternity. Symbolically, the specific site of the conception of Solaris is the windowless, womblike library, "the big circular chamber," where Kelvin relaxes: "I felt at ease in my egg, among the void of cabinets crammed with tape and microfilm" (p. 110). The world of Solaris is a conception of mind. The scientists who recommend a "withdrawal" from the "Solaris Affair" (p. 23) are putting the matter in its most accurate terms.

This interpretation may also serve to explain a difficulty that Darko Suvin perceptively notices regarding the theory that the "visitors" derive from the "deepest memory encoded in the brain's cerebrosides." Since that memory is, by Lem's not wholly convincing hypothesis, a trauma of erotic guilt, each scientist is visited by the woman he has in some way lost or slighted." Suvin observes that no convincing literal hypothesis is forthcoming. However, in terms of my procreation interpretation, it is utterly appropriate, on a symbolic level, that the succubi-like "visitors" are emanations of "erotic guilt." As Suvin accurately intuits, "Lem is on purpose unclear on this point" (p. 211).

I have already mentioned the connection between Solaris and one of her two suns. The double shadow cast by these two suns—the narrator repeatedly describes the dual sunrise—is one further indication of man's propensity for duplication, but more important is the emphasis on suns per se. Presumably, since Earth's sun was the primal object of man's veneration, man's first anthropomorphized image of god, Lem has a certain point in directing the reader's attention to the suns of Solaris. The name of the mother ship, *Prometheus,* is further evidence that beliefs linking gods with fiery bodies are relevant. The name Solaris, whether in English, French, or Polish, is more appropriately descriptive of a sun rather than a planet, the point being that Solaris is an illegitimate sun. Just as man originally applied anthropomorphic qualities to Earth's sun in order to identify it as a god, while in fact fashioning a god who was literally—and here the English pun is helpful—a son of man, so the confusion of the planet Solaris with a sun is but a further analogue of the same propensity. In this sense, all man's attempts to plummet unknown "new worlds," particularly the efforts of science-fiction writers, are genetically predetermined sons of man, illegitimate offsprings of an incestuous relationship.

It follows that the foregoing interpretation may be particularly worthwhile if it is totally untrue. The extent of my analysis is some measure of the degree to which the novel *Solaris* encourages all kinds of hypotheses, none finally provable, some undoubtedly incorrect. Yet the paradoxical nature of the novel is such that all ill-conceived interpretations can only heighten its impact.

V. IT'S A FLAT WORLD!

A clear line between man and reality, so *Solaris* tells us, is hard to draw. We can't finally know to what extent any interpretation of reality, however far out, is referable to man's phenomenological or anthropomorphic limitations. This is, of course, an extreme philosophical position; most science fiction bases itself generically on the opposite possibility, that a genuine distinction does exist between the empirical, scientifically measurable universe on the one hand and the subjective or a priori interpretation on the other. Nevertheless those science-fiction writers with whom I am concerned in this section, who, in the company of a variety of mainstream authors, attempt a radical reformulation of the nature of reality, do find themselves drawn into the realm of phenomenological discourse.

The new and true conception of reality—revealed reality, if you like—has been, it must be assumed, concealed and obscured by man's previous faulty world view. Reality, as commonly conceived, constitutes one vast web of deception, and its illusionary nature is a consequence of man's ignorance, which is, in turn, determined by his limited awareness of time and space, among many other forms of perceptual limitation. This brings us back to Poe, who sees an arabesque reality imprisoned within the forms of conventional reality. Most dramatic reorientations of reality, no matter how scientific the method of discovery, more or less necessitate Poe's assumption that the old world has only a phenomenological validity and requires an apocalyptic form of breakthrough to the new reality. Thus the issue of phenomenology arises in relation to radical revaluations of the nature of man and in relation to equally radical revaluations of the nature of reality. A distinction may be drawn in terms of recognition or breakthrough. In *Solaris,* the subjective determinant is placed in a context whereby it may be recognized, and this recognition serves to redefine man by equating his shape with that of the observable universe. In the case of Twain's *A Connecticut Yankee* and the Aldiss novels *Report on Probability A* and *Barefoot in the Head,* a phenomenological reality is both recognized and then, as with Poe, in some sense broken through.

To the extent that language creates or obscures reality, it is necessary to suppose that an Englishman, a Frenchman, a Russian, a Chinese, and the speaker of any other tongue inhabit different phenomenological worlds determined by the idiosyncrasies of vocabulary and syntax. In an extreme case, the learning of an alien language may occasion the revelation of an utterly new world. This possibility is explored in Samuel R. Delany's *Babel-17* (1968). The female protagonist, a linguist, solves the problem posed by the alien race by mastering its language, thereby experiencing a philosophical apocalypse: "She had felt it before with other languages, the opening, the widening, the mind forced to sudden growth."[1]

The dimensional-speculation theme in science fiction, which I consider in Chapter 10, makes in direct and obvious ways for the revaluation of new present realities. *Flatland: A Romance of Many Dimensions* (1884), by the mathematician and Shakespearean scholar Edwin A. Abbott, provides a convenient combination of scientific empiricism with the element of phenomenology. The two-dimensional world of Flatland is described in Part I. It is inhabited by a hierarchy of geometrical figures. Circular Flatlanders occupy the top position, while those whose shape corresponds to a scalene triangle form the base level of society. This hierarchical structure should not, however, be visualized as a pyramid, since all forms of existence are confined to the dimensions of a plane. Consequently,

[1] See *Babel-17* (London, 1968), p. 98.

individual Flatlanders experience considerable difficulty in appreciating the geometrical configuration of their fellows and thereby recognizing their place in the all-important social hierarchy. In Part II, the narrator, Mr. Square, tells of his experiences in other-dimensional worlds. In a dream visit to the one-dimensional Lineland, whose inhabitants form a connected straight line, Mr. Square is unable to convince the king of Lineland that the two-dimensional world of Flatland does exist. But Mr. Square is similarly incredulous when he, in turn, is subsequently visited by an emissary from a three-dimensional world, the Sphere. When Mr. Square is finally convinced of such a possibility, he is able, by an analogical exercise, to propose to the disbelieving Sphere the likelihood of a four- and even a five-dimensional reality. Clearly the Sphere, the king of Lineland, and the Flatlanders who finally imprison Mr. Square as a heretic are bound by the limitations of their phenomenological universes. The reader is invited to assume that the pseudoscientific business of arguing from analogy provides an objective way out of this phenomenological bind and is not, properly considered, an aspect of it.

An alternative and perhaps less "scientific" procedure than reasoning from analogy, once the deceptive nature of conventional reality is suspected, often depends upon a simple process of inversion. Poe's sense that reality is an illusion and Twain's belief that reality is a dream allow for the possibility that illusionary experience pertains to a genuine reality and that the dream world is reality. Much of William Burroughs' work, particularly *The Ticket That Exploded* (1962) and *Nova Express* (1964), appears to be based on the apocalyptic belief that reality is a drugged condition (in so far as we accept a film environment that is being beamed at us from outer space) and that the perception of the dope fiend is therefore more accurate:

As we have seen image *is* junk—when a patient loses a leg what has been damaged?—Obviously his image of himself—So he needs a shot of cooked down image—The

hallucinogen drugs shift the scanning pattern of "reality"
so that we see a different "reality"—There is no true or
real "reality"—"Reality" is simply a more or less constant
scanning pattern—The scanning pattern we accept as
"reality" has been imposed by the controlling power on
this planet, a power primarily oriented towards total
control—In order to retain control they moved to monop-
olize and deactivate the hallucinogen drugs by effecting noxious alterations on a molecular level—[2]

Burroughs' cut-up technique is intended as a means of
destroying the imposed "reality."

The image of reality as a movie, much exploited recently, particularly in Tom Wolfe's *The Electric Kool-Aid
Acid Test* (1968), encourages a similar act of apocalyptic
inversion. It becomes necessary to get out of the establishment film and escape into a personal and therefore more
viable and truthful movie. Similarly, Kurt Vonnegut, Jr.,
seeks to characterize reality as science fiction and science
fiction as reality.

A combination of phenomenology with the principles of
analogy and inversion might allow a science-fiction writer
to describe a genuinely flat earth and the consequences
of this condition. Present-day cosmology, with its understanding that Earth and other heavenly bodies are basically round, has displaced the Ptolemaic system and any
empirical sense of a flat earth. But it is surely possible that
our own cosmology may eventually be displaced both in
its particulars and fundamentally, and that our conception of reality will stand revealed as illusory, much as the
flat-earthers' conception of reality now appears illusory. It
might follow that when people believed that the earth was
flat, such in fact was the case!

Other writers have conveyed their revelatory conceptions of the true nature of reality less mechanistically by
pressure of intellect and sensibility and by power of

[2] See the Evergreen Black Cat paperback edition of *Nova
Express* (New York, 1965), pp. 51–52.

perception. Franz Kafka is an apocalyptic writer in this sense. Kafka is concerned with an observable present reality that alarmingly and consistently fails to make sense, unless it is assumed to operate within an alternative, perhaps demonic, context. Throughout Kafka's work there are indications of this unfamiliar reality breaking through and perhaps accounting for all the mysterious, unanchored circumstances. Kafka's technique has been successfully adapted to the kind of science-fiction story that attempts to present an alien situation from the "inside," as something utterly divorced from the ordinary world of the reader. Gradually the reader moves from a state of total bewilderment to a dawning awareness, as the alien condition that gives rise to the apparently inexplicable series of events becomes finally manifest. "Travellers' Rest" (1965), by David I. Masson, is an example of such a tale. Events make sense when the reader appreciates that they take place on a planet where time flows at different rates in different latitudes. This kind of Kafkaesque science fiction is usually confined to the short story because it is extremely difficult to write and would become maddeningly irritating to read at an extended length. As in the case of a Kafka story, the ultimate, if somewhat indirect, effect of "Travellers' Rest" and allied works is to convey the sense of conventional reality as an incomplete system of knowledge.

In *The Education of Henry Adams: An Autobiography* (1907), Adams offers a non-fictional interpretation of the reality of his times that is no less apocalyptic than Kafka's fiction. The dynamos that Adams saw at the Paris Exposition of 1900 provided the inspiration for Chapter 25, "The Dynamo and the Virgin," the apocalyptic high point of the autobiography. Writing of himself in the third person, Adams describes the effect that the dynamos at the Exposition had on him: "As he grew accustomed to the great gallery of machines, he began to feel the forty-foot dynamos as a moral force. The planet itself seemed less impressive, in its . . . revolution, than this huge wheel . . ." (p. 1,285).[3] The dynamos represent a "sudden eruption of forces totally new," whereby "man had translated himself into a new universe which had no common scale of measurement with the old" (p. 1,286). But this apocalyptic transformation, which includes the discovery of X rays, is comparable to others:

> The year 1900 was not the first to upset schoolmasters. Copernicus and Galileo had broken many professional necks about 1600; Columbus had stood the world on its head towards 1500; but the nearest approach to the revolution of 1900 was that of 310, when Constantine set up the Cross. The rays that Langley [the American physicist] discovered, as well as those which he fathered, were occult, supersensual, irrational; they were a revelation of mysterious energy like that of the Cross; they were what, in terms of mediaeval science, were called immediate modes of the divine substance (pp. 1,286–87).

According to Adams, the spiritual values symbolized in the Middle Ages by the Virgin were being replaced by a potentially destructive value system based on material power. Adams also speculates about the possibility that these forces might be used to blow up the world, and thus he anticipates a "day of the locust" different from but no less final than the one West describes.

There is little need to elaborate on the assertion that Nathanael West is an apocalyptic writer, although he doesn't fit neatly into any one of my categories. To the extent that *The Day of the Locust* argues that present history corresponds to the "last days" foretold by St. John, West is providing a radical reinterpretation of an observable reality and belongs in this section of my schematized argu-

---

[3] All parenthetical references to "The Dynamo and the Virgin" may be located in the one-volume edition of *The American Tradition in Literature*, ed. by Sculley Bradley, Richmond Beatty, and E. Hudson Long (New York, 1967).

ment. However, West's emphasis is not philosophic but satiric, and therefore his work might more appropriately be considered among those other satiric apocalyptic worlds in space and time—were it not that *The Day of the Locust* implies that the end is now. The truth, of course, is that my divisions are ultimately arbitrary and reflect heuristic models that actual works will never totally conform to. It is enough that the elements in West's stories that might be described as apocalyptic may be totally accounted for if considered within the entire framework of my definition of the apocalyptic imagination, and it is in no way necessary that they occur within one aspect of that framework. The matter of distribution of texts within this framework is, in every case, a matter of emphasis. West's work, more so than that of most apocalyptics, resists allocation within a single category.

Another writer who presents special difficulties in this regard is William Faulkner. The criticism of George Snell and Walter J. Slatoff attests to the general sense that Faulkner's work may be described with some accuracy as apocalyptic.[4] Yet the common associations of the term don't apply. The world is not coming to an end in any literal fashion in Faulkner's work; there are no worldwide catastrophes. There is some concern with transcendence and visionary awareness, but Faulkner's focus is primarily on man. Perhaps, in calling Faulkner's work apocalyptic, critics are merely commenting on the vast scope of experience the novels treat. However, as I have defined the word apocalyptic, Faulkner's work does claim consideration among those apocalyptic writers who seek to radically reinterpret our present reality. Faulkner's extreme emphasis on the relativity of truth—an emphasis that is also true of Melville—amounts to the discovery of a new, paradoxical, suspended reality typified by circular

[4] See Snell's consideration of Faulkner as an apocalyptic in *The Shapers of American Fiction*, pp. 87–104, and Slatoff's *Quest for Failure: A Study of William Faulkner* (Ithaca, N.Y., 1960), *passim*.

movement, which goes nowhere and is therefore more accurately perceived as non-movement. I would suggest that the temptation to label Faulkner an apocalyptic writer is an accurate response to this disorienting philosophical dimension in his fiction. In Faulkner's case, I believe that my segmented framework does allow for a relatively neat placing within a single category which makes readily apparent the sense, elsewhere only vaguely articulated, in which he is an apocalyptic.

Jorge Luis Borges' verbal dexterity and interest in recondite philosophical systems makes his work pre-eminently important among those apocalyptic writers who transform present reality by profoundly reinterpreting it. Richard Burgin's *Conversations with Jorge Luis Borges* contains this statement by Borges concerning the usefulness of philosophy: "I think that philosophy helps you to live. . . . I think that philosophy may give the world a kind of haziness, but that haziness is all to the good. If you're a materialist, if you believe in hard and fast things, then you're tied down by reality. So that, in a sense, philosophy dissolves reality, but as reality is not always too pleasant, you will be helped by that dissolution."[5] The imaginary world of Tlön in Borges' "Tlön, Uqbar, Orbis Tertius" is a nice example of the apocalyptic potential of a philosophical system. The world of Tlön has been imagined by a secret society with such completeness that it is at least as "real" as the "real" world. According to the narrator, "Contact with Tlön and the ways of Tlön have disintegrated this world."[6]

Tlön would not be out of place in the obscure universe of Thomas Pynchon, a contemporary American apocalyptic, in the philosophic sense. Pynchon's *The Crying of Lot 49*, a rather more accessible and considerably shorter

[5] See *Conversations with Jorge Luis Borges* (New York, 1968), pp. 142-43.
[6] See "Tlön, Uqbar, Orbis Tertius," translated by Alastair Reid in the Grove Press paperback edition of Borges' *Ficciones* (New York, 1962), p. 34.

work than his earlier novel V (1963) or his later novel *Gravity's Rainbow* (1973), suggests that reality may be an extended pun. Mrs. Oedipa Maas comes to understand the world-wide conspiracy known as the Tristero System as a functioning method of communication, postal and otherwise, which is everywhere in evidence but nowhere recognized. It coexists with conventional methods of communication just as the two meanings of a pun coexist. Like the mass of humanity, previously aware only of a surface meaning or a surface mail, as it were, Oedipa seeks some revelation—and this word is used repeatedly —of the underlying reality, "Another mode of meaning behind the obvious" (p. 137).[7] Pynchon's title makes his point. On coming across a description, early in the novella, of a sad-looking used-car lot, the reader assumes that "the crying of lot 49" refers, perhaps in some allegorical fashion, to the dismal condition of the cars in this particular lot. It is only on the last page of the book, during an auction, where "Oedipa settles back, to await the crying of lot 49" (p. 138) that the alternate import of the title is clear. The title, like reality, is an extended pun.

It would be easy but pointless to multiply examples of apocalyptic works that treat the present reality in startlingly other terms, but I'll conclude by mentioning Joseph Heller's *Catch-22* (1961). This book qualifies by virtue of the "catch-22" concept and the consequent absurdist vicious circle of a world that makes the exercise of free will pointless. The examples that are analyzed in detail in the next two chapters are all, more or less, works of science fiction. The various works instanced above, derived primarily from American literature, are for the most part not science fiction. Their number points to the fact that it is precisely within this area of the apocalyptic imagination, this concern with a redefinition of reality,

[7] All parenthetical references to *The Crying of Lot 49* may be located in the Bantam paperback edition (New York, 1966), p. 137.

that science fiction and "mainstream" fiction coexist most happily.[8] One might expect any future fusion of science fiction and the "mainstream" to proceed from this common ground.

[8] For example, the concept of entropy has obvious science-fictional possibilities, but recently this scientific theory appears to provide the basis for much mainstream fiction. See the chapter entitled "Everything Running Down," in Tony Tanner, *City of Words: American Fiction 1950–1970* (London, 1971), pp. 141–52.

9. Epoch-Eclipse and Apocalypse: Special "Effects" in A Connecticut Yankee

I

Hank Morgan's use of a solar eclipse in order to impress upon King Arthur and his court that a mighty magician—superior to Merlin—stands before them is undoubtedly the most impressive episode in *A Connecticut Yankee in King Arthur's Court*, Mark Twain's time-travel version of the international novel. Arthur is at least as affected as the reader, and as a consequence, Hank is transformed from being a prisoner into being the Boss. But the reader is perhaps not likely to fully appreciate, and Arthur not at all, that on a thematic and symbolic level, this blotting out and temporary displacement of one heavenly body by another parallels the "transposition of epochs—and bodies [human and stellar]" (p. 18),[1] which is the donnée of the novel—the displacement of nineteenth-century America by sixth-century Britain, and subsequently the displacement, tentative, then total, of sixth-century Britain by nineteenth-century America. By equating this "epoch-eclipse" with the apparent extinction of the sun, Twain is implying that the posited world transformation is conceivably an event of apocalyptic proportions.[2]

Because this revelation is a continuing process, the book

[1] All parenthetical references are to the Chandler Facsimile Edition of Samuel Langhorne Clemens' *A Connecticut Yankee in King Arthur's Court*, ed. by Hamlin Hill (San Francisco, 1963).

[2] Cf. the symbolic vision of an eclipsed and dying sun in H. G. Wells' *The Time Machine*.

is repeatedly given to fiery reminders of the epoch-eclipse
that has taken place. Indeed the work is remarkable for
the number of explosions that occur and for images that
draw on the sun's various qualities: its fieriness, its circularity, its color, and its role as a source of light. As I hope
to demonstrate, all these instances depend upon "The
Eclipse" chapter for their essential meaning.

If all the rather intricate connections I shall argue for
are not immediately obvious to the reader, they are even
less apparent to Hank, although, as the narrator, he is
the source of all the information. Hank, being a narrowly
pragmatic exhibitionist and something of a boor, is incredibly obtuse, unaware, and quite incapable of questioning his own attitudes. These limitations manifest themselves in a hackneyed and exaggerated speech which
admirably serves the purposes of comedy and burlesque
at the expense both of Arthur's England and of himself as
a representative nineteenth-century "Yankee." But what
Hank's style does not allow for, as James M. Cox has made
very clear, is enough "analytic intelligence or wit to dis-
charge his growing indignation" when the novel moves
from an essentially burlesque to an essentially satiric
stance.[3] In other words, because Hank cannot function
satisfactorily as a satiric norm, and because, outside of
the frame, there is no "Mark Twain" narrator, the novel
lacks an acceptable perspective on reality. All the reader
has is the very limited perspective implied by Hank's
style, a perspective that would certainly not generate
and would seemingly deny the possibility of any subtle
imagistic design. My analysis of imagistic patterning,
which follows, must, then, infer a sophisticated consciousness that is otherwise explicitly absent from the novel. An
explanation as to why Twain excluded from his satire a
normative and intelligent consciousness which might have
provided a convincing source for imagistic significance, in

[3] See James M. Cox, *Mark Twain: The Fate of Humor* (Princeton, N.J., 1966), p. 205, and Chapter IX, "Yankee Slang,"
passim.

favor of a philistine who is a most unconvincing source, must await the further development of my argument.

II

Lest the reader miss the sun's function as an apocalyptic image, Twain is careful to associate the eclipse with that biblical prefiguration of the Apocalypse, the Flood: ". . . when the silver rim of the sun pushed itself out, a moment or two later, the assemblage broke loose with a vast shout and came pouring down like a deluge to smother me with blessings and gratitude" (p. 79). It is assumed that Hank's incantation, timed with the astronomical process, is the causal factor. So it is that Hank escapes death at the stake by fire or, in symbolic terms, survives the apocalypse and successfully enters the new world. Previously, after being hit on the head in the nineteenth century, the old "world went out in darkness" (p. 21)—like a light. Now we learn that "the eclipse had scared the British world almost to death: that while it lasted . . . the churches, hermitages, and monkeries overflowed with praying and weeping poor creatures who thought the end of the world had come" (pp. 85–86). As Hank notices "my eclipse beginning," he exclaims, "I was a new man" (p. 75). During the eclipse he literally puts on the new man by donning the sixth-century clothes that befit his new status.

As a further exhibition of his power and in order to consolidate his position, Hank arranges the first of many explosions. His "magic" causes Merlin's tower, conceivably an apocalyptic symbol in its own right, to blow up: "I made about three passes in the air, and then there was an awful crash and that old tower leaped into the sky in chunks, along with a vast volcanic fountain of fire that turned night to noonday [previously, noonday had been turned into night, since the eclipse occurred at approximately twelve noon], and showed a thousand acres of human beings groveling on the ground in a general collapse of consternation" (pp. 90–91). I contend that the symbolic relationship between the eclipse and this explosion, pointed up here by the specific time reversal, is intended as applying to the remaining explosive fires in the book.[4]

No sooner has Hank adjusted to the displacement of the nineteenth century by the sixth than he attempts to reverse the process. It is his particular aim to replace the monarchy and the aristocracy with a democracy, and it is toward this end that the only title he is willing to accept is that granted by the entire nation: "THE BOSS" (p. 103). Just as, during the eclipse, the moon threw the sun into shadow, so democracy will eclipse monarchy. "I was no shadow of a king; I was the substance; the king himself was the shadow" (p. 96), affirms Hank. And in a voice very reminiscent of Huckleberry Finn, Hank continues, "It is enough to make a body ashamed of his race to think of the sort of froth that has always occupied its thrones without shadow of right or reason . . ." (pp. 97–98). Is it a mistake to deduce from the shadow image the light necessary to produce shadow and from there to recall the sun once more? However this may be, Dan Beard's illustrations, which accompanied the original text, frequently make overt what Twain only implies. In this case, a drawing of the solar eclipse has the sun symbolic of the "Divine Rights of Kings VI ceny," while the moon, which bears the legend "The Earth belongs to the People XIX ceny" (p. 101), casts the "shadow of right and reason."

Concurrently, Hank manages surreptitiously to install most nineteenth-century technical improvements, notably electric light, and thereby the emergent nineteenth cen-

---

[4] Henry Nash Smith notes an additional connection between the two events in that the thunderstorm Hank requires "to ignite his charges" "appears as fortuitously as the eclipse." See *Mark Twain's Fable of Progress: Political and Economic Ideas in "A Connecticut Yankee"* (New Brunswick, N.J., 1964), p. 53. See also p. 86.

tury is associated with explosive fire: "There it was, as sure a fact, and as substantial a fact as any serene volcano, standing innocent with its smokeless summit in the blue sky [the sun is shining!] and giving no sign of the rising hell in its bowels" (p. 120). Meanwhile, in his despair at turning Sandy, his traveling companion, into a pragmatic nineteenth-century American woman, Hank can conceive the transformation only by blowing her up: "It may be that this girl had a fact in her somewhere, but I don't believe you could have . . . got it with the earlier forms of blasting, even; it was a case for dynamite" (p. 132). The attention paid to Hank's pipe, which causes Sandy to faint, is not accidental. Its forceful effect may be more accurately attributable to its function as a symbol of the apocalyptic change associated with Hank. Surely the episode in which Hank, mistaken for "one of those fire-belching dragons" (p. 166), routs "half a dozen armed men and their squires" (p. 167) is a little too fantastic in anything other than symbolic terms. Hank should be seen as a Prometheus bringing to the Middle Ages the fire of the nineteenth century. Just as Prometheus is assisted by Hercules, so Hank's displacement depends upon being hit on the head by "a fellow we used to call Hercules" (p. 20). It should also be noted that Hank's father, like Vulcan, was a blacksmith.

Announcing, in his Tom Sawyer voice, "You can't throw too much style into a miracle" (p. 289), Hank takes pains that the restoration of the dry fountain in the Valley of Holiness doesn't lack the apocalyptic element: "Then I touched off the hogshead of rockets, and a vast fountain of dazzling lances of fire [here fire and flood are identified] vomited itself towards the zenith [the position of the sun at greatest strength and, in traditional symbology, a point of exit from the world of space and time—the eclipse, it will be recalled, occurred at midday on June 21, the time at which the sun is at its zenith in the Western Hemi-sphere[5]] with a hissing rush, and burst in mid-sky into a

[5] Hank is quite specific in his information "that the only total eclipse of the sun in the first half of the sixth century occurred

storm of flashing jewels!" (p. 294). The cry of exultation
that follows might be an appropriate response to a sight
of the jeweled New Jerusalem descending from the sky's
zenith, although mention of "flashing jewels" may not itself warrant such an extension. This event is written up in
the newspaper that Hank has founded, the *Weekly Hosan-
nah and Literary Volcano,* with the phrase "INFERNAL
FIRE AND SMOKE AND THUNDER!" (p. 339) in large
print. The column "Local Smoke and Cinders" (p. 340)
is presented as being representative of the rest of the paper. If Marshall McLuhan is right about the impact of the
Gutenberg revolution, and, at a later point, Gutenberg,
along with Watt, Arkwright, Whitney, Morse, Stephenson,
and Bell are credited, "after God," as "the creators of this
world" (p. 420), Hank could find no surer means than a
newspaper of displacing a sixth-century reality by a nineteenth-century reality. It is then meaningful that the newspaper by its titles and headline is associated with apocalyptic heat. No wonder that Hank, upon reading this first
edition, feels, "Yes, this was heaven" (p. 344).

---

on the 21st of June, A.D. 528, O.S. [presumably Old System,
hence the Julian Calendar], and began at 3 minutes after 12
noon" (p. 36). Because Twain has symbolic reasons for the
particular day and time, historical accuracy is not to be expected. However, given that Theodor Ritter von Oppolzer's
Canon of Eclipses (Vienna, 1887), which remains the standard
work on the subject, was, coincidentally, published during the
five years from December 1884 to May 1889, when Twain was
working intermittently on *A Connecticut Yankee,* it might be
expected that he would have checked for a year in the early-
sixth century in which a total eclipse of the sun was visible
from Britain. But not so, apparently. In A.D. 528, O.S., the
four eclipses that occurred, on February 6, March 6, August 1,
and August 30, were all partial. An eclipse of the sun that was
total and the nearest such to Twain's year did occur, according
to the *Canon of Eclipses,* on September 1 in A.D. 538, O.S.
Nevertheless, whether or not Twain checked this matter still
cannot be verified, because, as the later portion of my argument indicates, it is most appropriate that the eclipse cannot
be anchored to "reality."

III

The journey Hank and Arthur make through the kingdom is undertaken with the intention of opening Arthur's eyes to that reality of sixth-century England of which Hank has become aware in the earlier part of the book. There are two disconnected worlds or realms of experience in sixth-century England, since the romantic experience of Arthur, his knights, and the aristocracy is quite distinct from the actual living conditions of the majority of the population. The nineteenth-century experience is similarly dual: there is the technological utopia in which Hank believes, his own form of romanticism, and the dehumanized Armageddon that is much closer to a possible future reality. There are, then, essentially four worlds in *A Connecticut Yankee:* two negative visions—of the sixth century and of the nineteenth century—and two corresponding positive visions. Twain's purpose is to have Arthur undergo an apocalypse of mind in recognizing the negative reality of his time, and subsequently to have Hank experience a similar apocalyptic revelation concerning the negative reality of his epoch. The effect of this movement is of course to imply an essential lack of differentiation between the sixth century and the nineteenth century.

While traveling with the king incognito, Hank engineers another miracle, which consists of another explosion, in order to dispose of some troublesome knights. Thus we are provided with an objective correlative for Arthur's dawning realization about the sham of chivalry. By noting that the conflagration "resembled a steamboat explosion on the Mississippi" (p. 355), Hank associates it with a new and different world and consequently with the notion of apocalyptic transformation. A fifth instance of fire, the manor-house fire and the death of the lord of the manor, is intended as symbolic of the end of an old, feudal world. For accompaniment "there was an ear-splitting explosion of thunder, and the bottom of heaven fell out; the rain poured down in a deluge" (p. 383)—the mixture of fire and flood as before.

Hank's efforts to update the sixth-century economy allow Twain to draw symbolically on a further characteristic of the sun—its circularity. Dan Beard diagrams the revolution as a coinlike sun emerging over the horizon. Around its edges are the words "free trade" (p. 429). The new "currency" Hank introduces, plus the notion of "a trade union, to *coin* [italics mine] a new phrase" (p. 428), must be seen for the puns contained if these measures are to impart their total meaning; likewise the description of the "gun-purse," which uses different-sized shot for money and which Hank offers as an explanation for the phrase "Paying the shot." In other words, the new money and the new world of mind it signifies entail destruction. Revolutionary ideas must be circulated to be effective—hence the rather weird information, regarding the gun-purse, that "you could carry it in your mouth," wherefrom, of course, might issue that "Paying the shot" line, which "would still be passing men's lips, away down in the nineteenth century" (p. 438).

It is Arthur's experience as a slave—as a part of that slave band which Hank had witnessed earlier—that, more than anything else, encourages the emergence of his new awareness and heroic stature. Once again the revelation and reversal of fortune is accompanied by fire. The slave-holders smoke Arthur and Hank out of the tree in which they were hiding: "They raised their pile of dry brush and damp weeds higher and higher, and when they saw the thick cloud begin to roll up and smother the tree, they broke out in a storm of joy-clamors" (p. 445). One might here recall Hank's earlier experience, when "the fagots were carefully and tediously piled about my ankles, my knees, my thighs, my body" (pp. 74–75), just prior to the eclipse. I would incidentally not insist upon the addition of the symbolic dimension to all the incidents and images involving fire were it not for two factors: first, the apparently deliberate referral back to the eclipse that most of these fiery verbal details encourage, and second, the coincidence of these combustible elements with moments of major tranformation and revelation.

In a following episode Hank and Arthur, still slaves, witness the actual burning of a witch: "They fastened her to a post; they brought wood and piled it about her; they applied the torch, while she shrieked and pleaded and strained her two younger daughters to her breast; and our brute, with a heart solely for business, lashed us into position about the stake and warmed us into life and commercial value by the same fire that took away the innocent life of that poor harmless mother" (p. 459). Again we recall Hank's possibly similar fate at the stake, but the incident is particularly important to the process of revelation that Arthur is undergoing. In addition, this incident illustrates particularly well the dual nature of an apocalypse: it is both destructive and creative. Shortly afterward, Hank and Arthur witness a similar atrocity: the hanging of a young girl after a priest has pulled her baby from her arms. The priest pledges to look after the child: "You should have seen her face then! Gratitude? Lord, what do you want with words to express that? *Words are only painted fire; a look is the fire itself* [my italics]. She gave that look, and carried it away to the treasury of heaven, where all things that are divine belong" (p. 464). Here fire is specifically equated with divine will and thereby with apocalyptic revelation. Fire figures yet again in the next episode, which features "a man being boiled to death in oil for counterfeiting pennies" (p. 468)—for inability to adapt to Hank's new currency?

IV

Hank and Arthur are finally rescued, Arthur with his neck in a noose, when, in response to Hank's telephone call, five hundred knights come cycling to his aid, seemingly having harnessed the power and aggression of the sun itself: "Lord, how the plumes streamed, how the sun

flamed and flashed from the endless procession of webby
wheels!" (p. 490). It might be noted in passing, that the
idea of the sun as a fiery wheel goes back to antiquity.
Hank describes this spectacle as "the grandest sight that
ever was seen" (p. 490). Yet at a later point, when an
army, similarly sun-coated since "the sun struck the sea of
armor and set it all aflash" (pp. 553–54), aligns itself
against Hank, the impression is even more formidable: "I
hadn't ever seen anything to beat it" (p. 554). In between
these two moments Hank suffers a major reversal. The remaining action consists of an escalated series of violent
encounters between Hank, or the nineteenth century, and
Arthur's knights, or the sixth century. As I hope to demonstrate, the association of the knights with the sun is
not accidental. This climactic Armageddon is a kind of
literal equivalent to the solar eclipse, the symbolic import
of which I trust I have made sufficiently clear. But whereas
the solar eclipse seemingly signaled the displacement of
the sixth century by the nineteenth for the people of
Arthur's England and the displacement of the nineteenth
century by the sixth for Hank, the concluding Armageddon signifies, for the world of King Arthur, a final if costly
victory of the sixth-century reality over that of the nineteenth century and, for Hank personally, a displacement
of the sixth century by the nineteenth century. In a sense,
then, both sides win and both sides lose.

The tournament between Hank and Sir Sagramour,
motivated at the beginning of the book, is in reality "a
duel not of muscle but of mind," a "mysterious and awful
battle of the gods" (p. 497), because the real conflict is
that between two magicians, Hank and Merlin. It is described in terms of a conflict of the elements of fire and
air. To the repeated blasts of apocalyptic bugles, Sir
Sagramour, and after him other knights, engage Hank in
combat. All fall prey to the "snaky spirals" (p. 502) of
Hank's lasso, which is linked with a whirlwind. Thus
Hank "whirled" out of Sir Sagramour's path, which occasions a "whirlwind of applause," while, afterward, Lancelot falls "with the rush of a whirlwind." Sir Lancelot

is described as "the very sun of their shining system"
(p. 503), while one of his predecessors charges "like a
house afire" (p. 502). Sir Lancelot's fall is greeted with a
"thunder-crash of applause" (p. 503). After Merlin steals
his lasso, Hank is compelled to use his revolver to halt
the five hundred knights who then bear down upon him.
Hank's subsequent challenge to take on with fifty assist-
ants *the massed chivalry of the whole earth and destroy
it* (p. 512) is not taken up initially. However, the double
syntactic ambiguity of the italicized section of the challenge (the words "massed chivalry" may be a description
of the "whole earth," the "it" may refer back to the
"whole earth") allows for the implication that he will
destroy the whole world, and makes the cosmic and
apocalyptic nature of the upcoming conflict readily apparent.

Following the civil war between the king's party and
Sir Lancelot's over Guinevere, which began when Lancelot
thwarted the king's intention to "purify her with fire"
(p. 533) (we might well recall once more Hank's own experience at the stake), and the civil war between Arthur's
group and Sir Mordred's for possession of the kingdom,
during which Arthur is killed, both Hank and Mordred
find themselves bereft of power by force of the Church
Interdict. However, Clarence, Hank's chief helper, has prepared Merlin's cave for a siege, whereupon Hank declares
his republic. (Actually the cave is as much Plato's as
Merlin's, given Twain's concern with the nature of reality,
a concern I take up in section v.) At the battle of the
sand-belt, Hank, Clarence, and fifty-two boys, one for
each week of the solar year, prepare to take on the Church
army. The detailed description of Hank's fortification is, I
believe, meaningful. Twelve electrified wire fences circle
the cave concentrically, while, around the outer fence,
lies the mined sand-belt. The planetary, somewhat Copernican setup of this design, confused possibly with the
twelve signs of the zodiac *"belt,"* to create a mix of sixth-
century and nineteenth-century cosmologies suggests to me
that the sand-belt, which is presumably yellow in color,

should be symbolically identified as the path of the sun.
If this is the case, Hank's choice of analogy in the con-
gratulatory proclamation to his army is deliberate: "So
long as the planets shall continue to move in their orbits,
the BATTLE OF THE SAND-BELT will not perish out
of the memories of men" (p. 556). It would seem that
Twain intends some equation between the battle and
cosmological phenomena, an eclipse of the sun for example.

The ensuing holocaust has all the requisite apocalyptic
features. The knights first advance to "the blare of trumpets," only to be "shot into the sky with a thunder-crash,
and become a whirling tempest of rags and fragments"
(p. 554). The "smell of burning flesh" (p. 561) is noticeable first, and then the carnage itself becomes visible when
Hank "touched a button and set fifty electric suns aflame
on the top of our precipice" (p. 564). The solar eclipse
turned day into night; now Hank turns night into day.
(To our ears, incidentally, the reference to "fifty electric
suns" gains in intensity with its ominous implication of
megatonnage.) When the eclipse was total, the multitude
"groaned with horror" (p. 78). Now, as a host of knights
are electrocuted, "There was a groan you could *hear!*"
(p. 564). The "deluge" (p. 79) of congratulations that
Hank received for returning the sun, now becomes a "with-
ering deluge of fire" (p. 565) directed at the remaining
knights. The deluge here is both literal and metaphorical,
composed of both fire and water, since Hank opens the
sluice gates in order to fill the now-surrounding ditch
caused by the explosion of the torpedoes and thus drown
many of the knights like Pharaoh's army. But my point
here is that these ordered repetitions are purposeful.

Hank's victory is pyrrhic only. Merlin, disguised as a
woman, works his most effective enchantment—more truly
impressive than any of Hank's magical accomplishments—
and puts the wounded Boss to sleep for thirteen centuries.
(It may be recalled that Merlin's first accomplishment in
the novel is to send all of Arthur's court to sleep during
his droning rehearsal of Arthur's adventures with the Lady
of the Lake.) However, Merlin's victory, too, is short-lived.

A moment later, in the midst of a delirious cackle, he electrocutes himself. Subsequently, the remainder of Hank's followers gradually die off for reasons Clarence explains: "We were in a trap, you see—a trap of our own making. If we stayed where we were, our dead would kill us; if we moved out of our defences, we should no longer be invisible. We had conquered; in turn we were conquered" (p. 570). Following the end of Hank's manuscript, we obtain the truly apocalyptic revelation, a revelation indirectly hinted at throughout, namely that the sixth century does not displace the nineteenth century in any real sense, nor does the nineteenth century displace the sixth century, because there is no essential difference between them.

v

The eclipse of the sun is a false apocalyptic image, *at least in the sense that I have so far implied*. And the same goes for the related fiery, circular, luminous yellow elements I have been cataloging. They are all "effects" in so far as they relate to the usurpation of one historical world by another. Nevertheless, these elements, outside of Hank's usage of them, do have a "factual" and symbolic reality as apocalyptic imagery in so far as they herald the revelation that any apocalyptic transformation, from an Eden in the past to a utopia in the future, is all myth. Gradually we are made aware that the most startling fact about the sixth century in relation to the nineteenth is the lack of significant differentiation. It is no accident that Hank's story is inscribed on a palimpsest and that underlying his writing are "Latin words and sentences: fragments from old monkish legends" (p. 23). The common parchment is more important than the apparent differences imbedded in successive historical records. And it is this essential lack of differentiation that prepares the reader for the genuine apocalyptic revelation with which the book concludes.

Careful attention to the imagery associated with the sun is in itself revealing. Shortly after his spectacular demonstration, Hank draws attention to the current belief that "he could have blown out the sun like a candle" (p. 86). There is some irony to this statement, as the sun-candle world of mind comes, during the course of the book, to be associated with nineteenth-century America and not sixth-century Britain. This process gets under way with Hank's decision to wait for an opportune moment before *flooding* sixth-century England with nineteenth-century electric light: "I was turning on my light one-candle-power at a time, and meant to continue to do so" (p. 120). He was, nevertheless, ready, like God to "flood the midnight world with light any moment." Somewhat weirdly, except as a part of this process, Hank, in full armor, speaks of himself as being "snug as a candle in a candle-mould" (p. 135). And, at the end of the novel, when Hank appears to be losing ground to the Church, Dan Beard provides an illustration of a monk snuffing the candle of the nineteenth century, an illustration presumably based on this description of Camelot: "From being the best electric-lighted town in the kingdom and the most like a recumbent sun of anything you ever saw, it was becoming simply a blot—a blot upon darkness—that is to say, it was darker and solider than the rest of the darkness, and so you could see it a little better; it made me feel as if maybe it was symbolical—a sort of sign that the Church was going to *keep* the upper hand, now, and *snuff out* [italics mine] all my beautiful civilization just like that" (p. 528). Once again, snuffing out the candle and the eclipse of the sun are clearly related, although the import is completely reversed. But this confusion seems to imply that if the two transformations can be imaged in the same terms, perhaps the similarities between the two epochs are more important than the differences.

Similarities between sixth-century Britain and nineteenth-century America quickly assert themselves. The major common denominator is slavery. In large measure, Twain's source for the Old World of the sixth century is the pre-Civil War South. Furthermore economic thinking is as muddled in King Arthur's time as in Hank's day, due to the failure to realize that the important thing is not how much you earn but how much you can purchase with it.[6] Twain was fond of blaming Sir Walter Scott for causing the Civil War by romanticizing aristocratic behavior. It becomes apparent, in *A Connecticut Yankee*, that Scott has a predecessor in this activity in Malory, who presented a similarly romantic version of chivalry, which Twain derides by parody—witness Merlin's opening story, the style of which is later taken up by Sandy's rambling narrative.

From this comparison between Malory and Scott it is but a short step to the recognition that men are all the same under the skin. Hank refers with approval to a prisoner's critical assertion, "If you were to strip the nation naked and send a stranger through the crowd, he couldn't tell the king from a quack doctor, nor a duke from a hotel clerk" (p. 223). The later portion of the narrative, with the king and the Boss traveling incognito, effectively bears this point out. Nor is there any fundamental distinction between good and evil. The essential similarity between the sinister Morgan Le Fay and our hero, Hank Morgan, pointed to by their common name, becomes increasingly obvious as the book goes on. As Edmund Reiss suggests, Hank's surprise at Morgan Le Fay's beauty is a means of indicating the ambiguity of good and evil, but "what appalls the Yankee in the character of Morgan Le Fay are the same insensitivities Twain objects to in the Yankee's character."[7] A further distinction is eroded when we learn of Hank's factory, where he

---

[6] Tony Tanner notes that the Round Table "comes to have an uncanny resemblance to the stock exchange and the final civil war is precipitated by a shady deal reminiscent of the "railroad frauds of the Seventies." See "The Lost America: The Despair of Henry Adams and Mark Twain," reprinted in *Mark Twain: A Collection of Critical Essays*, ed. by Henry Nash Smith (Englewood Cliffs, N.J., 1963), p. 162.

[7] See Edmund Reiss' "Afterword" to the Signet Edition of *A Connecticut Yankee* (New York, 1963), p. 325.

plans "to turn groping and grubbing automata into *men*"
(p. 212), which raises, in the modern reader's mind, the
equal likelihood of turning men into automata. What
superficial distinctions do exist are all a consequence of
training and inherited ideas. Since man is essentially without free will, he might fittingly be considered allegorically as a slave, which is how Dan Beard presents him,
chained to two iron balls of debt (p. 339).

Clearly, since our recognition of material reality depends upon our ability to make meaningful distinctions, the discovery that meaningful distinctions do not
exist would tend to throw that state of reality into question. It is, then, a relatively small distance from demonstrating an essential homogeneity to asserting that there
is no reality or that reality is a dream—the truly apocalyptic revelation of the postscript. There is, however, one
further logical intermediary step: the business of eradicating any distinction between reality and appearance or
reality and unreality. It is all shown to be a matter of
phenomenology. Toward the end of the book, Hank's
entire conception of reality comes to depend upon the
health of his child. Thus this description of her recovery:

> Then our reward came: the center of the universe
> turned the corner and began to mend. Grateful? It isn't
> the term. There *isn't* any term for it. You know that,
> yourself, if you've watched your child through the
> Valley of the Shadow and seen it come back to life and
> sweep night out of the earth [like the sun?] with one
> all illuminating smile that you could cover with your
> hand (p. 526).

In the circumstances, this image of the creation is most
appropriate and in no way inflated.

Now is the appropriate time to recall Hank's status in
the novel as narrator, because the perceptual idiopathic
bias that his child's recovery highlights is endemic. To the
degree that all events are filtered through the hardheaded,
burlesque, "Yankee" consciousness of Hank, the entire

account is "unreal." Hank's idiosyncracies translate themselves into a style that is ultimately as "unreal" as the
Malory romance he ridicules. For example, although one
might speak descriptively of Hank's "ordeal" at the stake,
the use of quotation marks should be taken as ironic, because Hank is simply insufficiently serious and insufficiently aware to experience the incident as more than a
spectacular show, albeit somewhat uncomfortable.[8] Similarly, Hank's practical and rather callous application of
the energy expended by the bowing hermit on his pillar
to run a sewing machine reflects on his total incomprehen-
sion of the realities of religious ardor.

The image of this hermit standing against the "background of sky" (p. 292), producing energy at the rate of
"1244 revolutions in 24 minutes and 46 seconds" to make
shirts which "sold like smoke" (p. 281) shares certain
qualities with the sun, and now I can perhaps seek to
further justify my imagistic use of that body as a viable
approach to the novel. My point is that Twain's narrative
strategy blurs the distinction between an event or incident considered externally and the subjective image
whereby events and images are understood. Given that
Twain's aim is an impression of the unreality of reality, it
makes sense that a reader might find his bearings, or clue
to the novel's "reality principle," in the imagery, by definition unreal, particularly since the entire narrative, which is
a statement of Hank's consciousness, might be conceived
as having the same ontological status as imagery. There
is, then, good reason for the disjunction raised earlier.
Twain chooses to dissociate his intricate imagistic patterns from a poetic consciousness capable of comprehend-
ing them and instead locates them in the mundane,
"effective" rhetoric of a practical man, because such a
stance turns out to be an extreme but representative form
of unreality. Ultimately the form of Hank's narrative *is* the
primary reality of the novel, and it is there that the ambiguous imagistic import of the eclipse is appropriately if

[8] I am grateful to James M. Cox for this portion of my argument.

paradoxically "grounded." Indeed the "truth" of the novel
has much to do with what appears to exist but is independent of factual justification.

Twain's point about the idiopathic nature of perception
is more strongly made by dramatizing the weird conceptions of sixth-century humanity—of Sandy in particular.
Where Hank sees pigs in a sty, she sees enchanted prin-
cesses in an enchanted castle. Sandy ponders:

> And how strange is this marvel, and how awful—that to
> the one perception it is enchanted and dight in a base
> and shameful aspect; yet to the perception of the other
> it is not enchanted, hath suffered no change, but stands
> firm and stately still, girt with its moat and waving its
> banners in the blue air from its towers (p. 244).

Although men differ only in their training, such differences as do exist are sufficiently powerful to mold external
reality! It is indeed tempting, incidentally, to extend the
connotations of the sand-belt to the name Sandy!

To confuse swine with members of the aristocracy, and
then a few pages on to refer to the band of slaves that
perambulate through the novel as "bundled together like
swine" (p. 261), is not just a matter of being uncompli-
mentary to the nobility, nor is it just a means of pointing
to an essential lack of distinction between animals, nobles,
and slaves. It is, more especially, a further and final confusion of reality and unreality. The slave chain, as I have
argued, is an image of humanity. Hank and the king do
not suddenly become slaves toward the end of the novel to
be "sold at auction, like swine" (p. 449); this is but a concrete manifestation of their continual situation. But this
conception of human reality, by being linked to Sandy's
unique perception of swine, is, then, equally a picture of
human unreality. The swine image comes to stand for both
the aristocracy and the slaves, but primarily for the Circe-
like force of illusion.

The apocalyptic discovery with which the book is con-

cerned is the understanding that no apocalyptic transformation has occurred. The true apocalyptic revelation is
not that the sixth-century world is so different but that it
is identical and identically unreal. In this context, the
concluding doubt in Hank's mind as to which is the
dream, the sixth century or the nineteenth century, makes
perfect sense. Apparently back in the nineteenth century,
Hank, delirious, believes he is speaking to Sandy in the
sixth century: "I seemed to be a creature out of a remote
unborn age, centuries hence, and even *that* was as real as
the rest! Yes, I seemed to have flown back out of that age
into this of ours, and then forward to it again, and was
set down, a stranger and forlorn in that strange England,
with an abyss of thirteen centuries yawning [pun intended?] between me and you. . . ." He begs Sandy to
shield him from "these hideous dreams" (p. 574).

This revelation is in alignment with, but does not depend for justification upon, those other moments in the
book when the reality of a dream world is particularly
pressing. Can we be sure that everything is not merely the
narrator's dream—after all, Hank's second entrance occurs
after midnight and after the narrator has read a stretch of
Malory with the intention that it put him to sleep? In fact,
as Twain's notebook entry tells us, his original idea for the
story derived from a dream following his reading Malory, "a dream of being a knight errant in armor in the
middle ages."[9] Certainly Camelot is "as lovely as a dream"
(p. 27), and Hank "moved along as one in a dream"
(p. 28). Toward the end of the book, Hank's dreams are
of the nineteenth century: "In my dreams, along at first, I
still wandered thirteen centuries away, and my unsatis-
fied spirit went calling and harking all up and down the
unreplying vacancies of a vanished world" (p. 524).

The apocalyptic solution implied in *A Connecticut Yankee* and subsequently stated directly in *The Mysterious*

9 Notebook ⅍18, October 24, 1884–April 4, 1885, typescript,
p. 11, Mark Twain Papers, University of California Library,
Berkeley.

Stranger and in Twain's late symbolic writings is that all reality is a dream.[10] Apparently the inhabitants of sixth-century Britain were absolutely correct in their intuition that the eclipse of the sun betokens the end of the world. As an image, the eclipse and the related details chronicled earlier connote not the transformation of realities but the end of reality, the final apocalypse. The images of apocalypse that figure in Hank's final pronouncements suggest the impact of such an extreme philosophical position: "A bugle. . . . It is the king! . . . turn out the —" Are we not justified in hypothesizing the adjective "apocalyptic" before bugle, in identifying "the king" as God rather than Arthur, and, in completing the phrase as "turn out the light," recall, a final time, the episode detailing the extinction of the sun, which now darkens both the sixth century and the nineteenth century? The frame narrator interprets this as Hank "getting up his last 'effect'" (p. 575), but the quotation marks around "effect" are fortunate. In a reality that turns out to be a dream, a special effect must be granted its measure of actuality.

[10] See *Mark Twain's Which Was the Dream? and Other Symbolic Writings of the Later Years*, ed. by John S. Tuckey, (Berkeley, Calif., 1967). As H. Bruce Franklin indicates in his *Future Perfect*, there is the further connection that in *A Connecticut Yankee* and that unfinished symbolic work, *The Great Dark*, Twain has broken into the genre of science fiction, pp. 375-78.

10. New Dimensions of Time, Space, and Literature

I

But for the suit of armor with what appears to be a bullet hole in the breastplate, there exists no tangible evidence, in the present, that a time traveler from the nineteenth century ever visited the era of King Arthur. Thanks to the incredibly destructive battle that concludes *A Connecticut Yankee*, we may assume that none of Morgan's technological "innovations" survive to tell the tale. Time travel into the past raises all kinds of paradoxical and science-fictional possibilities centering on the problem of historical anachronism. That Twain realistically faces the anachronism issue constitutes a major point in any argument for considering *A Connecticut Yankee* an example of classic science fiction. The same problem does not usually arise in *Looking Backward* and other works in which the time traveler's voyage is into the future—unless, of course, he returns to a past prior to his own time or unless the future is technologically primitive as compared with his temporal point of origin. But a certain basic philosophical speculation as to the nature of time must attend all serious experiments with the theme of time travel, whether into the past or into the future: the past or the future must be understood as somehow constantly existent.

Most theoretical rationales follow Wells' suggestion that time is actually the fourth dimension, and thus, by analogy with the three dimensions of space, time travel becomes a possibility. However, time travel into the past has the edge over time travel into the future as far as credibility goes, perhaps because we already have the evidence that, the speed of light being finite, when we observe the night sky and witness a supernova we are actually looking at a situation and an event that occurred many years in the past. There are several stories— P. Schuyler Miller's "The Sands of Time" (1937) is an example—in which the past is photographed. In a recent variant, "Light of Other Days" (1966), by Bob Shaw, a product called "slow glass" retains images of the past because light travels through it extremely slowly. Actually, time travel, as compared to space travel, is very much a fantastic notion, and, since Wells, its importance as a science-fictional theme is the result of its acceptance as a convention rather than as a realistic possibility.

At the same time, there have been many scientific and philosophical attempts including Einstein's to explain the nature of time, and such attempts frequently suggest a fundamentally altered apocalyptic conception of reality, since we depend upon the co-ordinates of space and time to fix what we presently understand as reality. The books of J. B. Dunne, *An Experiment with Time* (1929), *The Serial Universe* (1934), *The New Immortality* (1938), and *Nothing Dies* (1940), have a particular science-fictional applicability.[1] Dunne produces mathematically consistent evidence to support his conclusion that the future exists, that at moments of choice and decision, alternate time tracks branch out, and that from the vantage point of the fourth dimension, into which a person may hoist himself, the best choice may be made. This, then, raises the possibility of alternative universes for each of the alternative decisions that can be made. Jorge Luis Borges' "The Garden of Forking Paths" (1956) presents a labyrinthine analogy for the reality conceived by Dunne, in which

[1] See Ivor A. Rogers, "The Time Plays of J. B. Priestley," *Extrapolation*, X (December 1968), pp. 9–16, for an account suggesting the relevance of Dunne's time theories, Ouspensky's philosophy and E. A. Abbott's *Flatland* to Priestley's work.

"Time is forever dividing itself toward innumerable futures. . . ."[2]

Temporal speculation, while implicit in all time-travel literature, has become increasingly more explicit in recent science fiction. Aside from the anachronism question, which has inspired plots concerned with the "Time Police" or "Guardians," whose job it is to keep history in place, there are stories concerned with the rate at which and the direction in which time flows. As I have already indicated, Masson's "Travellers' Rest" introduces the concept of time flowing at different rates in the different latitudes of a planet. Brian W. Aldiss has written an interesting story entitled "Man in His Time" (1966), about an astronaut whose temporal experience is slightly ahead of everybody else's after returning from an expedition to Mars, where the "time field" is 3.3077 minutes ahead of Earth's. In "Mr. F. Is Mr. F" (1961), by J. G. Ballard, time flows backward and the protagonist finds himself disappearing into the moment of his original creation. Ballard has a particular interest in the mysteries of time. In *The Crystal World*, for example, one of his metaphoric catastrophe stories, the end comes about because time congeals. The theme allows for a good deal of whimsicality. For example, the tourist business goes into time travel in Ray Bradbury's "The Sound of Thunder" (1953) and Robert Silverberg's *Up the Line* (1969). Robert Heinlein's *By His Bootstraps* (1946) is the best known of many stories that ring changes on the theme of what happens when a time traveler meets a younger or an older version of himself. Heinlein's particular wrinkle is to have his protagonist travel thirty thousand years into the future and meet himself not at some age in excess of thirty thousand, but as middle-aged!

The most fertile derivative of the time-travel theme, the parallel-worlds story, is anticipated by my earlier allusion to Dunne's theories and the Borges story. There must exist a string of worlds exactly like ours except that different

[2] See "The Garden of Forking Paths," trans. by Helen Temple and Ruthven Todd in *Ficciones* (New York, 1962), p. 100.

decisions were made along the way, with different results. In "Sail On, Sail On" (1952), Philip José Farmer presents a parallel world in which the Church, instead of opposing scientific research, encourages it. Consequently Columbus sails to America in a ship equipped with radio, but since the world turns out to be flat, there is no America and Columbus falls over the edge. Ward Moore, in *Bring the Jubilee* (1955), describes life in the twenty-six United States following a southern victory in the American Civil War. John Brunner's *Times Without Number* (1962) describes a world consequent upon the victory of the Spanish Armada. Nobody has yet written the parallel-worlds-story sequel to Twain's *A Connecticut Yankee*. In this story the current of history would divide following the victory of Hank Morgan and his followers at the Battle of the Sand-Belt. Perhaps Farmer, having written a sequel to *Moby-Dick* and resurrected Mark Twain for The Riverworld Series might try his hand at this one?

II

John Boyd's *The Last Starship from Earth* (1968) reads, for the most part, like a straightforward dystopia rather than a parallel-worlds story. But for the fact that the time is the late sixties, it would be easy to accept the sociopolitical situation as a plausible projection of present realities—except for a few striking anomalies. The part of the narrative that takes place on Earth is set in the San Francisco area of California, "Union of North America, World State" (p. 110).[3] Apparently, Canada does not exist. The Catholic Church and academe have inherited the earth. Under the ultimate control of an advanced computer called the pope, created by the famous Fairweather I, the administration of state falls to the various academic disciplines, particularly Sociology, which exer-

[3] All parenthetical references to *The Last Starship from Earth* may be located in the Science Fiction Book Club edition (London, 1970).

cises the judicial function, and Psychology, the police power. A system of selective eugenics forbids the professional academicians to mate either outside of their particular discipline or with a member of the proletariat, except in exceptional circumstances. Hence the existence of family dynasties and numbered descendants. Deviation from the norm is not tolerated, and extreme cases are exiled to a distant penal planet, light-years away, called Hell. None of these conditions depend exclusively on the parallel-worlds hypothesis. However, this hypothesis does become operational when we learn that Henry VIII is known as a notorious head sociologist and that Christ, who remains central to the religious system, died not on the cross at age thirty-three, but from a crossbow arrow while leading a revolutionary attack against Rome at age seventy.

The protagonist, Haldane IV, the fourth in a line of theoretical mathematicians, becomes the typical dystopian deviant. Confronted with a symbolic fork in the road (an aspect, doubtless, of a Borgesian labyrinth of choices) in the book's opening paragraphs, "on September 5, at two minutes past two, he took the wrong turn and drove down a lane to hell" (p. 1)—literally to Hell. The connection between an awareness of time, alternative choice, and parallel worlds is immediately apparent. As a result of turning down this lane, Haldane meets Helix, a beautiful arts student. They fall in love in the face of prohibitive eugenic regulations. In an attempt to legitimize their relationship, they propose a new interdisciplinary category of study involving literature and mathematics. It appears that the brilliant Fairweather I, aside from creating the computer pope in 1881 and the star drive— a method of laser propulsion enabling men to escape the confines of the solar system—was also a poet. Helix has a particular interest in Fairweather I the poet and has need of Haldane's mathematical knowledge in order to properly interpret Fairweather's imagery, which has an unexpectedly subversive content—a reference in one poem to the three "Weird Sisters" (p. 37) who have denied men

the stars appears to be an indirect attack on the three
powers of Sociology, Psychology, and the Church, which
have delimited the use of starships except for the two that
ferry undesirables to Hell. For his own part, Haldane con-
cocts a particular interest in researching possibilities for
perfecting the mathematical analysis of literary styles.
Matters are precipitated when Helix announces that she
is pregnant and when they discover that the ensuing conversation has been bugged. Eventually they are arrested.

During the course of this relationship, Haldane makes
a succession of discoveries about the nature of reality in
general and the nature of Fairweather I in particular.
This awakening is systematically compared to successive
ice ages. Goaded by Haldane's revelation that he plans
to marry Helix and beat the machine, his father, Haldane
III, states the facts about Fairweather I, whom Haldane
IV instances as a humanist. Fairweather I mated with a
member of the proletariat to produce a son, Fairweather
II, "who created more evil on this planet than any evil
since the starvation. Despite the evil of Fairweather II,
Pope Leo brought excommunication proceedings against
Fairweather I because he betrayed his own son to the
police"—ergo Pope Leo XXXV was genuinely the "last
humanist." Sociology and Psychology supported Fairweather I against the Pope and won. "Fairweather I sent
his own son to Hell" (p. 64) and began work on the
computerized pope. Haldane IV's rage subsides: "He
knew that it had been the last tropical storm before an
advancing ice age of his mind. The king was dead, destroyed by Haldane's sure knowledge that his father had
spoken the truth, and Helix was a snow maiden lost in the
frozen mists. Fairweather, that worse-than-filicide, was a
pope-building sycophant of the Church." But "even as he
adjusted to this subarctic of the spirit, an aurora borealis
flickered and then flared into a dazzling display of rustling light which sent his blood singing through his veins"
(p. 65). The "concept that had come to him, like an
aurora borealis" (p. 92), is explained later: "In that First
Ice Age of his discontent, he had discovered the incom-

pleteness of Fairweather's Simultaneity Formula" (p. 89)
—a formula that is bound up with the star-drive theory.
In a cell, separated from Helix, Haldane "knew he had
come to the Second Ice Age of his mind but he was getting acclimatized to the cold. His sensibilites were frozen
and all his problems were the problems of a corpse"
(p. 79). The "Third Ice Age" (p. 117) of the mind hits
Haldane during the trial, when he intuits that Helix, as an
agent of the state, has set him up.

The full import of the ice-age metaphor depends upon
the reader noting the relationship between this imagery
and Hell, which is not a fiery planet but, on the contrary,
a place of intense cold. In the early part of the book,
characters are repeatedly given to expletives like "Hell's
sleigh bells!" (p. 98), which emphasize the frigidity of
Hell. At one point, Haldane "cared not an icicle on Hell"
(p. 41). Given the imagistic sense of ice as illumination,
the reader is prepared for the revelation that Hell itself
will provide the ultimate reality underlying the situation
of the novel. As in Blake, it is Hellish wisdom to which we
must attend. After all, as we are later informed, "Hell
means light in German" (p. 152). As Haldane initiates
the sequence of events that leads to an ultimate illumination about the nature of reality, "He felt as Columbus must
have felt as he sailed past the Pillars of Hercules, or as
Iranorna must have felt as the particolored globe of her
native earth dwindled beneath her, a feeling of finality
tinged with death" (p. 59).

At the conclusion of a lengthy and complicated trial,
Haldane is convicted not so much for disregarding mating
regulations, but as an instance of the Fairweather Syn-
drome first exhibited by Fairweather II, the revolutionary.
Fairweather II and Haldane are, in fact "alter egos"
(p. 174). Haldane's mother may have accidentally fallen
from a window, but it is more likely that she jumped, like
Fairweather's mother. The plot parallelism here, like the
numerical naming system, is in some way analogous to
the parallel-worlds concept. For the same reason, an in-
ordinate number of characters in the book, particularly on

Hell, have names beginning with the letter H—a letter that might be considered an illustration of the image "parallel lines all meet in space" (p. 5), from one of Fairweather I's poems. In any event, Haldane, a possible "anti-Christ" (p. 97) in the eyes of the Church, is exiled to Hell and leaves on the next starship, the *Styx*.

Once on Hell, the revelations come thick and fast— rather too mechanically, in fact. Haldane discovers that Fairweather II, who is still alive in Hell, anticipated the further extension of the Simultaneity Formula that Haldane believed he originated and about which he became so excited. By traveling beyond the speed of light, a starship would achieve "minus time" or "Time in excess of simultaneity" (p. 91). The formula that Fairweather II originated and Haldane stumbles upon accidentally, allows for a star drive, which, utilizing the "chain reaction of light [symbolically analogous, perhaps, to the succession of illuminations with which the book concludes], triggered by the laser source, would mean speeds of infinite acceleration" (p. 167). In other words, by traveling the necessary distance at the necessary speed, it would be possible to arrive on Earth at various historical moments in the "past" and make the necessary adjustment. All is a plot concocted by Fairweather I and Fairweather II. The weather on Hell, as anticipated in the lines of a song sung by a black man in a cell opposite Haldane's, is fair during the summer. Only Fairweather I understood that Hell "swings in an ellipse" (p. 149) around its sun and, although the winter is severe, it is not the permanent condition. All in all, Hell is a pleasant enough place. Disgusted with the totalitarian system on Earth, Fairweather I and II did nothing to correct the impression that Hell's orbit was circular, in order to use the planet as a base for the time-travel experiment. The ultimate decision as to who goes to Hell comes from the cybernetic pope that Fairweather I invented "to keep his son in high-level bridge partners . . ." (p. 152). In addition, Fairweather I "set up the schedules of the prison ships so that they always arrive in winter" (p. 153). The Hellions need a theoretical mathematician, so Helix, Fairweather II's daughter born on Hell (the surprises are a bit overdone at this point), is sent down to set up Haldane or someone like him.

Fairweather II goes on to explain, ". . . there are few periods in history, and those come early, when one man could alter the course of nations" and "we needed a theoretical mathematician to make the drop, because hairline adjustments will have to be made during the approach to earth." Haldane, alias Judas Iscariot, is shipped back with his "cellular balance" stabilized "to prevent disease" (p. 173) or aging, and with a homing device in a tooth filling to guide him to the escape vehicle when his mission is completed—his mission being to get Christ out of the way, long before he reaches age seventy in a position to die by a crossbow, and become the founder of Christianity. In the "Epilogue: Earth Revisited," it is Earth back as we know it. Apparently "Judas Iscariot" was persuaded by Mary Magdalene to relinquish his seat "on the last starship from earth" (p. 179) to Jesus and remain behind as the ageless Wandering Jew—albeit a Christian Jew. The phrase "the last starship" contains a pun on last as "final" or last as "most recent," either the ship on which Haldane left Earth, or the smaller vessel carrying Christ. One of the more interesting effects in Boyd's novel is the implied sense of temporal simultaneity, which Jane Hipolito has explored.[4] Linear concepts of first and last are meaningless. As Haldane IV, alias Judas Iscariot, alias Hal Dane, comes to realize, "Patterns never change" (p. 179). The world he may be assumed to have made is a little better than the one he left, but he did not succeed in forestalling the development of Christianity. Maybe time is more correctly perceived as a circle or a

[4] See "The Last and First Starship From Earth" in SF: The Other Side of Realism, ed. by Thomas D. Clareson (Bowling Green, Ohio, 1971), pp. 186–92. Incidentally the Wandering Jew crops up as an art thief in Ballard's "The Lost Leonardo" (1964). See my analysis of Miller's A Canticle for Leibowitz in Chapter 6 for the Wandering Jew's further career.

helix—Mary Magdalene, Helix, and the new Greek girl
Helen Patrouklos appear to be different avatars of the
same type.

The subtle philosophical sense of time that the novel
proposes is genuinely apocalyptic. Haldane has real cause
to wonder whether he "had sidetracked history or de-
railed it when he laid the hissop-drugged body of Jesus
into the one-seater right after the Crucifixion. . . . If he
had triggered Armageddon when he launched the starship, then it was oblivion for him and he could use the
sleep" (pp. 180–81). That "last" starship might just have
"engineered the final merger of the ultimate thesis with
the ultimate antithesis . . . the great Jubilee" (p. 181) in
bringing an apocalyptic sense of time or eternity up
against a material sense of time. Certainly the world
Haldane left is nowhere in evidence. With such knowledge, for the Wandering Jew, the present earth can only
be "Purgatory" (p. 182), more like hell than the real
Hell. One could continue with such philosophical possibilities. Boyd's novel is a dazzling achievement in terms
of its suggestiveness alone. But it is the subtle play of wit
and humor deactivating what might otherwise be destructively far-fetched, overcoincidental plotting and softening
philosophical profundities, in a manner more usually associated with Kurt Vonnegut, Jr., that constitutes Boyd's
particularly outstanding achievement in this novel.

III

In parallel-worlds stories, the opening pages typically
present the reader with an incomprehensible jumble that
begins to make sense only when he has established the
point at which the "fictional" reality shears off from the
accepted "historical" reality. This is particularly so in
Philip K. Dick's subtle novel *The Man in the High Castle*
(1962). Only as the reader gradually becomes aware that
in the parallel world, World War II resulted in the defeat of the Allies by the coalition of Germany, Japan, and

Italy, does the situation in America, where the action occurs, become intelligible. Italy appears to have been sold out, but Germany and Japan have divided the United States between them. The Nazis occupy the eastern United States, while the Japanese dominate the Pacific States of America with some nominal German interference. Britain seems to have disappeared except for talk of British atrocities in the war. This is a world in which all dark-haired people—particularly blacks and Italians, but not, it would seem, the Japanese—are equated with the Jews as biologically inferior to the blond, Aryan race. Franklin D. Roosevelt has been assassinated. The smoking of marijuana cigarettes—"Land-O-Smiles" (p. 13)[5] is a popular brand—is legal and perhaps essential. Everybody, particularly in the Japanese sector, appears to be strongly influenced by two books. The Japanese have introduced the ancient Chinese *I Ching*, or *Book of Changes*. By means of this oracular work of divination, an individual is supposedly able to understand the nature of his present circumstances, to foresee the future, and to act accordingly. The other book, an underground best seller, is a parallel-worlds story entitled *The Grasshopper Lies Heavy*, by someone named Hawthorne Abendsen. One of Dick's characters describes the work as "an interesting form of fiction possibly within the genre of science fiction," adding that there are "Many well known science fiction novels" that deal with an "alternate present" (pp. 103–4).

In the alternate present of Abendsen's novel, Germany and Japan lose the war to the Allies. Not surprisingly, the book is banned in the German-occupied area of America while only tolerated in the Pacific States. The world that Abendsen describes appears to be the one that we, as readers of Dick's novel, know. Italy betrayed the Axis countries, and Roosevelt was not assassinated. There are, however, significant differences. Abendsen states, "In the U.S.A. the color problem had by 1950 been solved. . . .

[5] All parenthetical references to *The Man in the High Castle* may be located in the original, hard-cover edition (New York, 1962).

World War Two had ended discrimination" (p. 149). Everything is not perfect, but the over-all situation is somewhat closer to utopia than our "historical" reality. As the author of a subversive work, Abendsen realizes the danger of his position and, according to rumors, he has surrounded his hilltop cabin, or "high castle," with defensive fortifications. He is, then, "the man in the high castle."

It turns out that such defensive measures are justified, because one of the major plot elements in the novel involves the attempt of a Swiss agent, acting for the Germans, disguised as an Italian named Joe Cinnedella, to assassinate Abendsen. He is eventually forestalled by the woman whom he meets along the way, seduces, and travels with, Juliana Frink. The political situation is particularly urgent because Martin Bormann, Hitler's successor as the Reich's Chancellor, has died, and there is a good deal of nervous anxiety as to who, among a variety of unappealing possibilities, will be his successor. Some of these possibilities are more favorable than others to a conspiracy known as "Operation Dandelion," dedicated to serving Japan in the treacherous fashion already experienced by Italy. Another German agent, this one disguised as a traveling Swedish businessman named Mr. Baynes, and representing a faction opposed to "Operation Dandelion," has the mission of informing the Japanese of what is brewing. It is within this wider context of intrigue that a hysterical Juliana Frink, having discovered the true identity of her lover and his purpose in wishing to visit Abendsen, slashes him with a razor blade and leaves him to die in a Denver hotel. She decides to continue alone with the plan to visit Abendsen, in order to tell him of his narrow escape and to congratulate him on his remarkable novel.

There are certain apparently incidental details related to these circumstances that deserve scrutiny. It becomes apparent that "Joe" picked up Juliana as a means of gaining entrance to Abendsen's "high castle": "We have a folder on Abendsen and it seems he is attracted to a certain type of dark libidinous girl. A specific Middle-Eastern or Mediterranean type" (p. 195). To augment this image and play on Abendsen's libido, "Joe" buys Juliana a blue Italian dress with "a wildly low neck line" (p. 189). As Joe says, "When he sees you I'm certain he'll let us in, especially with that Italian dress cut as it is" (p. 196). Just before finally seeing Abendsen, she decides to wear the blue dress but discovers "that she had not brought any of the new half-bras from Denver" (p. 230). She tries a regular bra, but the straps show. Consequently, she settles for going braless and protecting her well-developed bust by collecting the front of the dress with a pin. Spilling out the contents of her jewelry box, "she spread out the pins, relics which she had owned for years, given her by Frank or by other men before their marriage, and the new one which Joe had gotten her in Denver" before selecting "a small horse-shaped silver pin from Mexico" (pp. 230–31). Shortly after Juliana and Abendsen have met, he innocently remarks, "What's that pin on your dress do? Ward off dangerous anima-spirits of the immutable world? Or does it just hold everything together?" (p. 234). In a sense that Abendsen does not realize but Dick unquestionably intends, this pin holds the entire novel together—hence the emphasis in the novel on Juliana's new dress.

Juliana's pins are described as "relics" (p. 230)—objects of personal historical interest. There are two plot lines that appear to be only incidentally related to the political action described above but do connect with the pin. The more dominant of these concerns Robert Childan, the owner of "American Artistic Handcrafts Inc." (p. 9), a store in San Francisco selling antique Americana, particularly prewar artifacts. Frank Frink, Juliana's now-estranged, Jewish husband, who figures in the other plot line, has recently been fired from his job at Wyndam-Matson Corporation, where he was involved in the production of imitation antique American artifacts, some of which make their way into Mr. Childan's store. Mr. Childan is not aware that many of the articles he sells are forgeries. There is a current boom in articles with "historicity." Frank and another ex-employee of W-M Corporation decide to set up their own business devoted to contemporary jewelry on the expectation that, once the forgeries are known, the bottom will fall out of the antique market. Quite simply, Juliana's pin relates the unfamiliar political situation to the eccentric plot lines involving Mr. Childan and her husband, and provides Dick with a subtle means of establishing the historicity of his parallel world by questioning the reality of historicity and, by extension, historical reality. The device is an original one and much more intriguing than the customary anachronistic, often unconscious, manipulations of bewildered time travelers. Just as Juliana's pin brings into relationship the different worlds occupied by the various characters who figure in the complicated plot lines Dick skilfully orchestrates, so the pin also relates alternate parallel worlds to a common concept of historicity.

When Childan eventually discovers that he has bought a fake Colt .44 from the W-M Corporation, he complains, and Wyndam-Matson himself is informed of the matter. Wyndam-Matson explains his position to his mistress: "This whole damn historicity business is nonsense. . . . I'll prove it." He shows the girl two Zippo cigarette lighters and invites her to pick out the one with "historicity in it," the one worth "maybe forty or fifty thousand dollars on the collector's market" because it "was in Franklin D. Roosevelt's pocket when he was assassinated. . . . One has historicity, a hell of a lot of it. As much as any object ever had. And one has nothing. . . . You can't tell which is which" (p. 63). When the girl doubts that either lighter belonged to Roosevelt, Wyndam-Matson exults, "That's my point! I'd have to prove it to you with some sort of document. . . . The paper proves its worth, not the object itself." In other words, "The word 'fake' meant nothing really, since the word 'authentic' meant nothing really" (p. 64). Later "Joe" explains to Juliana that Abendsen's book has "no history in it" (p. 151). The samples of EDFRANK contemporary jewelry that Ed McCarthy leaves with Mr. Childan make no claim to historicity. However, a prominent Japanese whom Mr. Childan is cultivating, on being shown one example of this contemporary jewelry, an oddly angled pin, declares, after a train of meditation, that the object possesses *wu* value "in opposition to historicity." "In other words, an entire new world is pointed to, by this" (p. 164). On reflection, Mr. Childan decides that he has been subtly insulted by the final evaluation that the pin would make a good-luck charm. However, when, following a frenetic series of events, Mr. Tagomi, representative of the Japanese Pacific Trade Mission, contemplates the silver, triangular EDFRANK piece, which he buys from Mr. Childan, he believes himself to be transported temporarily "Out of my world, my space and time" (p. 216).

Mr. Tagomi is in an agitated condition because of the confrontation that occurs in his office when the various political issues in the novel come to a head. "Mr. Baynes" arrives with his warning about "Operation Dandelion" shortly before two armed "Operation Dandelion" agents attempt to kill him. But Mr. Tagomi is able to kill them first with "his Colt .44 ancient collector's item" (p. 184). Goebbels, who favors Operation Dandelion, has taken over as Chancellor. Mr. Tagomi takes the gun back to Childan's store, where he bought it, hoping to trade it "in on more historicity sanctioned item." As he reflects, "This gun for me has too much subjective history . . . all of the wrong kind. But that ends with me; no one else can experience it from the gun. Within my psyche only." But by getting rid of the gun he can also free himself, for, as he goes on to conclude, the past "is not merely in my psyche; it is—as has always been said in the theory of historicity—within the gun as well. An equation between us" (pp. 208–9). On returning to his office, where all traces of the shooting incident have been removed, Mr. Tagomi is conscious of the same "Historicity bonded into nylon tile of floor" (p. 219). Obviously this sense of unseen historicity provides some plausible analogical basis for "Mr. Baynes's," or, rather, Captain Rudolf Wegener's, hope that, even if the Nazis succeed in destroying all life on Earth, "there must be other life somewhere which we know nothing of. It is impossible that ours is the only world; there must be world after world unseen by us, in some region or dimension that we simply do not perceive" (p. 226).

If, during Juliana's visit, Abendsen is struck by her pin designed to "hold everything together" (p. 234), she is most immediately surprised by the lack of the fortifications that the rumor of Abendsen's "High Castle" (p. 231) had led her to expect: "The house was ordinary, well maintained and the grounds tended. Apparently Abendsen did live in a fortress but, finding the environment uncomfortable, he gave it up. He has since discovered that the myth is as effective as the reality in turning the fear associated with the "SS fairies in those training castles in Bavaria" (p. 38), "the Castle System" of the "Reich's elite corps" (p. 177) and Hermann Göring with his "immense castle" (p. 89)—these being the only occasions where actual castles are referred to in the book—to his own advantage. As for Abendsen's provocative novel, it turns out, as Juliana guesses, that it was written with the oracular aid of the *I Ching*. Abendsen's wife explains, "One by one Hawth made the choices. Thousands of them. By means of the lines [in the *I Ching*]. Historic period. Subject. Characters. Plot" (p. 236). Juliana asks the oracle a final question, why it chose to dictate that particular story, and discovers, in Abendsen's words, "my book is true" (p. 237). But Juliana's earlier understanding that Abendsen "told us about our own world" (p. 230) is also true. To know of the existence of a parallel world where the succession of events took the ideal course predicted by the *Book of Changes* is to know the truth about her own world, where the succession of events was much less than ideal. The same applies to the reader's world, which follows the ideal history presented in *The Grasshopper Lies Heavy* only to a certain point. It is left to the reader to assume that both his world and Juliana's world have their places among a multitude of parallel worlds with less claim to "historicity" than the parallel world depicted in Abendsen's novel. However, the supposition that Abendsen was not personally able to arrive at these conclusions constitutes a strange weakness (dictated perhaps by the exigencies of dramatic plot construction) in an otherwise exceptionally fine novel. At the same time, it should be recognized that this kind of contrivance is a seemingly inevitable feature of the paradoxical implications prompted by dimensional speculation.

IV

Dick's novel, being less dependent on the time-travel gimmickry utilized by Moore and Boyd, may conveniently serve as a bridge to my corresponding survey of science-fiction works that generate alternate realities largely on the basis of spatial speculation. Although time and space, like form and content, may be separated only artificially, it is often, as here, convenient to do so. I used *A Connecticut Yankee in King Arthur's Court* as a means of introducing my discussion of time-centered speculation, and, by way of emphasizing Twain's importance to the development of science fiction, I can do no better than cite another work of his to introduce those works which play with unappreciated spatial dimensions. H. Bruce Franklin deserves credit for his presentation of Twain the science-fiction writer and, in so doing, for highlighting an unfinished and untitled work begun in 1898.[6] Bernard De Voto supplied the title by which the piece is now known, *The Great Dark*, from a phrase in one of Twain's notes. To claim, as does Franklin, fired by a pioneer's enthusiasm, "Even in its unfinished state *The Great Dark* . . . is a minor masterpiece which hints of a potential to have become Twain's finest creation" is something of an exaggeration, but despite problems of tone, it does have a notable place among those works which treat the notion

[6] See "Mark Twain and Science Fiction," in *Future Perfect*, pp. 374–79.

of spatial dimension in its most literal sense, as relating to size.[7]

The narrator-protagonist of this tale, Mr. Edwards, examining a drop of water through the microscope he has bought his daughter, Jessie, for her birthday, is amazed at the bizarre animal life thereby revealed: "An ocean in a drop of water—and unknown, uncharted, unexplored by man!" (p. 187).[8] Mr. Edwards then falls asleep, and after making arrangements with the Superintendent of Dreams to explore the unknown ocean, finds himself aboard a storm-tossed ship with his wife and two children. It is a starless, moonless night. The ship would seem to be somewhere near the edge of the drop of water under the microscope. As the Superintendent of Dreams explains, "All of the drop of water is outside the luminous circle of the microscope except one thin and delicate rim of it. We are in the shadow . . . of the brazen end of the lens holder" (p. 202). While originally looking through the microscope, Mr. Edwards had noticed that the light from the microscope illuminated only one area, a "great white sea" (p. 187), of the drop of water. Certainly the strange animals previously observed and now seen as monstrous spider-squids are very much in evidence. Within the microscopic world, time is correspondingly extended, and the Superintendent hints that the terrifying passage across the drop of water will take a considerable amount of time—years, as it turns out. But what most disturbs Edwards is the suspicion implanted by the Superintendent, a close relative of Satan in *The Mysterious Stranger*, that the present experience is not a dream: "I give you ten years to get over that superstition in!" (p. 204). Philosophically Mr. Edwards reflects, "We seldom really know the thing we think we know; that our best-built certainties are but sand-houses and subject to damage

[7] Ibid., p. 375.
[8] All parenthetical references to *The Great Dark* may be located in the Fawcett Crest Book paperback edition of *Letters from the Earth*, ed. by Bernard De Voto (Greenwich, Conn., 1962).

from any wind of doubt that blows" (p. 204). Such winds continue to blow strongly. Mr. Edwards turns out to be the only person on board who believes that it is all a dream experience. The only dream experience his wife acknowledges is of a mysterious existence on land. For her, their shipboard life is and always has been the reality: "The earliest thing I can call to mind was Papa's death by the sun heat and Mama's suicide the same day," when "we were in the edge of a white glare once for a little while" (p. 210). According to Twain's notes for continuing the story, as interpreted and summarized by De Voto, after a mutiny is settled and a treasure ship spirits away the Edwardses' new son, born aboard ship, and the captain's daughter, further misfortunes follow when the ship once again enters the region made unbearably hot by the "white glare," which, of course, derives from the light reflected on the microscope's mirror. The "new world" (p. 218), which the Edwardses piece together from dream fragments they experience in common, is ultimately agreed to be imaginary.

The first mate, who like the other crew members, believes that they are attempting to navigate one of the earth's oceans, can only explain the lack of celestial illumination by assuming "That the world has come to an end" (p. 200). In a metaphorical sense, the first mate is correct. Twain proposed to end the novel with a succession of catastrophes, leaving only the Edwardses alive. Mr. Edwards escapes from this tragic situation to what he understands as a dream of a former existence on land with his wife and two children. The reader may assume that Mr. Edwards has simply awakened from a nightmare, but it is Twain's purpose to end the world we know, to suggest that it is, in fact, a dream, and that, in its meaninglessness, our reality is equivalent to the microscopic world explored by Mr. Edwards.

The Great Dark is not the first American work to explore the science-fictional possibilities of microcosmic dimensions. Indeed there is an earlier American example, entitled "The Diamond Lens" (1858), by Fitz-James O'Brien,

which may or may not have influenced Twain. As in
Twain's case, the narrator/protagonist becomes obsessed
with the fascinating world in a drop of water made visible
by the electrically treated diamond lens he fits into his
microscope: "I stood trembling on the threshold of a new
world" (p. 328).[9] But where Twain's narrator becomes
aware only of a hellish existence, O'Brien's narrator sees a
paradisal Garden of Eden inhabited by an exquisitely
beautiful Eve, which causes him to lose "all note of time"
(p. 349). Evil in this symbolic tale (note the section entitled "The Bending of the Twig") is introduced by the
bent narrator himself, who has committed murder in
order to acquire the diamond lens. There is some suggestion that the light from the microscope is responsible
for the gestation of life within the globe of water. God's
command "Let there be light" is here at the volition of a
Satanic figure. The narrator falls hopelessly in love with
the enchanting Animula, as he calls her, in spite of the fact
that communication is impossible and she is not aware
of his existence. When she is lost irretrievably with the
evaporation of the drop of water, we may assume that
the rest of his existence is appropriately and unbearably
hellish. Although he then falls into a trance, to awake a
shattered man, there is no indication that the entire experience is to be taken as a dream.

Any complete history of microscopic or macroscopic
speculation would find its starting point considerably further back in time than Twain and O'Brien. The subject
should properly be related to various creation myths,
Homer's treatment of Ulysses' run-in with the Cyclops,
and to any number of fairy tales. Swift was the first
writer to accommodate this theme to the realistic treatment characteristic of science fiction. Indeed Book I of
Gulliver's Travels (1726), set in the microscopic world
of Lilliput, and Book II, set in the macroscopic world of
Brobdingnag, are of much greater science-fictional interest than the flying island of Laputa and the Struldbrugs

[9] Parenthetical references to "The Diamond Lens" may be
located in Franklin's anthology *Future Perfect*.

in Book III, which is usually pointed to as Swift's excursion into science fiction. In *Micromegas* (1753), Voltaire follows Swift's use of the contrasting-proportions theme as a vehicle for satire. Voltaire's Sirian and Saturnian are presented as giants both physically and intellectually, compared with the beings they converse with on Earth. Generally, giants have played a larger part in fantasy than in science fiction. Wells' monstrous children who digest *The Food of the Gods* (1904) provide rather weakkneed science fiction.

None of these works, however, qualify as the kind of dimensional speculation to which O'Brien and Twain point: the understanding either that the visible universe is but a molecular aspect of an incredibly vaster entity (the situation in Piers Anthony's *Macroscope*) or that an entire universe may exist in an atom. The latter possibility is approached in Ray Cummings' *The Girl in The Golden Atom* (1923), in which the hero is reduced to microscopic proportions; Theodore Sturgeon's "Microcosmic God" (1941), which is concerned with a scientist who creates a minuscule humanoid society; and Blish's "Surface Tension," part of *The Seedling Stars* (1952), in which a genetically designed microscopic race of men explore microscopic worlds. In addition, two films deserve mention. The potential for horror has been explored in *The Incredible Shrinking Man* (1957) and the potential for wonder in *Fantastic Voyage* (1966), novelized in the same year by Isaac Asimov. The fantastic voyage within the human body is made possible by techniques of miniaturization pressed into service for delicate internal surgery. As for inspired whimsy, W. H. Auden has written a poem entitled *A New Year's Greeting*, in which he addresses the microscopic beings who inhabit his own body as we inhabit the world: "I should like to think that I make/a not impossible world, but an Eden it cannot be." The poet goes on to wonder what colorful catastrophe myths might explain the twice-daily "Hurricanes" that attend his dressing and undressing, and anticipates "A Day of Apocalypse" and ecological horror coincident with his own death.[10] But Twain earlier explored this idea in his incomplete "Three Thousand Years Among the Microbes" (1905). The narrator, reduced to microscopic size by a wizard, inhabits the world-body of a diseased tramp and is therefore in a position to appreciate the transcendent organic unity of nature.

V

More often than not, alternate spatial dimensions, like alternate temporal dimensions, manifest themselves without any conscious, scientific experimentation on man's part. A brief piece by Ambrose Bierce entitled "Mysterious Disappearance" (1893) describes three cases of people who appear to have vanished in mid-stride, then concludes with the tentative theory that these people have accidentally fallen into holes of "non-Euclidean space . . . space which has more dimensions than length, breadth, and thickness—space in which it would be possible to tie a rubber ball inside out without 'a solution of its continuity,' or in other words, without breaking or cracking it."[11] The fictional possibilities of such an utterly alien dimension are radically limited. Bierce's holes in space seem akin to the more recent notion that space is wrinkled or warped. This dimensional anomaly is frequently used as a gimmicky transportation device in the kind of plot that spans an entire galaxy or universe. On other occasions the ploy of an alternate space-time continuum where all known natural laws are suspended is often invoked as a means of introducing fantasy material in a science-fiction context. John Brunner's *The Traveller in Black* (1971) and Poul Anderson's *Operation Chaos* (1971) are recent examples. Ray Bradbury's whimsical tale entitled "The Shape of Things" (1948) describes a woman who gives birth to a pyramid. On discovering that her child appears

[10] See W. H. Auden, *Epistle to My Godson* (New York, 1972), pp. 12–14.

[11] See *Future Perfect*, p. 361

to be a pyramid only because he was born into the fourth dimension, she and her husband opt to join their offspring in that other dimension. The discovery of anti-matter has opened up the possibility of a potentially destructive anti-matter universe. In *The Triumph of Time* (1958), by James Blish, the collision at the "megagalactic center" of the known universe with its corresponding anti-matter universe is the occasion for the death and rebirth of universes. Poul Anderson's *Tau Zero* (1970) involves a similar conception.

To conclude this survey of dimensional speculation in science fiction, I shall glance at two novels by Brian W. Aldiss that, like the universes in *The Triumph of Time*, exist in an antithetical relationship to one another. Although neither *Report on Probability A* (1968) or *Barefoot in the Head* (1969) is particularly successful, they, together with the work of J. G. Ballard, are culminating examples of the kind of technical experimentation associated with the so-called "new wave" of science fiction, a wave now fast disappearing among successive waves. On the assumption that a literature dealing in new versions of reality should be innovative technically and stylistically, "new wave" writers abandoned the prosaic and conventional narrative style of a Heinlein or an Asimov in favor of the equally dated but less popular stylistic devices of surrealism, Dada, and Joyce. Aldiss's mimicking of that super-precious objectivity favored by the practitioners of the French anti-novel in *Report on Probability A* does, it is true, have a newness that can't be claimed for his pastiche of super-subjective, late Joyce in *Barefoot in the Head*. The problem with both novels appears to be that Aldiss began with a particular style that he wished to imitate and then contrived a plot to allow for the extended use of that style. The result eventually makes for excruciating reading.

The totally objective style depends upon a disengaged and dispassionate narrator, and in *Report on Probability A* Aldiss has contrived this situation by supposing that observers in one space-time continuum are writing a report on events taking place in another space-time continuum which they call Probability A. This report consists of a minutely detailed factual account of the apparently mundane activities of five people and the banal but precise notation of elements in their environment. The observers have no knowledge of the subjective factors that might make the situation in *Probability A* intelligible. Four more probability worlds are successively involved, allowing Aldiss to achieve the verbal equivalent of the picture of a man painting a picture of a man painting a picture . . . except that the picture is more interesting. In fact Aldiss's point would seem to be made by a picture entitled *The Shepherd,* by Hunt, a copy of which everyone in *Probability A* seems to own. This painting, which, like everything else, is described in extreme detail, is of a frozen moment in time that would seem to promise a seduction scene if the other possibilities are ignored. The concluding paragraph of the novel, set in the italic type used to distinguish material relating to probability worlds other than the subject of the report, describes the probability world of the painting without answering the essential question. Is Aldiss implying stylistically that any understanding of experience based solely on objective data can have no more dimensionality than a painting?

The concern of *Barefoot in the Head* would appear to be omnidimensionality. This novel might well be the result of Aldiss's attempt to come up with a plot that could appropriately be presented in the multilayered, free-associational, stream-of-consciousness style employed by James Joyce, with touches of William Burroughs and Lewis Carroll. The plot solution represents a twist on the worldcatastrophe theme. Europe, where the novel's action takes place, is in a chaotic state following the Acid-Head War—hallucinogenic drugs were part of the military arsenal. The effect of this war, like the dimensional vista in *Report on Probability A,* is best represented pictorially—and the cover illustration of the Corgi Books paperback edition of *Barefoot in the Head* says it all more eloquently than over two hundred pages of surrealistic, pun-encrusted prose.

What appears to be a picture of a brain or an explosion is actually a picture of Earth as *earth,* with the land masses projected outward from the world's center—the seas and other areas of water, as prophesied in the Apocalypse, have disappeared. The images of the Earth, an explosion and a brain, combine to suggest a mind-bombed world or the world as a zonked-out brain. General Curtis Lemay's threat to the Vietnamese, "We're going to bomb them back into the Stone Age," which Aldiss reproduces as the book's epigraph, has become a world-wide actuality.

The result has been a very literal apocalypse of mind. The old world of "pre-psychedelic man" (p. 57)[12] has gone: "All the known noon world loses its old staples and everything drops apart" (p. 214). The protagonist, who calls himself Colin Charteris, after Leslie Charteris, the creator of the Saint and a reminder of the "straight" world, which is now no more real than the Saint himself, is persuaded to act as a messiah ushering in and interpreting the new reality. But the only new vision Charteris has to offer is that of the pothead, influenced and made somewhat impressive by his reading of the Russian philosopher P. D. Ouspensky, disciple of Gurdjieff, whose mystical mélange he dignified. Charteris believes, "Only the preceptual [presumably a neologism and not a typo] web was 'real'" (p. 19). This is the word that Charteris, at the head of a motorcade with his mistress, Angeline, brings to Europe: "The Escalation and I now setting out on a motor crusade down through Europe, the autobahns, the war, dislocation, to ultimate unity" (p. 91). But ultimate unity is not exactly where the crusade is headed. The "trip" "Northwards" in Book One, "Southwards" in Book Two, and "Homewards," in Book Three, takes place in a well-worn circular groove and ends up in a nowhere disaster area. The various car-crash sequences along the way culminate in a massive pile-up involving the entire motorcade.

Aldiss's argument would appear to be that we are pres-

---

[12] All parenthetical references to *Barefoot in the Head* may be located in the Corgi Books paperback edition (London, 1971).

ently in the midst of a new reality or a new dimension of experience, but that we fail to see it because of the Stone Age sensibility and mental equipment that cause us to re-tread circular patterns of behavior and thus avoid a genuine confrontation with the new. The world catastrophe and the traffic-accident motif should be seen as symbolic of Toffler's "future shock." Man's reaction to a reality he can't keep up with is to internalize it and thereby destroy it. The connection between speed and traffic accidents and between speed, the drug, and mental breakdown, is marvelously appropriate. In *Report on Probability A*, reality is mysterious because of a lack of subjective information; in *Barefoot in the Head*, reality is essentially unknown because of a lack of objective information—the result of an inability to distinguish objective elements from subjective elements. The difficult and densely associational verbal style, sliced at regular intervals with concrete and other experimental forms of poetry, reflects the confused response to reality. Literal and metaphorical statements become indistinguishable: "This infrasound really breaks people up" (p. 59), says one Charteris disciple.

In a poem entitled "Living: Being: Having," described as "An epic in Haiku," situated among the batch of poems that concludes the book, the acid-heads' dilemma is stated in the simplest terms:

World and mind two or
  One? Funny how the simplest
    Question blows your mind! (p. 226).

This is the question raised throughout the narrative. Just how mixed are objective and subjective reality? This is the dilemma that finally unsettles Charteris about his role. In spite of all his talk about unity, there are occasions when it would be useful to establish certain elements as external:

All possibilities and alternatives exist but ultimately
Ultimately you want it both ways (p. 220).

Report on Probability A has as its epigraph this quotation from Goethe: "Do not, I beg you, look for anything beyond phenomena. They are themselves their own lesson." In that book, the lesson would appear to be that phenomena require subjective content if they are to make sense. In *Barefoot in the Head,* Angeline is particularly troubled by one phenomenon: "Either that running dog wore a tie or she was going acid-head like the others" (p. 85). Goethe's direction finally settles the matter for her: "It surely can't really matter, can it, whether there was a dog with a tie or not; the essential thing was that I saw it and stand by that. A phenomenon's only itself, eh?" (p. 91). But what exactly *is* a phenomenon if its subjective and objective aspects cannot be distinguished? The apparently objective information that makes some sense of this particular phenomenon is that one of the acid-heads had a black-and-red tie that "really sent him. He thought he had tied it round the neck of a black dog proceeding down Ashby Road" (p. 88). As it is, the incident remains in Angeline's mind to subvert the entire enterprise. It undermines her faith in Charteris the Messiah: "You aren't indestructible any more than I really saw a dog in a red tie that time" (p. 113). It becomes mixed up with her other fantasies: "No flowers or fruit ever on the old entangled damson trees except the dripping mildew where their leaves curdled in brown knots perhaps she had seen them among the branches the new animal the fey dog with red tie and been inoculated with the wildered beauty of despair against this future moment's recurrence" (p. 152). Finally this phenomenon becomes a disturbing element among Charteris's fantasies: "Before real miracles he had to dislocate the miraculous in himself. New dogs shagged along alleyways with ties of flame" (p. 167).

Like *Report on Probability A, Barefoot in the Head* is a tour de force, with all the limitations that such a bravura display of technical virtuosity entails. The attention that Aldiss lavishes on form and style is not matched by a corresponding interest in clarity of content. As I have suggested, it rather seems as if the stylistic experiment came first and a plot was then engineered to accommodate the style. However, since most science fiction illustrates the other extreme—the plot is of primary importance, the style is rarely more than serviceable and often less—a swing of the pendulum cannot but be salutary. Science fiction is often too glib in tossing off new versions of reality, alternate dimensions, parallel and microscopic worlds, in a hackneyed style that is utterly lacking in depth and reverberation, in any sense of dimensionality beyond that of a flat plane. The stylistic experiments of Joyce, Burroughs, and Robbe-Grillet do succeed in capturing hitherto unsuspected dimensions of experience. In adapting these experiments to his own dimensional speculation as to the nature of reality, Aldiss is attempting that appropriate combination of style and content that may truly liberate science fiction from the ghetto of its own clichés.

VI. SOMEBODY UP THERE

There is no more startling manner of transforming reality than to suppose the existence of a previously unsuspected outside manipulator controlling or interfering with human affairs. The prevalence of this apocalyptic theme in science fiction points to the element of paranoia, which is a likely characteristic of any literature oriented toward subversion. Tony Tanner's lengthy study *City of Words* attests to the prominence of the same paranoid theme in contemporary American fiction: "Narrative lines are full of hidden persuaders, hidden dimensions, plots, secret organizations, evil systems, all kinds of conspiracies against spontaneity of consciousness, even cosmic takeover. The possible nightmare of being totally controlled by unseen agencies and powers is never far away in contemporary American fiction."[1] Thomas Pynchon's novels provide a particularly intriguing example of this conspiracy consciousness. That this anxiety has a science-fictional coloration is implied by Tanner's reference to "hidden dimensions" and "cosmic takeover." It would appear that the outside-manipulator theme provides for one kind of convergence between "mainstream" literature and science fiction.

As already suggested in Chapter 1, it is the outside-manipulator gambit that accounts for the science-fictional dimension in H. P. Lovecraft's work. I am referring to the "Cthulhu Mythos," a mythological structure that Lovecraft developed in fourteen of his tales, particularly in "The Call of Cthulhu" (1928), *At the Mountains of Madness* (1936), and "The Shadow Out of Time" (1936), but which he incorporated into the majority of his other

[1] See *City of Words: American Fiction 1950–1970*, p. 16.

tales.[2] Subsequently, other writers of "weird" fiction, such as August Derleth and Robert Bloch, have written tales in accordance with the Mythos and added to its development. Most of Lovecraft's fiction—the Dunsanyan fantasy pieces are the major exception—may be conceived as a totality based on the concept that Elder Beings from the stars once inhabited the earth, until, following a succession of other invaders from space, they were expelled by another alien race. Now the Elders, equipped with awesome powers, located on various worlds throughout the universe, await an opportunity to repossess Earth. The notion that the earth was once inhabited or visited by extraterrestrials has recently been lucratively treated as fact by Erich von Däniken, whose two books *Chariots of the Gods?* (1968) and *Gods from Outer Space* (1970) amass a good deal of circumstantial evidence.

But for the "Cthulhu Mythos," which, as Lin Carter indicates, "is essentially a science-fictional concept,"[3] Lovecraft's importance to the history of science fiction would be minimal. Only one tale, "In the Walls of Eryx" (1935), written in collaboration with Kenneth Sterling, qualifies as straight if rather unsatisfactory science fiction. This account of a mysterious labyrinth on Venus is disappointing, in that it hints at but fails to explore various intriguing possibilities. The bulk of Lovecraft's work suffers from a failure to work at fully realizing the details of a bizarre experience. The repetition of gnomic references to "Cyclopean masonry" and "alien geometry," along with an adjectival insistence on the terrifying, hideous nature of whatever, draws attention to a failure of imagination. It is the Mythos itself, the novelty and possibility of the concept, that gives substance to much of Lovecraft's output. That the Mythos continues to enjoy a life independent

[2] There is some disagreement as to how central or how tangential certain of Lovecraft's tales are to the Mythos. In specifying the number fourteen, I am accepting Lin Carter's analysis in *Lovecraft: A Look Behind the Cthulhu Mythos,* a Ballantine Books paperback (New York, 1972).
[3] Ibid., p. xvi.

of its creator suggests that the value of the Mythos is distinct from the tales in which it is embodied.[4] Perhaps the alien-manipulator theme touches on a prevalent human phobia, the sense that unseen baneful forces are at work in the world, and Lovecraft's particular achievement was to create the most compelling version of that theme. Certainly Colin Wilson was sufficiently impressed to adapt Lovecraft's evocation of alien malignant powers harmful to man's autonomy, in *The Mind Parasites* (1967), thereby placing the alien-manipulator theme in the fully developed science-fictional context that Lovecraft only implies.

In recent years, a large number of science-fiction writers have variously exploited the possibility of unsuspected control. This, as I have indicated in Chapter 1, is the situation in Vonnegut's *The Sirens of Titan*, a novel that comes in for detailed analysis in my final chapter. Variations on the theme frequently account for a paranoid quality in the work of Philip K. Dick. For example, in Dick's *Time Out of Joint* (1959), the protagonist, Ragle Gumm, and his "brother-in-law," Victor Nielson, move toward the discovery that they exist in a manufactured past. The year is actually 1998, when a war is in progress between the One Happy Worlders and the Lunatics, as Earth's colonists on the moon are termed. Gumm, on the side of the One Happy Worlders, has the job, thanks to his special expertise, of applying the Law of Probabilities to the random bombing patterns of the Lunatics, thereby providing some rationale for evacuating a given area. However, Gumm comes to sympathize with the position of the enemy and edges toward a nervous collapse. In order to forestall this breakdown, the One Happy Worlders concoct a scheme

[4] H. P. Lovecraft's own life, like that of a number of apocalyptic writers, was a relatively short one. He died aged forty. Brockden Brown died aged thirty-nine; Poe, aged forty; Bellamy, aged forty-eight; London, aged forty; and Crane was lost at sea, aged thirty-three. It might seem that an apocalyptic reality laid claim upon the physical existence as well as the minds of these writers.

that involves placing Gumm and Nielson in an artificially
created environment that corresponds in every detail to
the Earth of 1959. Within this environment, Gumm enjoys
a certain fame as the most successful contestant in a daily
newspaper competition that invites readers to find the
"green man." Because of his phenomenal success, Gumm
enters the competition every day. What Gumm does not
know is that, in locating the "green man," he is actually
providing the One Happy Worlders with random areas
where they might prepare for an attack.

Their suspicions aroused, Gumm and Nielson gradually
undertake a search for the reality of their situation. Vehicles assume a particular importance, both as objects of
manipulation and "objective" dating evidence. Gumm is
prompted to a series of reflections that relate specifically
to his own situation when he observes a truck being loaded
via a ramp: "Must be fun, he thought. Tossing cartons on
that ramp and seeing them shoot down, across the dock
and into the open door. [Note the unnatural sentence
break here.] Where somebody no doubt takes them off
and stacks them up. Invisible process at the far end
. . . the receiver, unseen, laboring away" (p. 159).[5]
Nielson has a symbolic experience that suggests more
clearly that reality may be a fabrication. He is on a bus,
and "through his half-closed eyes, he saw the passengers
fade away . . .":

> The sides of the bus became transparent. He saw
> out into the street, the sidewalk and stores. Thin support
> struts, the skeleton of the bus. Metal girders, an empty
> hollow bus. No other seats. Only a strip, a length of
> planking, on which upright featureless shapes like
> scarecrows had been propped. They were not alive . . .
> ahead of him he saw the driver; the driver had not
> changed. The red neck. Strong, wide back. Driving a
> hollow bus (pp. 96–97).

[5] All parenthetical references to *Time Out of Joint* may be
located in the Science Fiction Book Club edition (London,
1961).

Later, while protesting his occasional interest in philosophy, Nielson says, "The other night coming home on the bus I got a look at how things really are" (p. 164). Dick is inviting his reader to entertain the possibility that, as in the case of Gumm and Nielson, the world around him may be artificially created by outside manipulators for unsuspected purposes.

There is also the intriguing possibility that man has been interfered with during some stage of his development by superior beings and that our present condition is a consequence of that interference. The third and best of Nigel Kneale's Quatermass serials for BBC Television, *Quatermass and the Pit* (December 1958–January 1959), dramatizes the theory that insectlike Martians left their dying planet for a prehistoric Earth and that they imprinted their evil mental characteristics on the apelike beings they found wandering around—hence the "missing link." As descendants of the Martians, our bellicosity is then explainable. I have already cited, in Chapter 1, an example of a more positive form of alien interference during man's infancy, in Arthur C. Clarke's *2001: A Space Odyssey*. Clarke's *Childhood's End* (1952) describes the ultimate result of this interference. The Overlords have watched over and guided human evolution to make sure that man's destiny is fulfilled and he successfully completes the progress from ape to a non-material, cosmic entity. As an interesting Blakean twist, Clarke's Overlords, a midwife species who cannot themselves participate in the ultimate translation, physically resemble man's conception of devils.

The various facets of the apocalyptic imagination that I have attempted to isolate come together in Clarke's work. It is to my present purpose to stress the philosophical aspect of Clarke's writing, but the visionary and satiric qualities are equally present. To a greater or lesser extent, this is true of the apocalyptic works that are variously deployed throughout this study. My artificial distinctions are intended to reflect only a particular emphasis. In Clarke's case, the emphasis is simply less obvious than in most other cases. Certainly *Childhood's End* can only be inadequately pigeonholed as an example of of my outside-manipulator category. Clarke would seem to be talking about the ultimate outside manipulator, or God. Obviously, the closer the conception of an outside manipulator moves toward God, the more a philosophical orientation is displaced by a visionary orientation, or, if the broadest definition of philosophy is applied, the more a materialist philosophical position is displaced by a metaphysical philosophical position. A similar situation arises in Melville's *The Confidence-Man,* the subject of analysis in the next chapter. Melville's outside manipulator is some kind of God, but there is little evidence of what might commonly be appreciated as a transcendent reality. It is a God made very much in man's image.

11. Melville's The Confidence-Man *and the Fiction of Science*

I

Ishmael experiences a climactic moment of awakening in *Moby-Dick*. While on midnight tiller duty, he is hypnotized by the hellish brilliancy of the *Pequod*'s try-works: ". . . then the rushing Pequod, freighted with savages, and laden with fire, and burning a corpse, and plunging into that blackness of darkness, seemed the material counterpart of her monomaniac commander's soul." Entranced, Ishmael releases his hold on the "jaw-bone tiller" (Vol. VIII, p. 180).[1] The ship proceeds to turn about and is in danger of capsizing when the accidental impact of the uncontrolled tiller arouses Ishmael in time to remedy the situation and allows him to learn this lesson:

> Look not too long in the face of the fire, O man! Never dream with thy hand on the helm! Turn not thy back to the compass; accept the first hint of the hitching tiller; believe not the artificial fire, when its redness makes all things look ghastly. To-morrow, in the natural sun, the skies will be bright; those who glared like devils in the forking flames, the morn will show in far other, at least gentler relief; the glorious, golden, glad sun, the only true lamp—all others but liars! (Vol. VIII, p. 181).

[1] Except in the case of *The Confidence-Man*, all parenthetical references to Melville's work may be located in *The Works of Herman Melville*, Standard Edition, sixteen vols. (London, 1922–24).

Ishmael is making that distinction between empirical and a priori insight, absolutism and relativism, which underlies all of Melville's writings. The subjective, a priori, or transcendental outlook tends toward absolutism—absolute evil or absolute good, hell or heaven. Preceding his nightmarish glimpse of hell, Ishmael, while squeezing sperm, enjoys a corresponding daydream vision of heaven. Nowhere does Melville claim that absolutist interpretations are wrong, only that such interpretations appear as in Ahab's case, to invite destructive and suicidal consequences. In many ways, Melville admires Ahab's stand. From the empiricist's point of view, "truth" is invariably cloudy and ambiguously relative. But, whether accurate or not, such a perception makes for a certain domestic security.

This philosophical position has its consequences for Melville's practice as a writer. It dictates that Melville keep his hand on the tiller and write as an empiricist, on a basis of pragmatism and experience. This is the case with all of Melville's early work. It might be objected that Melville's allegorical cast of mind—very much to the fore in *Mardi* and *Moby-Dick*—militates against any designation of Melville as an empiricist. But the inconsistency here is more apparent than real. Although from our point of view the notion that there exists a one-to-one relationship between material reality and spiritual reality, that the entire world is a "great allegory,"[2] is wildly fanciful and unscientific, for Melville and his contemporaries this "doctrine of correspondences" was accepted as a matter of fact borne out by experience. It follows that an allegory such as *Mardi* is empirical if the "thesis" it illustrates derives from experience that the author believes he has interpreted empirically, and that an allegory, such as that which Ahab foists upon Moby-Dick, is a priori if its thesis derives from experience that the author believes has been interpreted in an a priori manner. The

[2] Melville to Hawthorne, at Pittsfield (Nov. 1851), quoted by Eleanor Melville Metcalf in *Herman Melville: Cycle and Epicycle* (Cambridge, Mass., 1953), p. 128.

empirical underpinning for the position presented in *Mardi*, for example, is provided by *Typee, Omoo, Redburn*, and *White-Jacket*, which are tied to Melville's sea experiences in a basically "realistic" manner. Ahab's understanding that the White Whale is totally evil, on the other hand, is arrived at intuitively and not borne out by any empirical evaluation.

During the writing of *Moby-Dick* and subsequently through the writing of *The Confidence-Man*, Melville adopted an increasingly a priori approach to the business of literary composition. There are at least three reasons for this. First, with *Moby-Dick*, Melville had used up most of his experiential material. Secondly, he began leading a withdrawn existence after retreating, in 1850, to "Arrowhead" farm, near Pittsfield, Massachusetts. Thirdly, while at "Arrowhead," Melville developed a seminal relationship with a neighbor named Nathaniel Hawthorne and was very much influenced by that writer's work and his essentially a priori mode of composition. Melville may be admitting as much in the title story to his collection *The Piazza Tales*, which bears in certain respects a striking resemblance to Hawthorne's artistic manifesto in "The Custom-House Sketch." Just as Hawthorne, observing the play of moonlight and firelight, is able to conjure up his "neutral territory, somewhere between the real world and fairy-land,"[3] so Melville, sitting on his piazza, facing the mountain range that includes Mount Greylock, converts an elusive "spot of radiance" into evidence of "fairyland." The witching conditions of light prevalent "late in autumn —a mad poet's afternoon; when the turned maple woods in the broad basin below me, having lost their first vermilion tint, dully smoked, like smoldering towns, when flames expire upon their prey," serves to encourage the sense that the close-packed mountain ranges "play at hide-and-seek . . . before one's eyes" and to equate the ranges and the flickering flames in Hawthorne's room. We are left, then, with this image of the seated figure of Mel-

[3] *The Centenary Edition of the Works of Nathaniel Hawthorne*, Vol. I, p. 36.

ville as a Hawthornesque a priori artist, lost in abstraction, gazing toward Greylock. *Pierre,* it may be noted, is dedicated to Greylock. Melville's eventual "voyage to fairyland" (Vol. X, p. 5) and his discovery of the grim facts leads to a decision to "stick to the piazza" (Vol. X, p. 17) in the future.

As Melville moves technically farther and farther from his experiential base and the zero world, now viewed increasingly as an "empirical" fiction on a par with a priori fictions, his central statement undergoes a process of metamorphosis until, in *The Confidence-Man,* he appears to be articulating an apocalyptic position very close to Ahab's. The same "inscrutable malice" that Ahab discovers in striking through the "pasteboard masks" of "visible objects" (Vol. I, p. 204) appears to be behind the masquerade in *The Confidence-Man.* Such a philosophical view is not easy to live with, and there is documentary evidence that, after writing *The Confidence-Man,* Melville contemplated suicide. However, during the final stage of Melville's career he appears to have worked toward the re-establishment of his experientially based method of composition with a corresponding re-establishment, in the poetry and in *Billy Budd,* of his earlier, relativistic, "empirical" understanding of the nature of reality.[4] The quotation marks around empirical are now necessary, because Melville maintained the position, established in *The Confidence-Man,* that all human formulations, whether arrived at "empirically" or by an a priori process, are equally fictitious. But, like Vonnegut, Melville finds some fictions easier to live with than others. Melville's return to "empiricism," like his prior movement toward the a priori, may be partially attributed to three factors that abetted his return to the world of experience. First, in 1856, for health reasons, Melville undertook a journey to Palestine, which furnished him with the material to write the long, moderately affirmative narrative poem *Clarel* (1876). Sec-

---

[4] This interpretation is elaborated at length in my "Some Coordinates in Billy Budd," *Journal of American Studies,* III (December 1969), pp. 221–37.

ond, after 1860, an estrangement occurred between Melville and Hawthorne, thus freeing Melville from Hawthorne's potent a priori example. Third, the outbreak of Civil War in 1861 demanded commitment, and, more than anything else, forced Melville to regain contact with the external world.

It would seem that, in a general way, the relationship between method and meaning operates as a directing principle in Melville, as the "hitching tiller" of his craft. When Melville writes empirically, he comes up, almost axiomatically, with his balanced, empirical thesis of ambivalence; when he turns to an a priori approach, he arrives, again seemingly axiomatically, at an extreme or idealistic, a priori, absolutist, and apocalyptic thesis. This overview provides a necessary context for my discussion of *The Confidence-Man: His Masquerade,* a work that gives full expression to the apocalyptic vision of Ahab. *The Confidence-Man* presents that unsafe understanding of reality that Melville perceived when he allowed his hand to slip from the tiller.

II

I have already indicated my disapproval of attempts to interpret the initials "SF" as speculative fiction rather than science fiction, while allowing an affinity between speculative fiction and the apocalyptic imagination. The distinction here is well illustrated by works such as *Mardi, Moby-Dick,* and *The Confidence-Man,* all of which might appropriately be described as apocalyptic or speculative fiction. But to label all or any of these titles as science fiction would be singularly inappropriate. While Melville shares with science fiction an abiding interest in the unknown, his conception of that unknown, symbolized by Moby Dick, is beyond the bounds of scientific inquiry. Indeed in *The Confidence-Man* there is a strong sense that all science, or supposedly established knowledge, is bogus, as fraudulent as that futuristic-sounding panacea, the Omni-Balsamic Reinvigorator, hawked by one of the book's cosmic swindlers.

Melville's primary concern in this novel is with the assumptions that are made about the nature and existence of an outside manipulator, or God. An empirical approach to the understanding of human existence is judged to be inadequate, because whatever we experience exists within a reality context that ultimately is beyond scientific verification. Assertions about the benevolence, malevolence, indifference, or non-existence of a Supreme Controller are all equally a priori acts of faith. Because our understanding of material reality is radically dependent upon whichever of these theological-philosophical positions is held to be applicable, that understanding, too, is essentially a matter of faith or speculation and not of fact or truth. In his search for meaning, man creates a multitude of alternative fictions, none of which can be proved to be true. Melville would agree with Vonnegut that, given this situation, it is man's responsibility to distinguish among these fictions not the more likely from the less likely, but the more humane and practical from the more inhumane and impractical. This is a situation in which a critic can say everything and nothing with confidence, as is evident from the tangle of criticism devoted to *The Confidence-Man* in recent years.

In the spirit of confidence and uncertainty, then, I propose the argument that, in *The Confidence-Man,* Melville is singling out and attacking Christianity as a particularly inhumane and impractical fiction because of the immense gap it establishes between material appearances and the supposed spiritual reality. A Christian God consistent with this dichotomy would have to be a confidence man not just in the sense that He elicits an act of faith, but in the sense that He exploits an act of faith. To characterize God as a swindler is to imply that God either is Satan, works through Satan, or, at the very least, embodies both good and evil. The evidence typing the Confidence Man as Satan is substantial. Presumably the association of the snake metaphor with the Confidence

Man signifies both Satan's presence and the slippery nature of truth. After an encounter with the Confidence Man, a Missouri backwoodsman named Pitch has his worst suspicions aroused when "Analogically, he couples the slanting cut of the equivocator's coat-tails with the sinister cast in his eye; he weighs slyboot's sleek speech in the light imparted by the oblique import of the smooth slope of his worn boot-heels; the insinuator's undulating flunkyisms dovetail into those of the flunky beast that windeth his way on his belly" (p. 183).[5] In context, the word "dovetail" recalls the biblical injunction concerning the compatibility of serpents and doves.[6] If the reader applies the image of the Holy Ghost as a dove, this passage serves not only to characterize the Confidence Man as Satanic but also to incriminate God. The Black Rapids Coal Company, for which John Truman, one of the Confidence Men, is president and transfer agent, is highly suggestive of Hell, but the New Jerusalem, another pie in which Truman has a finger, is clearly Heaven. Perhaps someone identified as a "gentleman with gold sleeve-buttons" (p. 50) has something to tell us about the relationship between God and Satan. This gentleman, who, "like the Hebrew governor" (p. 51), Pontius Pilate, keeps his hands clean by acting through a negro surrogate, embodies certain Godlike qualities. As in the case of the lamblike man of Chapter 1, the gentleman wears a garb emblematic of purity and is a stranger. In fact all the material confounding God and Satan sheds a crucial light on the much-vexed question as to the nature of the lamblike man.

In the opening chapter of *The Confidence-Man,* Christianity is presented from a human point of view as an ineffectual, unconvincing, and unreliable fiction. At St. Louis, as April Fool's Day dawns, a mute boards a Mississippi steamer named for the Christian faithful, the

[5] All parenthetical references to *The Confidence-Man* may be located in H. Bruce Franklin's heavily and helpfully annotated edition (New York, 1967).
[6] Ibid., p. 188, n. 13.

Fidèle. Dressed in "cream-colors, . . . his hair flaxen,
his hat a white fur one, with a long fleecy nap" (p. 3),
this gentle, "lamb-like figure" (p. 9) is apparently an
incarnation of Christ, the first of a succession of supernatural figures encountered during the voyage downriver.
His arrival is described as an "advent," and his appearance
resembles that of Christ in the Book of Revelation: "The
hair of his head was white as snow-white wool (1:14)."
The question arises, is his figure intended as a virtuous
contrast to the various avatars of the seemingly Satanic
Confidence Man, or is he the first such avatar? Both
R. W. B. Lewis and Ray B. Browne treat the mute as the
genuine savior. In neglecting and mistreating this Christ
figure—"they made no scruple to jostle him aside" (p. 7)
—it is argued that the passengers aboard the *Fidèle*
indicate their preference for evil rather than good and
hence, in the various Satanic avatars, get the kind of
Confidence Man they deserve.[7]

But the case for interpreting the hermaphrodite Christ
as the first avatar of the Confidence Man, a wolf in
lamb's clothing, is convincing. Franklin has assembled
"eight pieces of circumstantial evidence" incriminating the
mute, to which might be added the various hints throughout the book (and enumerated above) that God is Satan.[8]
Also suspicious is the fact that the barber couples this
first stranger with the concluding avatar of the Confidence
Man, the philanthropical Cosmopolitan: "Very odd sort
of man the philanthropist. You are the second one, sir,
I have seen" (p. 318). The mute's chalked messages of
Christian charity, which "thinketh no evil," "endureth
all things," and "never faileth" (p. 6), constitute an
idealistic fiction that is either inoperative or disruptive.
The mute establishes the biblical injunctions regarding

[7] See R. W. B. Lewis' "Afterword" to the Signet edition of
The Confidence-Man (New York, 1964), p. 272; and Ray B.
Browne, *Melville's Drive to Humanism* (Lafayette, Ind.,
1971), pp. 305–13.
[8] *The Wake of the Gods: Melville's Mythology* (Stanford,
Calif., 1963), pp. 155–57.

faith, hope, and charity by which the Confidence Man operates. Absolutes in Melville somehow create or necessitate their opposites: in the pursuit of Yillah, or absolute good, Taji, the protagonist in *Mardi*, is himself pursued by the Satanic forces of Hautia; Billy Budd and John Claggart are metaphysically akin. Ahab's intransigent position has some basis in the lessons that Father Mapple derives in his sermon. Man does not choose the Satanic Confidence Man; he is, from Melville's point of view and Blake's, the implicit basis of the Christian fiction, if that fiction is to be consistent and convincing.

III

Because men live by fictions, they create what is understood as reality. The relationship between fiction, reality, lies, and evil—one way of arriving at the Satanic Confidence Man—is implied in the first chapter by the incidental figure of someone hawking written material about "the lives of Measan, the bandit of Ohio, Murrel" (p. 5), and other unsavory characters. Melville's conception of a universe in which God is Satan or in some way allied to Satan is, then, descriptive of the reality of the Christian world. This point about the informing relationship between fiction and reality is made in three seemingly incidental chapters. These chapters defend the book against the charge that it is unrealistic by arguing essentially that the book is unrealistic in the same sense that reality is unrealistic. Throughout the novel, attention is drawn to the inconsistent attitudes of various personages. The first such instance, a merchant's sudden loss of confidence following a hitherto unrevealed capability for "philosophic and humanitarian discourse" (p. 88) on the part of the fifth Confidence Man, occasions a discussion in Chapter 44 of the consistency question in fiction. Far from being unrealistic, it is claimed that because "in real life a consistent character is a *rara avis*" (p. 94), inconsistent characters in fiction are more realistic than consistent ones. Of course a surface inconsistency may be the manifestation of an underlying consistency. *The Confidence-Man* is an exercise in reasoning from known inconsistencies to the nature of an unknown consistency. From a thesis and an antithesis it is possible to derive a synthesis, from two parts of a syllogism a third may be deduced. Hence the triangular logic and triangular structure of the book.

The Confidence Men who succeed the lamblike man fall into three groups, depending upon whether their appeal is to the Christian doctrine of charity, of hope, or of faith, the means by which Satan gains a purchase on the world. The Negro cripple Black Guinea, John Ringman (the Man with the Weed), and the "man in a gray coat and white tie," who acts as the agent for "a Widow and Orphan Asylum recently founded among the Seminoles" (p. 42), all use the lever of charity to prize money away from their victims. The next three Confidence Men, John Truman, the Herb-Doctor, and the man from the Philosophical Intelligence Office, play on the possibility of hope—hope of financial gain, hope of a return to health, and the hope that an employee may prove an asset. In each case, the enticement is that of investment, financial speculation. The eye of John Truman is "beaming with hope" (p. 106). Faith or confidence, in a general sense, is peddled by the Cosmopolitan, the final avatar of the Confidence Man. This Cosmopolitan appears to embrace all the previous confidence men, just as faith is integral to acts of hope and charity. A tripartite design coalesces into unity.

Much the same kind of development occurs if we consider the gamut of character types presented in the novel. Argument concerning the true nature of Black Guinea enables Melville, near the beginning of the book, to present in a tableau form the three basic categories of characters aboard the *Fidèle*: the apparent Confidence Man, the apparent skeptic, and thirdly, the apparent gulls, who would seem to constitute the majority. In this initial situation, the apparent skeptic is the sour-tempered man with the wooden leg. The figure of the apparent skeptic subsequently reappears in the shape of the "invalid Titan in homespun" (p. 118), the misanthropic Pitch, and Colonel Moredock. Presumably all the remaining characters involved in the confrontation with Black Guinea, including the Episcopal clergyman and the Methodist minister, are to be categorized as gulls engaged in a masquerade of naïveté. It would seem, then, that three masquerades are concurrently in progress. But a perspicacious reading soon reveals the unreliability of these three categories and the ultimate difficulty of meaningfully distinguishing among any of the *Fidèle*'s passengers. Black Guinea's list of people who can vouch for him is highly ambiguous, because of the thick dialect in which he speaks and because of the incidental manner of identification. In the case of the eight figures specified, more often than not, the avatars of the Confidence Man that I have enumerated are only the most obvious among several possible identifications. Black Guinea's list concludes with the embracive reference to "ever so many good, kind, honest ge'mmen more aboard what knows me and will speak for me, God bress 'em; yes, and what knows me as well as dis poor old darkie knows hisself" (p. 20). In other words, everybody is suspect. Because the nature of reality is finally unprovable, all attitudes, all philosophical, political, and religious systems, skeptical or otherwise, are essentially acts of faith. All men are confidence men. After enumerating the passengers in opposing pairs, the narrator finally conflates them as "a piebald parliament, an Anacharsis Cloots congress of all kinds of that multiform species, man. . . . Here reigned the dashing and all-fusing spirit of the West, whose type is the Mississippi itself, which, uniting the streams of the most distant and opposite zones, pours them along, helter-skelter, in one cosmopolitan and confident tide" (p. 14). Here is evidence, then, that the hearty, wine-imbibing Cosmopolitan, ruled by a "fraternal and fusing feeling," who "federates, in heart as in costume, something of the various gallantries of men" (p. 186), embodies not only all the previous Confidence Men but the entire human race.

There are consequently many indications that the apparent skeptics and the apparent gulls are actually confidence men, whether of the supernatural or material variety. Cripples and a related group, men with canes —the man with the "ruby-headed cane" (p. 42) and the "auburn-haired gentleman . . . with his cane" (p. 125), —abound in this book. As a cripple, the man with the wooden leg would appear to have something in common with Black Guinea. The next cripple, Mr. Fry, the soldier of fortune, is certainly a confidence man on the human level, but in literally buttonholing the herb-doctor, "with his horny hand catching him by a horn button" (p. 131), he may be confessing to a more immediate relationship. "Much such a case as the negro's" (p. 138) is the herb-doctor's comment on the soldier's disability. An old miser's tarnished coins look like "old horn-buttons" (p. 104). Given the Confidence Man's snakelike associations, the narrator's use of the word "rattle" or "rattled" may be seen as subtly incriminating. The Cosmopolitan condemns a line in Shakespeare in which trust is "rattlingly" (p. 246) ridiculed. Pitch's dark name may be indicative only of his bleak, skeptical view of life and imply nothing Satanic, but he does take to "rattling down his rifle" (p. 173). The "rattling" (pp. 294, 302) manner of Orchis types him as a confidence man. The barber, whose message of "NO TRUST" would seem to put him in a position of diametrical opposition to the initial manifestation of the Confidence Man as a lamblike advocate of charity, is spoken of as "having rattled down his shutters." Perhaps his name, William Cream, at the same time as it recalls the "man in cream-colors," is some indication of how he treats his customers.

The possibility that the barber and the Confidence Man are working in collusion is further reinforced by a syntactic ambiguity in this sentence concerning the barber and the Cosmopolitan: "In after days, telling the night's adventure to his friends, the worthy barber always spoke of his queer customer as the man-charmer—as certain East Indians are called snake-charmers—and all his friends

united in thinking him QUITE AN ORIGINAL." (p. 328).
Most immediately, the "him" refers back to the "queer
customer," the Cosmopolitan, but syntactically, it may
also refer to the barber. The "mysterious impostor" equated
with the lamblike man is described as "quite an original
genius" (p. 4); so, too, is the herb-doctor (p. 127).
Certainly the Cosmopolitan, Frank Goodman, and his
"acquaintance," Charles Noble, are birds of a feather.
During their lengthy conversation in Chapter 30 the
alternating speakers are frequently not identified, causing
the reader to confuse the two characters and causing
Frank and Charlie to lose their separate identities. The
technique of beginning a chapter in the middle of a conversation, as in Chapter 19, serves a similar purpose,
leaving the reader to puzzle over the precise relationship
between the conversationalists.

It would appear that the theoretical chapter arguing
for the realism of inconsistent characterization provides
not only for the basic identity of the ten shape-shifting
Confidence Men and the inconsistent nature of God but
also for the possibility that all the characters in the book
are seemingly inconsistent aspects of the composite, cosmopolitan Confidence Man. One can infer, then, that
whenever the narrator draws attention to some form of
inconsistent behavior, the character concerned is revealing an underlying consistency with the nature of the
Confidence Man. In the chapter devoted to inconsistent
characterization, the narrator resorts to the following analogy: "That author who draws a character, even though
to common view incongruous in its part, as the flying-
squirrel, and, at different periods, as much at variance
with itself as the butterfly is with the caterpillar from
which it changes, may yet, in so doing, be not false
but faithful to facts" (p. 95). This caterpillar-butterfly
metaphor may be subsequently applied to the culminating metamorphosis of the Confidence Man into the re-
splendent Cosmopolitan. An avatar of the Confidence
Man asserts that it is a mistake to "visit upon the butter-

fly the sins of the caterpillar," to which Pitch replies:
"The butterfly is the caterpillar in a gaudy cloak; stripped
of which, there lies the impostor's long spindle of a body,
pretty much worm-shaped as before" (p. 172).

As a Satanic identifying trait, the accelerating incidence
of inconsistency to behaviour gains a particular focus
in the person of Mark Winsome, kin to the deputizing
gentleman with gold sleeve-buttons, "a man of more than
winsome aspect" (p. 50). Winsome appears to be a portrait of Ralph Waldo Emerson—Egbert, his practical disciple, cannot be so conclusively identified with Thoreau.[9]
The Confidence-Man involves a general attack on the easy
optimism of Transcendentalism. Emerson's statement in
"Self Reliance" (1841), "A foolish consistency is the hob-
goblin of little minds. . . . With consistency a great mind
has simply nothing to do"[10] finds its echo in Winsome's
assertion "I seldom care to be consistent" (p. 271),
after the Cosmopolitan has caught him in an inconsistency.
Egbert shares his master's penchant for inconsistency. On
being accused of "an inconsistency," Egbert retorts, "Inconsistency? Bah!" Whereupon the Cosmopolitan drops his
easy manner and, after condemning Egbert's philosophy,
"turned on his heel, leaving his companion at a loss to
determine where exactly the fictitious character had been
dropped, and the real one, if any, resumed" (p. 311).
The reader has a similar problem in determining the real
nature of any single character in The Confidence-Man

[9] For different views on this question of identification, see
Egbert S. Oliver, "Melville's Picture of Emerson and Thoreau
in The Confidence-Man," College English, VIII (November
1946), pp. 61–72; Elizabeth Foster, "Introduction to The
Confidence-Man," pp. xxiii–xxix, xxxi–xxxii; Sidney P. Moss,
"'Cock-A-Doodle-Doo!' and Some Legends in Melville Scholarship," American Literature, XL (May 1968), pp. 192–210;
Hershel Parker, "Melville's Satire of Emerson and Thoreau: An
Evaluation of the Evidence," American Transcendental Quarterly, VII, 2 (summer 1970), pp. 61–67.
[10] See The Complete Works of Ralph Waldo Emerson (Boston
and New York, 1968), Vol. III, p. 57.

and so distinguishing one character from another. Shakespeare's line "One man in his time plays many parts" (p. 311) is quoted in *The Confidence-Man* with a new relevance.

IV

Chapter 33, the second authorial digression concerned with literary theory, further advances the case for the subversive relationship between fiction and "reality." Although the position argued in this chapter, coming as it does before the interpolated "story of Charlemont," in Chapter 34, appears to apply particularly to the four self-contained stories that apparently digress from the main narrative line of *The Confidence-Man*, the stated occasion is the "unreality" of the Cosmopolitan, who is about to tell "the story of Charlemont" (p. 258). The narrator argues that a "severe *fidelity* to real life" (my italics, p. 259) is not required of a work of fiction that exists primarily as a form of escapist entertainment. However, a fantasy world may tap an underlying "reality" more real than the surface dullness of daily life: "As, in real life, the proprieties will not allow people to act out themselves with that unreserve permitted to the stage [hence the dramatic characteristics of *The Confidence-Man*, mixing the morality-play form with a Jonsonian comedy of humors and Expressionism]; so, in books of fiction, they look not only for more entertainment, but, at bottom, even for more reality, than real life itself can show" (pp. 259–60). Here Melville is approaching something very close to my definition of apocalyptic literature, with its emphasis on other worlds that exist in a credible relationship with the "real" world. The desire is to see nature "in effect transformed": "It is with fiction as with religion: it should present another world, and yet one to which we feel the tie" (p. 260). For further, related augmentation the reader is referred back to the chapter on inconsistency of characterization.

The "tie" with "reality" is provided most immediately by that fourth masquerade, which cuts across and further serves to combine the other three: the masquerade involving Melville's contemporaries, who appear in the book under a variety of guises. Edgar Allan Poe figures as "a haggard, inspired-looking man," who wanders in to peddle "a rhapsodical tract" (p. 273), most probably *Eureka*. The figure of the "gentleman-madman" (p. 261), for this is what Poe's portrait amounts to, recurs in the character of Charlemont. However, the shape of Charlemont's career, with its interim period of depression followed by a kind of recovery, conforms loosely to the pattern of Melville's life. It is germane to my present argument, concerning the area of the book illuminated by the theoretical statements in Chapter 33, that each of the various identifications, aside from the more extended cases of Thoreau and Emerson, either occurs in or "ties" in with one of the four interpolated stories. There is evidence to suggest that Goneril, the wife of the unfortunate man in his interpolated story, is a caricature of the famous actress Fanny Kemble. The Missouri backwoodsman Pitch may be a portrait of James Fenimore Cooper, but Cooper's presence is most strongly felt in the two chapters devoted to the interpolated story of Colonel Moredock, the Indian-hater, especially given the references to "Pathfinder" (p. 205) and "Leather-stocking" (p. 212) in the introductory chapter on "The Metaphysics of Indian-hating." The final injected story, concerning China Aster, appears to be, in part, an allegorical account of Melville's career and his relationship with Hawthorne, Orchis playing the Hawthorne role.[11] This particularly fanciful tale may, then,

---

[11] For identifications in *The Confidence-Man* thus far, aside from material cited in footnote 9, see Egbert S. Oliver, "Melville's Goneril and Fanny Kemble," *New England Quarterly*, XVIII (December 1945), pp. 489–500; Harrison Hayford, "Poe in *The Confidence-Man*," *Nineteenth-Century Fiction*, XIV (December 1959), pp. 207–18; connections between Pitch and James Fenimore Cooper have been drawn by Edwin Fussell in *Frontier: American Literature and the American West* (Princeton, N.J., 1965), pp. 313–19; Fussell also sees Orchis as a

be the one most directly allied to the reality of Melville's experience. Of course Melville, as author, presents himself as a Confidence Man. Consider that the story of China Aster is told by Egbert, who may represent Thoreau, while he and the Cosmopolitan are engaged in restaging the confrontation between Frank Goodman and Charlie Noble (Egbert playing Charlie's role) and as an immediate response to Frank's suggestion that "Charlie" put himself in his position: "Were the case reversed, not less freely would I loan you the money than you would ask me to loan it" (p. 290). This extreme equivocation of roles allows the realistic element, in this case the figures of Thoreau and Hawthorne, to contaminate the entire gamut of characterizations in the book and thus to provide the world "to which we feel the tie" (p. 260). Most immediately, perhaps, it relates Orchis as Confidence Man and the suppositious free-loaning Cosmopolitan as caricatures of Hawthorne.[12]

The four interpolated stories are similar in that they all claim or suggest a basis in fact but are told at second or third hand, never as personal experience. Charles Noble explains "The Metaphysics of Indian-hating" and the story of Moredock not in his own words but, thanks to an "impressible memory" (p. 201), in those of a judge named James Hall, from whom he heard the account and who in actuality was the author of *Sketches of History, Life, and Manners, in the West* (Philadelphia, 1835), from which Melville has taken Moredock's story, with some omissions and some alteration of emphasis, but often verbatim.[13] Egbert tells about the experience of China Aster in Winsome's words: "I wish I could do so in my own

_____

portrait of Hawthorne in the China Aster story, which he takes to be "a rather transparent allegorical parody of Melville's disastrous literary career and its relations to Hawthorne's" (p. 314n.).

[12] See John D. Seelye, "'Ungraspable Phantom': Reflections of Hawthorne in *Pierre* and *The Confidence-Man*," *Studies in the Novel*, I (winter 1969), pp. 436–43.

[13] For Melville's use of Hall, see Fussell, pp. 320–25.

words, but unhappily the original story-teller here has so tyrannized over me, that it is quite impossible for me to repeat his incidents without *sliding* into his style" (my italics, p. 290). The Cosmopolitan does tell the earlier story of Charlemont in his own words, although the experience is not his. Indeed he claims that the story is not true but "told with the purpose of every story-teller— to amuse," its strangeness "is what contrasts it with real life; it is the invention, in brief, the fiction as opposed to the fact" (p. 264). This comes after the chapter pointing to the basic reality of the most fantastic fiction, and after a story that is perhaps the most "realistic" of the four.

The uncertain distance between the teller, the tale, and any experienced basis seems to be the primary issue in the first interpolated story, which concerns the "unfortunate man" (p. 81). Told originally by John Ringman (the Man with the Weed), the third avatar of the Confidence-Man, this hard-luck story is, in context, a means of extorting money from Mr. Roberts, "the country merchant" (p. 25). At that time, the reader learns only of the history's effect on Mr. Roberts and not the account itself, although he has every reason to suspect it is a fabrication. Seven chapters later, Mr. Roberts has occasion to retell the sad tale, to another Confidence Man, Mr. Truman. "But," interjects the narrator, "as the good merchant could, perhaps, do better justice to the man than the story, we shall venture to tell it in other words than his, though not to any other effect" (p. 81). Given that the tale is clearly divorced from the original teller, this direction serves to further estrange the fiction from its possible basis in "reality."

The story is about a man reduced to misery and penury as the result of a disastrous marriage to an Indian shrew, of ambiguous witchlike appearance, named Goneril. Only when the reader has become aware of the metaphoric equation between the Indian and the Confidence Man established in Charles Noble's subsequent story, can he see that Goneril is in fact a Confidence Woman and that the unfortunate man's problems stem from his attempt to protect his child, "a little girl of seven" (p. 85), from her corrupting influence. Because the merchant cannot defend the story as his own experience, Mr. Truman is able to equivocate its meaning and proportion the blame between Goneril and her husband. With the appearance, five chapters after the tale is told, of someone identified as an "invalid Titan in homespun" (p. 118), we begin to suspect some particular purpose to the seven-chapter interval between tale and teller. The designation of the story's victim as the "unfortunate man" rather than as the "unfortunate man with a weed" is one clue that the experience described is not, and cannot be, that of the Confidence Man. Because the story is unanchored from its original teller, the reader is in a position to "tie" it to a character from whom the experience may have been appropriated: the skeptical "invalid Titan."

This character leads by the hand "a puny girl, walking in moccasins, not improbably his child, but evidently of alien maternity, perhaps Creole, or even Comanche" (p. 118). Surely this is the man who married Goneril? It is apparent from the Titan's attack on the herb-doctor that he knows all about the Indian/Confidence Man mentality and presumably hopes that, away from her mother, his daughter may not go the same way. A "hypochondriac" (p. 122) where Indians are concerned, the Titan's reaction is particularly violent when the herb-doctor cites the case of "a Louisiana widow" cured "of neuralgic sorrow for the loss of husband and child" (p. 122). There is some doubt, however, as to whether this identification of the unfortunate man points to the experiential reality of that man's story or whether the implied identification between the man with the weed and the Titan points to a more crucial reality. After all, "invalid" may be read as "in-valid," or untrue, and the black-bearded Titan is not without diabolic associations.[14] He emerges from a dark forest road that "presented the vista of some cavernous old gorge in a city, like haunted Cock Lane of London" (p. 117), in the company of a girl who looks like an In-

[14] See Franklin's edition, p. 118, n. 3.

dian. It seems reasonable to conclude that the unfortunate
man's story is tied particularly to a reality in *The Confidence-Man* that I have already attempted to explicate. It
is a significant aspect of Melville's over-all strategy for revealing the distinctions among the three masquerades of
gulls (like the unfortunate man), skeptics (like the invalid
Titan), and Confidence Men (like the Man with a Weed)
as fictitious.

The distance between the teller and any experience
upon which his tale may draw, functions in all the interpolated tales as a pointer to the unreliability of experience
as a guide to truth. Whatever lessons may be drawn
from experience have only relative validity. They may
change with subsequent experience and cannot be absolutely depended upon. To present an experience at second hand is to immediately equivocate the truthfulness of
the account, to make it appear utterly fabulous. Experience enters ambiguously into the discussion of inconsistent
characterization. Echoing the student's "Experience, sir,
. . . is the only teacher" (p. 70), the reader is informed:
"Experience is the only guide here; but as no one man
can be coextensive with *what is,* it may be unwise in
every case to rest upon it" (p. 95). "Philosophy, knowledge, experience" constitute an unreliable trinity—the
"trusty knights of the castle" are "recreant" (p. 182).
The Cosmopolitan fears that Pitch's misanthropic view of
humanity comes of reading Zimmerman's book *On Solitude,* which "will betray him who seeks to steer soul and
body by it, like a false religion" (p. 190). One might
align this direction with Ishmael's advice concerning the
hitching tiller and with the distinction between true and
artificial lights, which I take up presently. Pitch replies,
"Had you experience, you would know that your tippling
theory, take it in what sense you will, is poor as any
other" (p. 191). Just previously, however, Pitch, in spite
of "an immense hereditary experience" (p. 161) and "fifteen years' experience" (p. 162) of rascally servant boys,
has agreed to try one more boy.

The last three interpolated tales, which all occur in the

second half of the book, where the Cosmopolitan dominates, serve to isolate alternative responses to a world created by a Satanic God or, rather, created by the creation of a Satanic God. There is no one positive response, given the perversions to which any kind of absolutism, Christian or otherwise, is heir in the pragmatic, "empirical" world. Either God doesn't exist and man's position is absurd, or God is Satan and man's position is equally absurd. The various skeptics, most notably Pitch, in their hatred of the Confidence Man, are the most telling witnesses of this God's presence. But a bleak, self-consuming opposition to the Confidence Man is one possible response, perhaps more romantic than most others. The interpolated story concerning the career of John Moredock, who "hated Indians like snakes" (p. 198), illustrates the response of defiance. It is in this story that the Indian is equated with the Confidence Man as a symbol of pure evil. But that is not the only reason why this story, with its companion chapter on "the metaphysics of Indian-hating," is of particular relevance to what appears to me to be a correct interpretation of *The Confidence-Man*.

Moredock's career corroborates the interpretation I have already offered regarding the Christlike deaf-mute. Man does not find himself confronted with a choice between accepting God or accepting Satan; for all practical purposes, in accepting God, he in effect accepts Satan. Moredock's Ahab-like hatred of the Indian/Confidence Man is a "vocation" (p. 213), an expression of a deep Christian belief.[15] In a real sense, the skeptics, as represented by Moredock, are responsible for the existence of the Confidence Men. Even an Indian, on becoming "a genuine proselyte to Christianity" (p. 208), comes to abhor the Indian. Moredock is likened to "a Spaniard turned monk." Reference is made to his "cloistered scheme of . . . vengeance" (p. 212). Although for the most part he is a dedicated Indian-hater, "Soft enticements of domestic

[15] See Hershel Parker, "The Metaphysics of Indian-Hating," *Nineteenth-Century Fiction*, XVIII (September 1963), pp. 165–73.

life too often drew him from the ascetic trail; a monk who apostatizes to the world at times." Only when he is killing Indians is he a genuine Christian: "It is with him as with the Papist converts in Senegal; fasting and mortification prove hard to bear" (p. 213). The story concludes with the lesson, "To be a consistent Indian-hater involves the renunciation of ambition, with its objects—the pomps and glories of the world; and since religion, pronouncing such things vanities, accounts it merit to renounce them, therefore, so far as this goes, Indian-hating . . . may be regarded as not wholly without the efficacy of a devout sentiment" (pp. 219–20). Thus the trait of apparent inconsistency, "that nearly all Indian-haters have at bottom loving hearts" (p. 218).

The story of Charlemont as related by the Cosmopolitan provides a second response to the Satanic reality of God. As with St. Augustine, whose case is mentioned in Chapter 22, and Egbert, Charlemont, a gay-bachelor type, undergoes a major conversion around age thirty. Charlemont at twenty-nine chooses for reasons unspecified to withdraw from society. Years later, he suddenly reverts to his former, social self. Applying the theoretical pronouncements of the previous chapter and reading between the lines of this perplexing and seemingly fanciful tale, we catch a glimpse of that reality, more real "than life itself can show" (p. 260). Charlemont's metamorphosis is a consequence of his awareness of God's malignity. He subsequently decides to disregard this "knowledge" as far as possible and go on living as before. Instead of gloom and defiance, Charlemont chooses the alternative of self-imposed illusion.

China Aster's story presents a third alternative, that of the dupe. Named for a common field flower, China Aster, a poverty-stricken candlemaker, is persuaded by his friend Orchis, named for a tropical plant, to accept a friendly loan. The eventual result, when China Aster, unable to repay the loan, borrows more money at high interest rates, is destitution and death. As the "jeremiade" (p. 307) engraved on China Aster's gravestone has it, he was ruined because he allowed "himself to be persuaded . . . into the free indulgence of confidence, and an ardently bright view of life, to the exclusion of that counsel which comes by heeding the opposite view" (p. 306). A fourth alternative is presented by the unfortunate man's story, at least as I have interpreted it, and by the complete book; and that, of course, is to ape the Confidence Man. Given a universe in which the "morality" of Satan operates, no single one of the four possible attitudes that Melville isolates is necessarily better than any other. But however superficially unrealistic the four interpolated tales and *The Confidence-Man* as a whole may appear, they are allegorically and pragmatically tied to the realistic Christian fiction.

v

Chapter 44, "a dissertation" on the phrase *"Quite an Original"* (p. 331), is the third and final theoretical intrusion in the narrative. The phrase has just occurred as the concluding words of the previous chapter and serves, as I have indicated, to unite the barber, the Cosmopolitan, the lamblike man, and the impostor on the WANTED placard. In that first chapter, the "advent" of the lamblike man "At sunrise" (p. 3) consolidates his equation with the impostor "recently arrived from the East" (p. 4). We may further assume that the impostor, disguised as the lamblike man, shares his apparent point of origin in the East with the sun because the sun and the Confidence Man are mutually representative as means of illumination. Thus the lamblike man is compared with Manco Capac, an incarnation of the sun. It is appropriate to recall at this point the distinction made by Ishmael in *Moby-Dick* —apparently with Melville's approval—which I quote as an introduction to this chapter. Ishmael concludes that it is beneficial to steer one's course through life by the light of "the natural sun," "the only true lamp"; all other forms of illumination are equivalent to "the artificial fire" and, as "liars," should not be believed. In context, this advice points to the value of an empirical approach toward the problems of existence, as opposed to the suicidal potential of an a priori approach. But, in *The Confidence-Man,* which expresses Melville's growing sense that all man's conceptions of reality are fictional, a distinction between the empirical and the a priori can be only a very theoretical one. Consequently in the later book the sun is as much an "artificial fire" as the lamp with which it is confused and which the Cosmopolitan extinguishes on the final page. In *The Confidence-Man* the natural and the artificial light both fail.

It is the contained word "origin" that gives rise to the special meanings of the word "original" in the book. As Franklin notes, "original" derives from *oriri,* "to rise," the root word of Orient.[16] This, combined with the sense of the East as a point of origin, serves to relate the "original" with the sunrise and further equate the Confidence Man and the sun. The Confidence Man's singularity has less to do with his novelty—although as a Satanic portrait of God he is "an original" in that more immediate sense— than it has to do with his function as an originating or creating character. The world in which man lives is a world created by belief in God, a God who inevitably translates as the Confidence Man. It is this idea which is behind the narrator's exposition of the original character in Chapter 44. The original character occasions a philosophical apocalypse: "In short, a due conception of what is to hold for this sort of personage in fiction would make him almost as much of a prodigy there, as in real history is a new law-giver, a revolutionizing philosopher, or the founder of a new religion." The Confidence Man, whether as Manco Capac or the lamblike, Christlike man, is certainly the founder of a new religion.

Like a new form of illumination, the original character creates a new world, as did God with his direction "Let there be light" (Genesis 1:3). "Furthermore, . . . the original character . . . is like a revolving Drummond light,

16 See Franklin's edition, p. 4, n. 10.

raying away from itself all round it—everything is lit by it, everything starts up to it (mark how it is with Hamlet), so that, in certain minds, there follows upon the adequate conception of such a character, an effect, in its way, akin to that which in Genesis attends upon the beginning of things" (p. 330). In these circumstances it is inevitable that all the characters in the book should appear, as I have demonstrated, to partake of the reality of the Confidence Man, in whose image man is made.

If a genuinely original fiction may be seen to create reality, then the reality we accept must be the result of such a fiction. This third theoretical chapter brings to a culmination that inversion of fiction and reality which is progressively underway in the two previous theoretical chapters. Necessarily, the inspiration to produce original characters involves a chicken-and-egg problem: "There would seem but one point in common between this sort of phenomenon in fiction and all other sorts: it cannot be born in the author's imagination—it being as true in literature as in zoology, that all life is from the egg" (p. 331). This ambiguous formulation is somewhat clarified by a contrasting statement in *Pierre*, where the distinction between the inner and outer, the empirical and the a priori, which appears to hold in Melville's work through to *Moby-Dick*, is shakily maintained: "For though the naked soul of men doth assuredly contain one latent element of intellectual productiveness; yet never was there a child born solely from one parent; the visible world of experience being that procreative thing which impregnates the muses; self-reciprocally efficient hermaphrodites being but a fable" (Vol. IX, p. 361).

The Confidence Man's relationship with sources of ambiguous illumination is stressed periodically throughout the novel. For example, the meeting between the Cosmopolitan and Charles Noble takes place in a setting that allows for the metaphorical equation of a lamp with the sun: "It was in the semicircular porch of a cabin, opening a recess from the deck, lit by a zoned lamp swung overhead, and sending its light vertically down like the sun at noon." The light catches and defines the similar natures of both figures, highlighting Charlie's "violet vest" with its "sunset hues" (p. 196). But the relationship between the Confidence Man and the sun is presented most literally during the ensuing convivial discussion. The Cosmopolitan is speaking: "In the press, as in the sun, resides, my dear Charlie, a dedicated principle of beneficent force and light. For the Satanic press, by its coappearance with the apostolic, it is no more an aspersion to that, than to the true sun is the coappearance of the mock one. For all the baleful-looking parhelion, god Apollo dispenses the day" (p. 237). Parhelions, or mock suns, are created in bands on either side of the sun when the sun's rays are refracted by ice crystals. This seems to imply that the Confidence Man, as an incarnation of the sun, is a Satanic parhelion. The figure also implies that the existence of God necessitates the existence of Satan. Subsequently the sun and Satan are metaphorically related in the description of the rattlesnake, with its "lithe neck and burnished maze of tawny gold, as he sleekly curls aloft in the sun . . ." (p. 266).

In the chapter about original characters it is argued that certain fortunate writers are in a position to dispense new suns. Earlier, Frank has occasion to speak of Shakespeare in this regard. He is "a queer man," presumably because of one inconsistency: "There appears to be a certain—what shall I call it?—hidden sun, say, about him, at once enlightening and mystifying. Now, I should be afraid to say what I have sometimes thought that hidden sun might be." "Do you think it was the true light?" (p. 246), innocuously asks Charlie. Like the writer, China Aster, the candlemaker, whose surname is Latin for "star," or sun, is a provider of illumination, "one whose trade would seem a kind of subordinate branch of that parent craft and mystery of the hosts of heaven, to be the means, effectively or otherwise, of shedding some light through the darkness of a planet benighted" (p. 291).

The sun, as the original character, the Confidence Man, the writer, and God, is a ball of fire that produces light, but the fire itself signals destruction and apocalypse. For Black Guinea, "The sun is the baker" (p. 16). In the final chapter, "The Cosmopolitan increases in seriousness," that destructive apocalypse is apparently upon us. The Cosmopolitan enters the gentlemen's cabin, where he remembers seeing a Bible. He wishes to check a distrust-advising passage in the Book of Proverbs brought to his attention by the barber. The description of the cabin suggests a universe coming to an entropic end. Although the central "solar lamp" still burns and illuminates the cabin in radiated circles of "ever diminishing distinctness," the other lamps are "barren planets, which had either gone out from exhaustion, or been extinguished by such occupants of berths as the light annoyed, or who wanted to sleep, not see." The design on the shade of the central lamp, "the image of a horned altar, from which flames rose, alternate with the figure of a robed man, his head encircled by a halo" (p. 333), symbolizes, in Elizabeth Foster's words, "the light of the Old and New Testaments" of the Bible, a copy of which, as it happens, rests on the sacrificial, altarlike, marble table beneath the lamp.[17] Clearly the Bible is to be equated with the lamp as an artificial, or false, light. The gentle old man who is reading the Bible and whose countenance would be appropriate "to good Simeon" (p. 333) appears to be awaiting the second coming of Christ.

The old man's vigil is rewarded when he encounters the Cosmopolitan as a Christlike "bridegroom tripping to the bridal chamber" (p. 334) who checks the Bible to discover, to his relief, that the offending passage is located in a central section categorized as apocrypha. In the light of *The Confidence-Man* as a whole and the centrality of this section, the New and Old Testaments might more accurately be termed apocrypha, and the apocrypha inspired revelation. Mishearing the word but not misjudging the situation, a voice from one of the surrounding berths asks, "What's that about the Apocalypse?" (p. 337). The unpleasant boy who presently appears may

[17] See Foster's "Introduction," p. lxxiv.

be Anti-Christ. His appearance betokens Hell and fiery destruction: "All pointed and fluttering, the rags of the little fellow's red-flannel shirt, mixed with those of his yellow coat, flamed about him like the painted flames in the robes of a victim in *auto-da-fé*" (p. 339). The Norton edition of *The Confidence-Man* includes "a perhaps whimsical note Melville made on a page of trial titles for chapters": "Dedicated to victims of Auto da Fé."[18] I would suggest, however, that this unofficial dedication, pointing to acts of fiery destruction committed in the interests of Christianity, has a more than whimsical relation to the subject matter of *The Confidence-Man*.

The masquerade and April Fool's Day are now over, and the evil-looking boy is the first avatar of the Confidence Man to promote distrust as a basis for confidence. In place of salvation, this apparent Anti-Christ, before beating a fast retreat, sells the old man a door lock, a money belt—"a peddler of money-belts" (p. 5), it may be recalled, is referred to in the first chapter—and a Counterfeit-Detector, which is designed to test false bills but is too complicated to be of any practical use. Hopelessly confused, the old man whimpers for a life preserver, something equivalent to Queequeg's coffin in *Moby-Dick*. Instead the Cosmopolitan hands him a tin chamber pot. Observing, "We are being left in the dark here" (p. 349), the Cosmopolitan makes sure of that fact by extinguishing the solar lamp on his way out.

The concluding line of this perplexing narrative, following the many indications that the end of the universe is taking place, "Something further may follow of this Masquerade" (p. 350), should not be taken as any indication that Melville had it in mind to write a sequel, albeit Twain's "The Mysterious Stranger" may be so regarded.[19] I would suggest that it was Melville's intention to indicate

18 See the Norton Critical Edition of *The Confidence-Man*, pp. xi, xiv.
19 See Howard C. Horsford, "Evidence of Melville's Plans for a Sequel to *The Confidence-Man*," *American Literature*, XXIV (March 1952), pp. 85–89.

by the concluding line that, in spite of the apocalyptic
trimmings of the last chapter, a literal apocalypse has not
occurred. What has occurred during the course of the
book is a metaphysical revolution that is on such a total
and lasting scale that it can be adequately appreciated
only by means of apocalyptic imagery. The "apocalyptic"
conclusion is Melville's method of demonstrating the full
import of the mental revolution attendant upon his perception of the reality of a Satanic universe.

12. Vonnegut's Spiral Siren Call: From Dresden's Lunar Vistas to Tralfamadore

I

Kurt Vonnegut, Jr., more than any of his contemporaries, has explored the full scope of the apocalyptic imagination. Three of his novels to date draw on basic science-fictional themes. His first novel, *Player Piano* (1952), details, in somewhat conventional fashion, the futuristic, mechanized dystopia of Ilium, New York. *The Sirens of Titan* (1959), his second novel, the closest to "hardcore" science fiction and the subject of this chapter, involves the philosophical and metaphysical impact of the discovery that the entire span of human history has served the ends of alien manipulators on the planet Tralfamadore. Another discovery, in the indeterminate future of *Cat's Cradle* (1963), of a substance called *ice-nine* brings life on Earth to a frigid conclusion. The invention of a new form of religious consolation and the coming of a new messiah, a dominant theme in Vonnegut's novels and one associated with the utopian concerns of science fiction, receives its fullest treatment in *Cat's Cradle*. However, in *Mother Night* (1961), the earliest of Vonnegut's non-futurist novels, the religious or messianic element is notably absent, perhaps because this novel, more completely than any of the other five, is given over to Vonnegut's polarized interest in chaos and the horror of war, particularly World War II. In this case we follow the bleak, bewildering career and eventual suicide of Howard W. Campbell, an American double agent living in Germany during the war. Equally traumatic experiences during the Second World War have left their impression on Mr. Rosewater and Billy Pilgrim, the protagonists, respectively, of *God Bless You,*

Mr. Rosewater (1966) and *Slaughterhouse-Five* (1969). Largely through the example of Kilgore Trout, a prolific but financially unsuccessful science-fiction writer and Christ figure, Rosewater is able to assuage his guilt at having killed three German firemen in the war by dedicating his life to the creation of a philanthropic utopia. Billy Pilgrim, perhaps because of his appalling experiences during the fire-bombing of Dresden, perhaps through reading Trout, or maybe because it's true, believes himself to have come "unstuck in time" thanks to the example of his captives on the planet Tralfamadore; thus the account of his life is a temporal-switchback ride.

To observe that these three non-science-fictional novels hinge largely on the guilty interaction of the past and present, while the three science-fiction stories project the same forces, of mechanization, meaninglessness, and destruction, into the future, is one way of saying that Vonnegut's work presents a temporal totality—a clue that Vonnegut's vision has much in common with that of the inhabitants of the planet Tralfamadore, who see all of time laid out spatially. And spatially considered, there is no doubt that Vonnegut regards his work as a totality in the Faulknerian manner. What appear to be the same locations and the same people or families with a few seemingly deliberate discrepancies—Tralfamadore and Kilgore Trout are examples of this—slip in and out of his fictions. *Slaughterhouse-Five*, in particular, reads rather like a compendium of motifs from the earlier novels and is the only one in which the past, present, and future function in concert. The disappointing *Breakfast of Champions* (1973), composed apparently of what would not fit into *Slaughterhouse-Five*, only serves to emphasize this sense of finality. It would follow from this that the novels are mutually illuminating in a direct fashion and that *The Sirens of Titan* provides an outside perimeter or a cosmic backdrop against which the action in all of Vonnegut's works is played. *The Sirens of Titan*, then, has an importance that has not been recognized—except by Vonnegut himself, who has designated it his favorite novel.[1] The conclusion seems inescapable that *The Sirens of Titan* has been neglected because it is Vonnegut's most overtly science-fictional work. "It is a growing awareness of the seriousness of Vonnegut's inquiries which has made people realize that he is not only the science-fiction writer he first appeared to be," maintains Tony Tanner, thereby revealing that myopic critical assumption which has obscured the recognition that *The Sirens of Titan* is certainly Vonnegut's finest novel and perhaps the best work of science fiction in recent years.[2] This analysis of the role of science fiction generally and of *The Sirens of Titan* in particular in Vonnegut's fictional universe is intended as a corrective refocusing.

In the first of the three non-futurist novels, the science-fictional element is absent except for my assumption of *The Sirens of Titan* backdrop, but in the other two the science-fictional interest comes increasingly into the foreground. In a drunken address, Mr. Eliot Rosewater tells a group of science-fiction writers whose conversation he has crashed, "I love you sons of bitches":

> You're all I read anymore. You're the only ones who'll talk about the *really* terrific changes going on, the only ones crazy enough to know that life is a space voyage and not a short one, either, but one that'll last for billions of years. You're the only ones with guts enough to really care about the future, who *really* notice what machines do to us, what wars do to us, what tremendous misunderstandings, mistakes, accidents and catastrophes do to us. You're the only ones crazy enough to agonize over time and distances without limit, over mysteries that will never die, over the fact that we are right

---

[1] "Every mother's favorite child is the one that's delivered by natural childbirth. *Sirens of Titan* was that kind of book," according to Vonnegut as quoted by Richard Todd in "The Masks of Kurt Vonnegut, Jr.," *The New York Times Magazine* (January 24, 1971), p. 22.

[2] *City of Words*, p. 181.

now determining whether the space voyage for the next billion years or so is going to be Heaven or Hell (p. 18).[3]

If this is the inventory of Vonnegut's fictional themes that it seems to be, the logical deduction would be to include him, by his own admission, among Rosewater's audience of science-fiction writers. But to arrive at such a cut-and-dried conclusion is to ignore the fact that, while Rosewater's themes are science-fictional, such themes may be treated in works that are not: *Mother Night* and Twain's *The Mysterious Stranger*, for example. Grand-scale themes of this nature form the subject matter of what I have been calling apocalyptic literature, of which science fiction forms a readily identifiable subdivision. Although it is the science-fictional aspect of Vonnegut's work I shall examine, I should emphasize that I regard him as essentially an apocalyptic writer who utilizes a major science-fictional component.

II

It is in *Slaughterhouse-Five* that the relationship of this component to Vonnegut's larger, apocalyptic design becomes apparent. In this novel, Vonnegut attempts to confront the psychic wound that tenses his artistic bow. During World War II, while serving as a battalion scout, he was captured by the Germans and put to work in a Dresden factory that made malt syrup for pregnant women. Within "a cool meat locker under a slaughterhouse" on February 13, 1945, he survived the Allies' fire-bombing of the city—an atrocity, strategically unwarranted, that resulted in "one apocalyptic flame" and the death of 135,000 people, a record massacre considerably exceeding the number of lives lost when an atomic bomb

[3] All parenthetical references may be located in the 1966 Dell paperback edition of *God Bless You, Mr. Rosewater*.

was dropped on Hiroshima.[4] No analogy on Earth could adequately express the effect the devastated city had on Vonnegut: "Dresden was like the moon now, nothing but minerals" (p. 153).[5] To Billy Pilgrim, too, "It was like the moon": anyone who was to survive would "have to climb over curve after curve on the face of the moon" (p. 154). This, Vonnegut has done. Although we are now all familiar with that ashen, pitted, and sterile landscape from our television screens, the extent to which the silence of the moon, the solar system, maybe the entire galaxy, proclaims the absence of life is an imaginative conception that cannot be electronically transmitted. In an article about American youth Vonnegut concludes: "Their problem is this: the next holocaust will leave this planet uninhabitable, and the Moon is no Switzerland. Neither is Venus. Neither is Mars. In all the rest of the solar system, there is nothing to breathe."[6] These crushing imaginative implications are solely the province of science fiction.

Paradoxically, much as that ugly Dresden slaughter-house became a form of protection at the same time that a science-fictional analogy provided Vonnegut with a way of conceiving his shattering experience, it also furnished him with a mental strategy to cope with the tremendous guilt he experienced as an American of German extraction who survived the holocaust unleashed by his compatriots. Science fiction is often attacked because it characteristically lacks human interest and emotional involvement. But this seeming weakness can be regarded as a strength. The point is that, like St. John's Apocalypse, the cosmic scope of science fiction and the magnitude of the events or phenomena it treats causes the individual human being to shrink from view. In the science-fictional perspective, earthly problems become utterly inconsequen-

---

[4] See the "Introduction" to the 1967 Avon paperback edition of *Mother Night*, p. vi.

[5] Parenthetical references to *Slaughterhouse-Five* may be located in the 1969 Delta paperback edition.

[6] See "Why They Read Hesse," *Horizon*, XII (spring 1970), p. 31.

tial. As it is explained to Malachi Constant in *The Sirens of Titan,* space travel will give him "an opportunity to see a new and interesting planet, and an opportunity to think about your native planet from a fresh and beautifully detached viewpoint" (p. 93).[7] That such thinking was indeed an important aspect of Vonnegut's survival and perhaps an explanation for the strong science-fiction emphasis during the early part of his career following the Dresden experience may be inferred from two successive sections in *God Bless You, Mr. Rosewater.* In the first of these sections, Eliot, while riding a bus, is reading Kilgore Trout's *Pan-Galactic Three-Day Pass*—one of his seventy-five unsuccessful science-fiction novels. In the second section, "palms sweating" (p. 175), he reads a "description of the fire-storms in Dresden." The juxtapositioning here is important and central to *Slaughterhouse-Five.* Trout's "Earthling" protagonist, who is a member of an expedition, "supported by about two hundred galaxies," that has reached the "rim of the Universe," is offered a three-day pass "because of a death back home." After inquiring which of his relatives it might be, the "Earthling" is told, "It isn't *who* has died. It's *what* has died," and "What's died, my boy, is the Milky Way" (pp. 173–74). Presumably, Billy Pilgrim's fear in *Slaughterhouse-Five* that Earth might endanger the universe is doubly groundless: when a Tralfamadorian test pilot, experimenting with a new flying-saucer fuel, accidentally blows the universe up, Earth not only "has nothing to do with it" (p. 101), but is not even there. Extrapolating from the Trout tale that "Rosewater County was gone," Eliot discovers that he "did not miss it" (pp. 173–74). This cool perspective comes in handy as a response to the description of the Dresden fire storms. When the bus reaches the outskirts of Indianapolis, he hallucinates a fire storm, but it becomes transformed into a majestic and aesthetically beautiful column of fire: ". . . helixes of dull red embers turned in stately harmony about an inner

[7] All parenthetical references to *The Sirens of Titan* may be located in the 1959 Dell paperback edition.

core of white. The white seemed holy" (p. 176). Here
a science-fictional outlook functions as a form of consolation that is almost religious. Following this vision, "everything went black for Eliot, as black as what lay beyond
the ultimate rim of the universe." He awakes "to find
himself sitting on the flat rim of a dry fountain," much
like the dry fountain in *The Sirens of Titan*, listening to
a bird going "Poo-tee-weet?" (p. 177), rather like the
bird that goes "Poo-tee-weet?" in *Slaughterhouse-Five*
near a "green and coffin-shaped" wagon (p. 186). For
Vonnegut, science fiction not only provides a visual image
for death, but it evokes a setting in which regeneration
may take place.

Aside from life and death, there are no fixed criteria
for Vonnegut. Reality is of an ultimately unknowable
complexity. Lies, or *foma*, to use the term introduced in
Cat's Cradle, are all we can appreciate. The only useful
distinction to be made is that between fictions that encourage the forces of death and those which abet the
forces of life. As applied to literature, works of realism,
science fiction, and fantasy are all equally true or untrue.
However, works of realism depend upon a certain faith-
fulness to the kinds of rigid mental systems and patterns
that inhibit life. The life/death process suggests that
the most helpful designs will be loosely structured, fluid,
if only so one system may easily metamorphose into
another. Science fiction, as a convincing form of fantasy,
allows for this open structuring—hence its presence in
Vonnegut's work. As applied to the universe at large in
Cat's Cradle a distinction is drawn between a *granfalloon*,
or form of "fictional" organization such as the Communist
party, Daughters of the American Revolution, and nations,
which are rigidifying, meaningless conglomerations, and a
karass, which, being "as free-form as an amoeba" (p. 14),
is a more effective "fictional" pattern because the relationships are subtle and often completely mysterious, making
it impossible to establish cause and effect.[8] Of course

[8] All parenthetical references to *Cat's Cradle* may be located
in the 1969 Delta paperback edition.

both a *granfalloon* and a *karass* are *foma,* but the notion of a *karass* configuration, being much less identifiable and in no way subject to collective assent, cannot be challenged as *foma* in the often catastrophic fashion in which a *granfalloon* may be challenged. As a consequence, *karass* forms, such as personalized religions as opposed to organized religions, provide a much more reliable form of consolation for dealing with the business of life and death. Science fiction, in short, serves Vonnegut as a plausible *karass* form.

Vonnegut's use of science fiction as a form of substitute religion would explain why he has Trout take a skeptical view of Christ in two of his novels. In one of them, a time traveler rather like the protagonist in Michael Moorcock's *Behold the Man* seeks to verify the humanity as opposed to the divinity of Christ. Another Trout story, *The Gospel from Outer Space,* also summarized in *Slaughterhouse-Five,* derives from the conclusion of "a visitor from outer space, shaped very much like a Tralfamadorian" (p. 94), that what the Gospels imply is *"Before you kill somebody, make absolutely sure he isn't well connected"* (p. 84)—a *carte blanche* to lynch people who are not well connected. The replacement, outer-space gospel corrects this undemocratic teaching by making Christ a real nobody who is only adopted by God after he has been crucified, allowing God to draw this moral: *"From this moment on, He will punish horribly anybody who torments a bum who has no connections!"* (p. 95). This Trout tale provides an appropriate lead-in for my analysis of *The Sirens of Titan,* which reveals Vonnegut's "gospel from outer space" and seeks to identify the *karass* association that structures his fictional universe.

III

Among the more readily identifiable members of the *karass* encompassing the planets Earth and Tralfamadore in *The Sirens of Titan* are three members of Earth's rich

set, Winston Niles Rumfoord, his wife Beatrice, and
Malachi Constant, Beatrice's second husband; plus Salo,
a Tralfamadorian robot. Presumably millions of other
beings, from both Earth and Tralfamadore, are also involved. The nature of a *karass* is such that one simply
can't be sure as to who is in it and who isn't, who is
central and who is peripheral. In the Bokononist terminology of *Cat's Cradle*, we are informed that the *wampeter*,
or pivot of a *karass*, may be anything at all, animate or
inanimate, and "At any given time a *karass* actually has
two *wampeters*—one waxing in importance, one waning"
(p. 51). For most of the novel, Winston Niles Rumfoord
appears to occupy the controlling position, although it
turns out that he is the waning *wampeter*. Sometime in
the presumably near future, during a period known as
the "Nightmare Ages . . . between the Second World
War and the Third Great Depression" (p. 8), Rumfoord,
with his dog Kazak, accidentally(?) runs "his private
space ship right into the heart of an uncharted chrono-
synclastic infundibulum two days out of Mars." This
dimensional warp causes Rumfoord and Kazak to exist
"as wave phenomena—apparently pulsing in a distorted
spiral with its origin in the Sun and its terminal in
Betelgeuse" (p. 13). When the orbits of Earth and Mars
intersect this spiral, in the case of Earth every fifty-nine
days, in the case of Mars every one hundred and eleven
days, Rumfoord and Kazak materialize as their old selves.
For the same reason, they also materialize on Titan, one of
the moons of Saturn, where Rumfoord comes across the
marooned Tralfamadorian robot messenger Salo, whose
superior knowledge he exploits.

With the help of Salo's "Universal Will to Become"
(p. 270), an instantaneous power source, and his crippled
flying saucer, which is good only for junkets around the
solar system but functions as the prototype for simpler
models, Rumfoord kidnaps hundreds of people from Earth
to serve in the army he amasses on Mars. Malachi Constant and Beatrice are among these people. Known as
Unk and Bee after their Earthly identities have been

erased for purposes of martial conditioning, they mate to produce Chrono—as earlier prophesied to them, to their mutual horror, by Rumfoord during one of his materializations on Earth. In his infundibulated state Rumfoord knows all about the past, present, and future. All these arrangements are a part of Rumfoord's plan to establish a new religion, "The Church of God the Utterly Indifferent" (p. 180), based on the belief that everything happens accidentally. To prepare the ground, Rumfoord has his hopelessly ill-equipped Martian army—surely the puniest "threat from space" in all science fiction—attack Earth in order to suffer a catastrophic defeat. Earth's mass conversion to Rumfoord's new religion is made easy because of the postwar guilt. Rumfoord has arranged that, during the war, Unk/Malachi and another kidnapee, Boaz, be trapped on Mercury so that Unk can be subsequently brought back to Earth as the Space Wanderer at a climactic moment and function as a self-sacrificing scapegoat figure representing all that was bad about the old, hierarchical world. To finally consolidate the hold of his new religion, Rumfoord has Malachi, Beatrice, and Chrono, in an act of self-sacrifice, climb into a flying saucer to begin a lifelong period of exile on Titan.

Given the extreme complexity of this book's plot, I suspect that very few readers are likely to notice the "real" relationship between Rumfoord's religion and Salo's situation on Titan. We learn eventually that Rumfoord's design, in isolation, is a *granfalloon*, but, in the context of a much larger pattern, may be considered part of a *karass* formation. At the dawn of Earth's history, Salo, who might be described as a clockwork tangerine, was charged by his fellow mechanical beings on the planet Tralfamadore, in a distant galaxy, with the job of carrying a secret message from one end of the universe to the other. En route, mechanical difficulties and "the complete disintegration of a small part of his ship's power plant" (p. 270) force Salo to land on Titan. Salo's message to Tralfamadore explaining his plight takes "one hundred

and fifty thousand Earthling years" to arrive, and there-
after the Tralfamadorians have used Earth as a communications system. It transpires that most of Earth's large
architectural constructions are actually Tralfamadorian
messages. For example, looking through his telescope,
Salo reads Stonehenge as saying, *"Replacement part being
rushed with all possible speed."* When Malachi, Beatrice,
and Chrono finally arrive on Titan, we discover that the
fragment of junk steel Chrono picked up on Mars to
wear around his neck as a good-luck piece will serve as
the spare part for Salo's space ship. Apparently, all that
is important about Earth's history has been manipulated
for Tralfamadorian ends. Salo, who has become friendly
with Rumfoord, has not told him about this, *"because he
was sure that Rumfoord would be offended—that Rumfoord would turn against Salo and all Tralfamadorians"*
(my italics, p. 273). This devilishly subtle detail points
to the "true" relationship between Rumfoord's religion
and Salo's situation. The point is that Rumfoord, being
chrono-synclastically infundibulated and therefore aware
of the past, present, and future, of everything, in fact,
must know about the Tralfamadorian context. And in a
showdown before an attack of sun spots blows Rumfoord's
infundibulum out of the solar system, he indicates to
Salo that he was aware all along of the Tralfamadorian
hand in Earth's affairs and sees himself "as one of the
principal victims of that influence" (p. 284). "Tralfamadore," says Rumfoord bitterly, "reached into the Solar
system, picked me up and used me like a handy-dandy
potato peeler!" (p. 285). His incident with the chrono-
synclastic infundibulum was no accident.

Presumably, then, Rumfoord concocted his religion of
accidental causality as a form of compensation or consolation protecting mankind from the sad knowledge that
there has, indeed, been a purposeful design directing
human affairs, but one that does little to advantage
man's sense of dignity. In a book that generally calls
cause-and-effect relationships into doubt, this is one of
which we can be fairly sure. The question now is why

Vonnegut has failed to state this relationship directly, preferring instead to leave it up to his readers' powers of inference. The answer may be located in the brief prologue that provides a confusing frame for the novel. Appropriately enough, *The Sirens of Titan* is told by an "omniscient" but unidentified narrator sometime in the far future, long after the events he describes have occurred. This narrator is living in an age of religious renaissance. Instead of launching futile explorations into outer space to learn "who was actually in charge of all creation and what all creation was all about" (p. 7), man now looks inward, toward his own soul. It would seem that some refined variant of Rumfoord's religion has taken hold. Rumfoord's design has been at least as successful as he might have hoped. In view of the narrator's claim that the outward investigation resulted in "a nightmare of meaninglessness without end," it is surely curious and slightly contradictory that he should introduce as "a true story" (p. 5) an account that shows Tralfamadore to be the controlling factor in Earth's history. This somewhat schizoid logic is the clear consequence of the narrator's unwillingness to accept, and here he is presumably acting for his contemporaries, that the inner spiritual salvation man has arrived at is, in all likelihood, directly attributable to Rumfoord's discoveries concerning Tralfamadore. Consequently we may infer that the narrator's spiritual beliefs have resulted in a blind spot that causes him, probably subconsciously, to edit out that bit in which Rumfoord's motivations for launching his new world religion are stated directly. The parallel, of course, is that statement I italicized earlier, which indicates that Salo has edited out his knowledge of Rumfoord's prescience in the interest of their mutual friendship and trust. Since all that we know is a lie, and what truth there may be cannot be distinguished from lies, and since most of the lies to which we give assent are so unpleasant, uncomfortable, and destructive, lies that make for happiness or contentment, such as Salo's or the narrator's, are to be encouraged. Vonnegut is a propagandist for the virtues of schizophrenia.

So the narrator is wise to take the myth of Tralfama-dorian control as "a true story" (p. 8) of error, as is Beatrice Rumfoord, who concludes her life on Titan by writing a book entitled *The True Purpose of Life in the Solar System.* "It was a refutation of Rumfoord's notion that the purpose of human life in the Solar System was to get a grounded messenger from Tralfamadore on his way again" (p. 308). She does, however, see fit to conclude, "The worst thing that could possibly happen to anybody . . . would be to not be used for anything by anybody" (p. 310). And certainly there is every possi-bility that the Tralfamadorians are not the ultimate con-trollers but rather that they function as a metaphoric analogy for such beings. If the name Tralfamadore is a nautically consistent contraction of Trafalgar and commo-dore, it might be noted that a commodore is only the head of a yacht club or boat club; it is not the top naval rank. Maybe the "accident" that forced Salo to hole up on Titan, like Rumfoord's "accident," is actually part of someone's design. The central point Vonnegut is making in *The Sirens of Titan* is that a genuine cosmic controller must have dominion over time, whether he be God or a writer such as the unidentified omniscient narrator or Beatrice Rumfoord.

IV

The clearest metaphor for Vonnegut's conception of wheels within wheels, plots within plots, is the structure of the universe itself, in which every movement is caught up in a larger movement. Moons revolve around planets, planets around suns; suns partake of the wheeling move-ment of the galaxies around other galaxies and of the entire heavens around maybe some "still point" of the universe, while the universe itself is perhaps involved in some utterly inconceivable, larger orbit dancing to the

pull of other universes. The outermost movement we can
ascertain is that of the galaxies, hence Tralfamadore, as
a representative of that moving force, is located in a galaxy far from our Milky Way, the Small Magellanic
Cloud. In *Cat's Cradle* it is stated that the members of
a *karass* revolve around their *wampeter* "in the majestic
chaos of a spiral nebula" (p. 51). Because every orbital
movement is part of larger movement, the course that
every heavenly body describes is actually a spiral. Vonnegut does make this point about Titan:

> Saturn describes a circle around the Sun.
> It does it once every twenty-nine and a half Earthling
> years.
> Titan describes a circle around Saturn.
> Titan describes, as a consequence, a spiral around the
> Sun (p. 266).

Saturn with its "nine moons" (p. 265) may be regarded
as a microcosm of our solar system with its nine planets.
We are given to infer the further analogies and the particular point that the movement of Titan is representative of the movement of the universe. The information
that the chrono-synclastically infundibulated Rumfoord
and Kazak exist as a spiral wave and that this spiral and
that of Titan coincide exactly, causing this "one man
and his dog" to materialize permanently on Titan, is a
way of saying that Rumfoord and Kazak are in total
sympathy with the movement of the universe.

It would seem that all the spirals in the book, and
there are enough of them to be considered aspects of a
"controlling" image—a fortuitous phrase—are symbolic of
universal movement and—since the DNA spiral is surely
relevant—of life itself. For example, Chrono's good-luck
piece, for want of which Salo's ship will not move efficiently, is part of "a spiral of steel strapping, a type of
strapping that was used for binding shut the packaged
flame-throwers" (p. 143) for use by Rumfoord's "Martian"
army. Its connection with a destructive power is borne

out by the scratch it leaves on the factory manager's leg. In retaliation, the manager stamps on it and cuts it up into four-inch pieces, one of which Chrono pockets. If we can assume that the movement patterns of heavenly bodies convey ultimate meanings and purposes, this incident involving a spiral is not particularly optimistic, and, aside from Chrono's perversity, would seem to have little to do with good luck. Unfortunately the thing about spirals is that they can mean almost anything, good or bad. What should be made of Rumfoord's yodeling voice (p. 129) and the "Toodleoo" (p. 135) of the flying saucers considered as aural spirals? As a symbol of universal meaning, spirals are indeterminate. But there are four basic possibilities. Whether as a plane, a cone, or a tunnel—ultimately forming a line, a circle, or some other shape—spiral movement implies an extremely indirect progress. The extremely indirect and complicated methods that Rumfoord resorts to in order to launch his religion and that the Tralfamadorians use to rescue Salo are thus analogous to a spiraling form of progression. Indeed the entire technical strategy of the book relies upon every conceivable kind of indirection, and it should be remembered that *karass* formations favor connections that are indirect and subtle. Malachi, in journeying from the Earth to Mercury, back to Earth, and then on to Titan, describes a spiral that is particularly erratic. Given such indirection, it is no wonder the lure of linear progress is so appealing. Thus Malachi Constant, whose name means Faithful Messenger, "pined for just one thing—a single message that was sufficiently dignified and important to merit his carrying it humbly between two points" (p. 17). Apparently the Tralfamadorians also favor the linear direction in having Salo carry his "sealed message from One Rim of the Universe to the Other" (p. 269). That the message turns out to be simply a dot, which in English means a conclusion or nothing and in Tralfamadore means *"Greetings"* (p. 301), and is thus in accord with the suggestion that the name Salo is a contraction for "say hello," only seems to underscore the point that linear movement is a desirable end in itself.[9]

The three other possibilities depend upon whether the spiral movement is understood as creative or destructive or both. Metaphorically considered, whirlpools and whirlwinds might be regarded as integrative, and therefore creative, spirals moving toward unity. Thus Unk/Constant, looking down the bore of his rifle, sees heaven: "He could have stared happily at that immaculate spiral of the rifling for hours, dreaming of the happy land whose round gate he saw at the other end of the bore. The pink under his oily thumbnail at the far end of the barrel made that far end seem a rosy paradise indeed" (p. 109). Beatrice, who increasingly does become Dante's symbolic Beatrice, is related to this integrative spiral when she first greets Constant "from the top of the spiral staircase" (p. 39): "She wore a long white dressing gown whose soft folds formed a counter-clockwise spiral in harmony with the white staircase. The train of the gown cascaded down the top riser, making Beatrice continuous with the architecture of the mansion." Constant, at the foot of the staircase, "so low in the composition, so lost in architectural details as to be almost invisible" (p. 40), is also caught up momentarily in Beatrice's harmonious design. But, at the end of the interview, Constant "sensed that the spiral staircase now swept down rather than up. Constant became the bottommost point in a whirlpool of fate" (p. 42). It would seem we are to infer that assimilation may be viewed as destructive or that the destructive potential is primary.

Beatrice's cascading gown and Constant's whirlpool point to a connection between integrative, life-enhancing, or unifying spirals, and water, particularly the fountain that occupies a prominent place on the Rumfoord estate. Constant arrives at it via a spiral path—"The turns in the path were many, and the visibility was short" (p. 16)— that forks at the fountain: "The fountain itself was marvel-

[9] The suggestion about Salo's name is made in *City of Words*, p. 185.

ously creative. It was a cone described by many stone
bowls of decreasing diameter. The bowls were collars on
a cylindrical shaft forty feet high" (p. 16). The arrangement of the bowls, while not exactly spiral-like, does
suggest the system-within-system design of the universe,
and it is perhaps worth remembering the equation mentioned earlier, which is made in *God Bless You, Mr. Rosewater*, between the rim of the universe and the rim of
a fountain. (When, on Mercury, Unk experiences brief
recollections of his previous identity, the image of a "bone
dry" fountain is paired with a spiral image: "Unk imagined
again the three beautiful girls who had beckoned him
to come down the oily bore of his Mauser rifle" [p. 188]
—the girls being the three sirens in the hologram picture
Rumfoord handed Constant to convince him of the pleas-
ures of Titan.) Rather than going round the fountain,
which is dry, Constant climbs "to the top to see whence he
had come and whither he was bound" (p. 17). Constant is
indicating his desire for integrating the past and the future,
for a sense of wholeness. That the fountain is working
when, much later, Constant returns to Earth to become
the sacrificial Space Wanderer, suggests that this desire
for coherence has been, in some way, fulfilled. Indeed his
return is a very wet business. It is raining on arrival. The
firemen who, as ministers of a jejune revelation, announce
the Space Wanderer's coming with the fire-engine siren—
the only genuine siren in the book, incidentally—direct one
of their hoses skyward to create "A shivering, unsure
fountain" (p. 225). Firemen and fire engines are always a
strongly positive element in Vonnegut's fiction, particularly
in *God Bless You, Mr. Rosewater*, presumably a reaction
to the Dresden holocaust. The narrator speaks of the
watery welcome as "an enchanting accident. No one had
planned it. But it was perfect that everyone should forget
himself in a festival of universal wetness" (p. 225). And
water is very much in evidence on Titan, with its "three
seas," "a cluster of ninety-three ponds and lakes, in-
cipiently a fourth sea," and "three great rivers" (p. 265),
which unlike the seas and ponds, are moodily turbulent,

suggestive of the forces of creation. As a waterlogged Constant anticipates his second climb, this time up the ladder to the ship that will take him to Titan, he pointlessly "rubbed his left thumb and index finger together in a careful rotary motion" (p. 256).

The sense of a spiral as both creative and destructive, or perhaps of spirals concurrently creative and destructive, brings to mind Yeats's interpenetrating gyres. A spiral may be viewed as destructive when, in Yeats's line, "the center cannot hold," when centrifugal forces overcome centripetal forces, or, in terms of the dynamics of Poe's universe, when the reverse occurs. Certainly all the spirals in *The Sirens of Titan* have this propensity, although one, in particular, seems more darkly destructive than any of the others. The twenty concessionary booths that have been set up outside the wall of the Rumfoord estate to cash in on the materializations "were under one continuous shed roof" (p. 231). Five minutes before a materialization, the owners are required to close the shutters:

> The effect of the closing inside the booths was to turn the line of concessions into a twilit tunnel.
>
> The isolation of the concessionaires in the tunnel had an extra dimension of spookiness, since the tunnel contained only survivors from Mars. Rumfoord had insisted on that . . . (p. 236).

Admittedly, this spiral image is camouflaged somewhat, although a comparison with the infundibulum funnel and the rifle bore makes an identification of the spiral motif here at least plausible. It is hardly coincidental that this description, which implies the spiral's melancholy disintegrative potential, should involve the Martians, since Mars is the major source of destructive *granfalloon* formations in the novel. Rumfoord himself appears to be the victim of such forces at the novel's conclusion. First, an explosion on the sun causes Kazak's infundibulum to be separated from Rumfoord's. It is pointed out, "a universe schemed in mercy would have kept man and dog

together" (p. 295). Before long, Rumfoord, too, takes
his leave of the solar system: "The fizzing twig of electricity on Rumfoord's finger grew, forming a spiral around
Rumfoord. Rumfoord considered the spiral with sad con-
tempt. 'I think perhaps this is it,' he said of the spiral"
(pp. 297–98). Since Rumfoord has been speaking of the
replacement part for Salo's ship and Salo's secret message,
the "it" in Rumfoord's quietistic statement might be taken
as referring to either or both these things, but for the
specification that the spiral is the referent. The effect, of
course, is to conflate the message, the spare part, and the
spiral, as a way of emphasizing the all-embracing importance of the spiral motif in this book.

Indeed, the very possibilities and ambivalent meanings
that may be attributed to the spiral—the principle of indirection, integrated and disintegrated structuring, whether
functioning alternatively or simultaneously—determine the
entire thematic and imagistic development of *The Sirens
of Titan*, to suggest new philosophical worlds coming together and old philosophical worlds falling apart. And
once again, the analogy is with the American experience:
"The state of mind on Earth with regard to space exploration was much like the state of mind in Europe
with regard to exploration of the Atlantic before Christopher Columbus set out" (p. 30). But the feared cataclysm
diminishes to a gentle rain such as that which "fell on a
New World country churchyard" (p. 216) in Barnstable,
Cape Cod, to greet the returning Space Wanderer.

v

The book is a Byzantine labyrinth of crosshatched in-
terconnections, some subtle and devious, some obvious or
crass, some integrative and some disintegrative, which is
to say that some are apparently meaningful, others are
apparently not. It all depends upon whether a particular
image complex is judged to be part of a centrifugal or a
centripetal spiral. While I believe the imagistic material I

have been piecing together so far to be part of Vonnegut's conscious intention, I am much less confident about many of the interrelationships, where meaning literally spirals, that I am about to touch on. To some degree, this "openness" seems to be a consequence of Vonnegut's creative technique. In elaborating a plot, I would venture to suggest, Vonnegut relies a good deal on a process of free association, allowing a certain amount of anecdotal material to be suggested by a preceding phrase, image, or word, even. Obviously, within a thematic context of control versus accident, the existence of whimsical elaboration is hardly out of place. In terms of both thematic and imagistic structure, the novel keeps begging the question "Is this a matter of accident or design?" and in this fashion the whole subject matter, as to who is manipulating whom and who or what is in control, becomes part of Vonnegut's technical strategy. Aside from the spiral business, which is a central if utterly ambivalent and contradictory motif, the reader's search for a "controlling" design, or image, or analogy, or philosophical position is seemingly systematically encouraged and then called into doubt. With an art product, as with a scientific experiment, the validation of meaning depends upon a controlled environment. Vonnegut offers a reading experience in which the degree of control is either questionable or apparently variable, making the search for meaning often truncated or tentative at best.

There is an additional feature of Vonnegut's style that abets this condition. I am referring to the somewhat self-conscious and flashy use of imagery that Goldsmith has usefully noted in his study and takes, I believe wrongly, as a negative element. Using descriptions of people as an example, Goldsmith complains that Vonnegut's images, while striking, "tend to call attention to themselves and to exist outside the basic characterization rather than add to it."[10] He quotes, in an illustration, the description of Billy Pilgrim in *Slaughterhouse-Five*, italicizing the similes comparing his chest and shoulders with "a box of kitchen

[10] See *Kurt Vonnegut: Fantasist of Fire and Ice* (Bowling Green, Ohio, 1972), p. 40.

matches" and his over-all appearance with "a filthy fla-
mingo" (pp. 28–29). It seems to me entirely appropriate
that such similes should be only loosely attached to a
particular subject in order to facilitate their attachment
elsewhere, thus forming alternate configurations. The
surface of a Vonnegut novel thereby becomes a kaleidoscopic mosaic or a jigsaw puzzle allowing multiple possibilities for the placement of each piece. As a precondi-
tion for this flexibility Vonnegut attempts to jiggle out of
position the various pieces that might form fixed patterns
in his readers' heads. Goldsmith's conclusion that the
images are never "expanded into conceits nor are they used
in some thematic pattern" and that "Vonnegut seems unaware of the *leitmotiv*, or else, does not choose to use it,"
aside from the impression of absurdity, depends upon a
rather narrow and conventional conception of the function
of imagery that, if my analysis of the spiral motif is acceptable, is inaccurate even within its own terms.[11] A
similar point might be made about Vonnegut's over-all
style of writing, which is engagingly simple, almost child-
like, in its lack of qualifying, subordinating, or causal
phraseology. In technical terms, Vonnegut's style is *para-
tactic*, characterized by a succession of direct statements
that do not imply hierarchical distinctions. The effect is to
minimize immediate connections while maximizing the
possibility of more distant connections—the more distant
connections being the operative ones in *The Sirens of
Titan*.

Two tricky control panels specified in the novel might
be applied to Vonnegut's artistic strategy in support of
my argument here. The space vehicles manned by Rumfoord's Martian troops were essentially controlled by
"fully automatic pilot navigators" set by technicians on the
ground:

> The only controls available to those on board were
> two push-buttons on the center post of the cabin—one
> labeled *on* and one labeled *off*. The *on* button simply

11 Ibid., p. 41.

started a flight from Mars. The *off* button was connected to nothing. It was installed at the insistence of Martian mental-health experts, who said that human beings were always happier with machinery they thought they could turn off (p. 167).

This is analogous to the system of effective command within the army itself. The true controllers are not the ranking officers but plain soldiers like black Boaz, who are equipped with control boxes that issue commands or inflict pain through the radio antennas implanted in the heads of the other soldiers. Naturally enough, Boaz is disconcerted when he discovers that the buttons of his control box, like the Martian ships' *off* buttons, don't connect after Unk tears the insides out. The control panel of Salo's ship presents a different problem, being "far more complex than those of the Martian ships":

Salo's dash panel offered Constant two hundred and seventy-three knobs, switches, and buttons, each with a Tralfamadorian inscription or calibration. The controls were anything but a hunch-player's delight in a Universe comprised of one-trillionth part matter to one decillion parts black velvet futility (p. 303).

My point is that, in interpreting the thematic and imagistic patterns of *The Sirens of Titan*, the critic either draws some of the more obvious conclusions, in which case, likely as not, he is pushing buttons that have been disconnected, or else he finds himself enmeshed in a system of such complexity that, as with Salo's control panel, no conclusions are possible. Throughout the following attempt at this exercise, relating briefly some of the more conspicuously unanchored elements, the serendipity element I have been discussing should be borne in mind.

The rough summary I have already given of the book's plot is necessary background here, because only on a second reading, when the reader is in command of the main line of the narrative, are many of the subtleties I now wish to emphasize apparent. One can see for example why, given the scale of control, the Town of Newport is placed in an unusually wide reference system, which includes "Rhode Island, U.S.A., Earth, Solar System, Milky Way" (p. 9). The opening scene is replete with images of control. The crowd waiting outside the walls of the Rumfoord estate for a materialization they will not see is a supremely manipulatable entity. For example, the police exercise crowd control by spreading the rumor that the materialization has already occurred outside the walls two blocks away, thus causing a mass movement toward the specified area. "At the tail end of the crowd was a woman who weighed three hundred pounds." She had a little girl, named Wanda June, "by the hand and was jerking her this way and that, like a ball on the end of a rubber band" (p. 9). The image of control here and her position "At the tail end of the crowd," combined with the information that a man *and his dog* are to appear, surely encourages the idea of the tail wagging the dog. And recalling the book's title, the woman's weight surely qualifies her as a female Titan. The underlying sense of an unknown source of control is symbolized by the high blank wall itself, which effectively shields from view the mysteries within. The ball, here introduced as a simile, may be related to the many other spherical objects in the novel: "the hard, ball-like knot known as a *monkey's fist*" (p. 27), which describes the familial structure of Rumfoord's class, the suggestion that Rumfoord is a "screwball" (p. 28), Constant's distress because his father never threw him a ball, the game of German batball, which Rumfoord introduces on Mars, and Salo's feet, which may be inflated "to the size of German batballs" (p. 277). Further examples include the "cannonball" (p. 40), which might be substituted for Beatrice's face, and Constant's head "as heavy as a cannonball" (p. 312); mankind's advance agents flung into space "like stones" (p. 7); Boaz imagining his "stone deathbed" (p. 214) in the caves of Mercury; Constant's final if illusory meeting with the friend he has strangled, *Stony* Stevenson; the important "blue stone" (p. 123) on Mars under which Unk has hidden his letter; and the other "turquoise boulder" behind which Unk watches his son; Boaz's eyes like "diamonds" (p. 110) to which may be related the diamond-shaped Harmoniums of Mercury. Which, if any, of these circular objects is the prime mover?

The fat woman's imaginary ball is on the end of an imaginary rubber band. This rubber band, like the various strings (of a cat's cradle?), reins (the horse reins Beatrice holds in the picture of her as a young girl), leads (the one constraining Kazak), chains (the dog's skeleton within the Rumfoord estate wears a spiked collar chained to the wall, and the bowls of the fountain are described as "collars" [p. 16]), and wires and ropes used throughout the novel, is a means of manipulation. The suggestion of a puppet on a string gives way to a sense of the deathly reality of such a predicament and finally to the notion of suspension as a form of preservation, a means of escape from the unfortunate consequences of time. The materialization the crowd has come to watch at the opening of the novel is likened to "a modern, civilized hanging" (p. 8). At the end of the novel, Constant insists on being taken to Indianapolis, the scene of a true hanging, as it is "the first place in the United States of America where a white man was hanged for the murder of an Indian" (pp. 314–15). At the conclusion of the war with Mars, Martians are strung up on lampposts. Afterward adherents of Rumfoord's religion symbolically hang Malachi puppet dolls. The chapter entitled "Cheers in the Wirehouse" might lead the attentive reader to expect that this is where the wires and pulleys, the various control mechanisms, are situated. It turns out that the phrase derives from the inability of the President of the United States to recognizably pronounce the words "chairs in the warehouse" during an anecdote about a manufacturer who has overestimated the demand for his chairs. On the other hand the spooky floating furniture in Constant's office—suspended not by wires but by magnetism—is expected to "sell like hotcakes" (p. 70). On Titan, however, this floating furniture turns out to be impractical.

The "scaffold" that Rumfoord has constructed for the ceremony involving the Space Wanderer's return and that may be appropriately connected with the hanging motif, given that it is designed to facilitate Constant's sacrificial act, depends, like the floating furniture, on an unseen "system" of control:

> The system was not suspended magnetically, though it looked like a miracle of levitation. The seeming miracle was achieved by means of a cunning use of paint. The underpinnings were painted a flat black, while the superstructures were painted flashing gold (p. 244).

This "gilded system" enables Rumfoord to put a distance between himself, the puppet master, and Bea, Chrono, and the Space Wanderer, "a distance made tortuous by rococo and variously symbolic hazards" (p. 248). From this description it is apparent that the entire system is intended as an analogy for Vonnegut's artistic methodology in this novel, all the more so in view of Rumfoord's plan to stage a *"fast reverse"* (p. 247) because an audience loves the dramatic contrast. The novel is full of such "fast rareness," as the reader progressively becomes aware of all kinds of unexpected relationships: the discovery that the man Unk strangles on Mars was his best friend, and Unk's and the reader's discovery that Unk himself has written the informational letter hidden under the blue stone. Only the most unlikely relationship systems work. For example, Constant's father, in using the Bible as a profitable investment system, may be the only person to discover the book's true value. Rumfoord emphasizes the importance of the right connections—in a familial sense, to be sure—when, anticipating Chrono's importance, he tells Constant, "You can reproduce and I cannot" (p. 23); an emphasis he shares with his class, who depended "on marriages based cynically on the sorts of children likely to be produced" (p. 27). The novel sets up all kinds of connections and controls that may or may not apply. As part of the definition of a chrono-synclastic infundibulum, the child who doesn't know what a funnel is is directed to "*get Mommy to show you one*" (p. 15). Are we to intuit some genuine relationship between an infundibula and Mommy's vagina?

One thing the infundibulum/funnel does seem genuinely related to is the well down which Alice falls in *Alice in Wonderland*. Entrance to the Rumfoord estate is through a low, "Alice-in-Wonderland door" (p. 18). Just as Lewis Carroll's Cheshire cat "vanished quite slowly, beginning with the end of the tail, and ending with the grin, which remained some time after the rest of it had gone," so, in almost the same words, Rumfoord "vanished slowly, beginning with the ends of his fingers, and ending with his grin. The grin remained some time after the rest of him had gone" (p. 39).[12] This parallel with a familiar fantasy is obviously appropriate in the context of a novel that asks the reader to understand reality as simply an unusually plausible form of fantasy, and should be seen in relation to other details that serve to equivocate the status of reality. We are told for example that Constant takes drugs: "hallucinations, usually drug induced, were almost all that could surprise and entertain Constant any more" (p. 19). He hallucinates a running fountain in place of the dry one, and until he discovers otherwise, he looks "upon his Newport adventure as one more drug-induced hallucination—as one more peyotl party—vivid, novel, entertaining, and of no consequence whatsoever" (p. 46). Presumably the Moon Mist Cigarettes, manufactured by a company recently bought by Malachi Constant, contain marijuana and are therefore appropriately advertised in conjunction with Rumfoord's picture of the devastatingly desirable but illusory sirens of Titan. The goofballs required as part of the Schliemann Breathing

[12] I am grateful to one of my students, Karen Wood, for pointing out the exactness of this parallel. See the Penguin Books edition of Lewis Carroll, *The Annotated Alice*, ed. by Martin Gardner (London, 1960), p. 90.

Technique on Mars, in combination with blocked ears and
nose and closed mouth, breaking "every link with air and
mist" (p. 152)—to quote from Bea's poem on the subject—
would appear to point to the deathlike quality of Moon
Mist-induced fantasies. However, when it is Constant's
time to die, Salo arranges a heavenly apocalyptic vision:
"A golden space ship encrusted with diamonds came skim-
ming down the sunbeam, landed in the untouched snow
of the street." Out steps Stony Stevenson to vouchsafe the
particular fantasy of luck that has enabled Constant to
make sense of his life: "Somebody up there likes you"
(p. 319). What better form of consolation than the idea
of a divine manipulator working in one's own interests?

VI

All these errant imagistic and thematic details convey
the sense of an interrelated totality, but mythological
structures, more so than any other type of fantasy, abet
the sense of a coherent universe. They have therefore a
unique plausibility. The galactic setting of this tale allows
Vonnegut to specify heavenly bodies with an eye to their
relationship to that mythological unity and control system
the ancients saw written in the night sky. According to
classical mythology, the first forms of creation were giants,
or Titans, of which Cronus, or in Latin, Saturn, was the
most important. (Cronus, or Chronos, means time and is
particularly relevant as a pointer to the extratemporal
dimension of mythology itself.)

Hence Vonnegut's selection of Saturn, Titan its satellite,
and the name Chrono is not accidental. Nor is it accidental
that Rumfoord's spiral pulses between the Sun and Betelgeuse. Betelgeuse means "shoulder of the giant" (specifically of Orion) and can therefore be related to the
anthropomorphic conception of the universe as a gigantic
form. The foyer floor of the Rumfoord mansion "was a
mosaic, showing the signs of the zodiac encircling a golden
sun" (p. 20). In standing on the sun, Rumfoord merely

reveals his place in the system of things. The negative mythological idea of Mars as the god of war is consistently elaborated in Vonnegut's narrative. Vonnegut's Mars presents the ultimate image of control oriented toward patterns of deathly rigidity: conditioned soldiers marching to the programmed sound of snare drums in their skulls. The Martian Commandos, with "their dog tags," were "experts at killing sentries with loops of piano wire" (p. 123)—this pathetically linked with the shabby tendency of some soldiers "to skip loops in lacing up their puttees" (p. 122) and one drunk guard who *can't even tie his shoelaces so they will stay tied*" (p. 126). We learn, long after the Martian episode is over, that Phoebe, the main town on Mars, was named for a moon of Saturn. Always we have this sense of pieces locking into place.

Opposed to the destructive mechanistic patterns of Mars are the creative fluid patterns of Mercury. Mercury, mythologically speaking, is the messenger of the gods, the very kind of messenger Constant would like to be. And the message Constant ultimately delivers, "that a purpose of human life, no matter who is controlling it, is to love whoever is around to be loved" (p. 313), is the one he receives on Mercury. But, while on Mercury, Boaz is more attuned than Unk to the song of Mercury, and although he is not in the midst of Hollywood nightclubs, as he originally hoped, he does find the fulfillment he associated with such nightclubs. Mercury sings because of the tension between the bright, white-hot side of the planet that constantly faces the sun, and the other side, which is a dark, icy forest. In other words, contraries harmonize on Mercury. Since the planet is without an atmosphere, the song is experienced tactically rather than aurally, by the planet's only form of life, flat, kite-shaped creatures called Harmoniums, who cling to the walls of Mercury's caves with their four suction cups. They exist in order to eat the siren song of Mercury and like to arrange themselves in pleasing patterns "of jonquil-yellow and vivid aquamarine diamonds. The yellow comes from the bare cave walls. The aquamarine is the light of the

walls filtered through the bodies of the creatures"
(p. 187). It would appear that the "blue and gold"
(p. 180) flag of Rumfoord's new religion is attuned to the
colors of light on Mercury. On Titan, Constant replaces his
worn-out yellow Space Wanderer's suit with "an old blue
wool bathrobe" (p. 306), presumably a further act of
fidelity to Mercury's message. The Harmoniums come in
particular to enjoy the good vibrations emanating directly
from Boaz's pulse beat (they become "stuck on" his arm
in a dual sense) and indirectly from the taped music con-
certs he arranges. When Unk discovers that they can
leave the caves by turning their ship upside down, Boaz
prefers to be "stuck on" Mercury, especially after reading
one of the messages the Harmoniums spell out "every
fourteen Earthling days" (p. 197): "BOAZ, DON'T GO
. . . WE LOVE YOU, BOAZ" (p. 209). What Boaz does
not know is that these messages have been slapped on by
Rumfoord, who materializes on Mercury at fourteen-day
intervals. The vision Unk has of the jailers, "the masters
of creation" (p. 208), who live on the crystalline surface
of Mercury is at least half correct. Unk leaves Boaz turning the pages of a *Tweety and Sylvester* comic after
noting how the "muscles in Boaz's back slid over one another in slow patterns that were counterpoint to the quick
movements of his page-turning fingers" (p. 210). It is this
message of reciprocal, fluid patterns of empathy and love
that he takes with him. The opposition is between dignified patterns of love (Constant finally comes to love Beatrice) and disruptive patterns of hate or control. Even
the sirens of Titan are not totally fraudulent. As part
woman and part bird, the reality of the sirens could be
connected with the Titanic bluebirds, which Chrono attempts to emulate. From a mythological point of view,
Venus rather than Mercury might have been the more
appropriate location for this understanding, except for the
messenger relationship I have mentioned between Constant and Mercury. However, an equation is made between Mercury and Venus via the recipe from *The
Beatrice Rumfoord Galactic Cookbook*: "For a delicious

snack, try young Harmoniums rolled into tubes and filled with Venusian cottage cheese" (p. 196).

The coherent mythological structure should now be counterpointed with the erratic movement of the spiral motif in terms of the different temporal dimensions implied. The Newtonian notion of a clockwork universe still has a good deal of metaphorical vitality, and I would hope that I have conveyed some sense of the way in which the convolutions of plot in *The Sirens of Titan* are intricately and beautifully linked rather like the parts of a watch. Certainly the interdependent spirals of the universe do tell us one thing with a certain clarity: the time. It is important to notice that Malachi Constant is presented in the first chapter as very much time oriented. Mrs. Rumfoord has asked that he be punctual, and he is. As the sun sets, Constant passes through the Alice-in-Wonderland door set "in the west wall" (p. 10) and checks the time by his solar-powered watch. In other words, the time and his movement are correlated with the movement of the heavens. But the thing about punctual, linear Earth time is that it is not a constant. It does not truly apply anywhere else in the universe. And Vonnegut is very careful to specify, in the case of Mars, Mercury, and Titan, the differing lengths of the hours, days, months, and years. For example, in three Earthling years "Mercury had carried Unk and Boaz twelve and a half times around the Sun" (p. 198). A different space implies a different sense of time. Since nine Earth years are somehow lost when Unk is on Mars, and three or more when he is on Mercury, and an unspecified number when, back as Constant, he is on Titan, with each temporal disjunction we are presented with a rather different, rather older Constant. The effect of time is maximized, while the Earthly calibration of time is minimized or called into question. Thus Rumfoord complains about "being caught up in the monotonous clockwork of the Solar System" (p. 287).

Because any idea of control must invoke the principle of cause and effect, which is possible only given a linear conception of time, the understanding that the nature of time is relative goes some way toward undercutting most conceptions of control. This is the paradox Rumfoord signifies. He seems to be, in turn, controller and controlled, but he does not exist in linear time. What we have here is the central religious mystery of fate or determination and free will, given God's omniscience, in science-fiction garb. Depending upon the circumstances, as a source of consolation one may choose to emphasize either the knowledge that man has freedom of choice or that an unhappy event is God's will. This is the contradiction, or rather paradox, at the heart of Vonnegut's fiction, which he accepts as the dualistic *wampeter* ordering that system of *foma* which makes up his *karass* organization. *Granfalloon* systems, on the other hand, are characterized by a hostility to paradoxical dualism.

The religious notion of time and eternity becomes for Vonnegut punctual time and infundibulated time. The contrast is made in the first chapter, which is entitled "Between Timid and Timbuktu," after the title of Beatrice's slim volume of published poems: "The title derived from the fact that all the words between timid and Timbuktu in very small dictionaries relate to time" (p. 12). The operative phrase here, since it implies the limits of our perception, is "in very small dictionaries." Presumably *A Child's Cyclopedia of Wonder and Things to Do,* which provides the definition of a chrono-synclastic infundibulum as a rather larger way of seeing time, may be regarded as a larger dictionary. According to the *Cyclopedia,* "These places are where all the different kinds of truths fit together as nicely as the parts in your Daddy's solar watch" (p. 14). The same might be said of the contradictory parts of Vonnegut's fictions and is said about the way in which Chrono's good-luck piece slips into place to function as a spare part for Salo's ship: "The good-luck piece conformed to close tolerances and surrounding clearances in a way that would have pleased a Swiss machinist" (p. 303). The spare part is spiral-shaped and might even be viewed as the mainspring of a watch. In any event, the spiral motif, in addition to the meanings I have elaborated on, is associated with time. There is the "counter-clockwise spiral" (p. 40) of Beatrice's white gown, already noted, and Chrono's black bristly hair, which "grew in a violently counter-clockwise swirl" (p. 141). Rumfoord compares his own temporal perspective with the shape of a "roller coaster" (p. 57). Even the riddle about the man who "eats dates from the calendar and drinks water from the springs of the bed" (p. 72) in order to survive in a locked room that contains no other objects, serves to relate time and the spiral motif. Ransom K. Fern, too, in providing the book with an epigraph, connects time and heavenly movement: "Every passing hour brings the Solar System forty-three thousand miles closer to Globular Cluster M13 in Hercules—and still there are some misfits who insist there is no such thing as progress" (p. 5). Had Fern stopped to consider the larger spiral form of this "progress," he might have substituted the less optimistically loaded word "movement."

When we first meet Chrono on Mars, he is one of "fifty-two children" (p. 139), one for each week of the solar Earth year. I have already pointed to Chrono's mythological relationship to Saturn and time, a reading that is further pointed up by his rather more obvious connection with the chrono-synclastic infundibulum. It would seem that his survival in the novel may have something to do with his ability to exist in both punctual and infundibulated time. In consorting with the blue birds, Chrono, like his mythological counterpart who is sometimes portrayed with four wings, two outspread temporal wings and two at rest in eternity, reveals his interest in flight. When Salo commits suicide after discovering the nature of the message he has been carrying, Chrono, with equanimity, tosses his good-luck piece among Salo's scattered parts:

Sooner or later, Chrono believed, the magical forces of the Universe would put everything back together again.

They always did (p. 301).

And Salo's parts do come together again, in a manner that is left ambiguous unless we conclude that the spiral movement of time, after pulling things apart, brings them together again. Time or whoever can control time is the real agent of change, the true manipulator. Thus Chrono makes models of Saturn with her rings and moons and "spent hours moving the elements of the system about" (p. 305).

Although man can move about in space and seek desirable locations, he cannot so move about in time. The secret presumably is to be able to spatialize time, to see it all at once like God, to see all the possible truths, as Rumfoord does in his infundibulated state, and then make one's choice. The creative artist, the writer in particular, is able to do this. From Vonnegut's point of view, the writer has a duty to pick picturesque spots in time even at the risk of sentimentality, to make dissonance or contradiction a form of mystical paradox. Consequently the contradiction that the omniscient narrator of *The Sirens of Titan* seems to be guilty of in his prologue should now be viewed simply as a generative paradox. By distancing this narrator in time from the events of his narrative, Vonnegut puts his narrator in control of the plot, because, like Rumfoord, he is aware of its total shape. The reader is in a similar position when he takes up the book for the second time, and more so when he becomes aware of the multiplicity of imagistic and thematic configurations, which reflect in spatial terms the omnitemporal understanding that all things are true because all things are one. The Tralfamadorians, in manipulating our reality in order to form messages of consolation for one of their stranded kind, are Vonnegut's best writers. There is no evidence, however, that they enjoy that freedom of choice which comes from the writer's spatialized awareness of time. Salo claims that he exists punctually, and we are given to infer that all other Tralfamadorians are like him since the time when the machines took over, the creatures who made the machines being willing partners in their own extinction. However, this information is contradicted by the Tralfamadore of *Slaughterhouse-Five*. In that book the Tralfamadorians do not appear to be robots, and they experience time in something like Rumfoord's infundibulated fashion. From their point of view, we are suspended eternally like bugs "trapped in the amber of this moment" (p. 66). Have we caught the selective narrator of *The Sirens of Titan* out in another revealing contradiction, which might again indicate the fear of being involved in some one else's plot, or are we dealing with another temporal or mystical paradox? Certainly both Salo's third eye and the one-eyed heterotopic (the eye is placed in the one hand) Tralfamadorians, "shaped like plumber's friends" (p. 22) in *Slaughterhouse-Five*, betoken mystical awareness.

Although the Tralfamadorians' concept of time, like most concepts of God, would appear to deny free will, it does provide a useful form of consolation in periods of distress, and a final science-fictional rationale for coping with an event like the destruction of Dresden. Billy Pilgrim explains this apocalyptic view of reality:

> The most important thing I learned on Tralfamadore was that when a person dies he only *appears* to die. He is still very much alive in the past, so it is very silly for people to cry at his funeral. All moments, past, present, and future, always have existed, always will exist. The Tralfamadorians can look at all the different moments just the way we can look at a stretch of the Rocky Mountains (p. 23).

Seeing life as a matter of ups and downs, they wisely choose to concentrate on the ups. Their vision, incidentally, makes very evident the spiraling movement of the star-tracked heavens, which appear "filled with rarefied luminous spaghetti" (p. 75).

It should come as no surprise that the writers of this writer-orientated race produce telegrammatic books very like Vonnegut's own, "laid out—in brief clumps of symbols separated by stars":

each clump of symbols is a brief, urgent message—describing a situation, a scene. The Tralfamadorians read them all at once, not one after the other. There isn't any particular relationship between all the messages, except that the author has chosen them carefully, so that, when seen all at once, they produce an image of life that is beautiful and surprising and deep. There is no beginning, no middle, no end, no suspense, no moral, *no causes, no effects* (my italics). What we love in our books are the depths of many marvelous moments seen all at one time (p. 76).

There are many paradoxes here. Images of fixity or rigidity in Vonnegut—Dresden corpses or the victims of *ice-nine*—signify death and destruction. But aesthetic control largely rests on the rigid principle of determinism. Vonnegut distinguishes as creative the aesthetic fixity or timelessness of words on a page or statues like those of the sirens and others that Salo carves on Titan. Thus Constant, in order to avoid being manipulated, says, "I will freeze" (p. 289), so that anyone who wants to use him "will be a lot better off trying to get a rise out of one of these statues" (p. 290). It so happens that one of the statues just described "had a shocking erection" (p. 289). I make this rather delicate point in view of the rather too easy opposition that at least one of Vonnegut's critics has made between positive forces, which flow, and negative, rigidifying forces.[13]

In the total context of the argument I have offered, there is one episode in *The Sirens of Titan* that appears particularly loaded. It takes place in Skip's Museum, the chimneylike room under the spiral staircase. The room was Rumfoord's favorite retreat as a child, when he was called Skip. This somewhat doggy name provides some connection with Kazak, the suspiciously irrelevant Hound of Space. Among the mortal remains housed in this museum is "the long spiral tusk of a narwhal, playfully labeled by Skip *Unicorn Horn*" (p. 24). The possible imaginative ex-

13 See *City of Words*, p. 196.

tensions of this spiral might be seen as embracing the *Whale,* a large space vehicle owned by Constant, which in turn prompts Constant to adopt the pseudonym of Jonah Rowley when he discovers that the *Whale* might indeed be the means of conveying him to a fate no less appetizing than Jonah's. But the *Whale* also prompts that more fruitful image that Buckminster Fuller has made so familiar: "Evangelist Bobby Denton's image of Earth as God's space ship" (p. 87). Skip's creative naming of the narwhal tusk points to the survival value of pleasant fantasies. The museum itself is such a fantasy. It represents the attempt to freeze time and so order reality.

Shortly after the episode in which Constant passes himself off as Jonah Rowley and after Constant's visit to the Rumfoord estate "disguised by dark glasses and a false beard" (p. 11), a genuinely bearded young man named Martin Koradubian (his initials are close to Malachi Constant's) had identified himself as the bearded stranger who had been invited into the Rumfoord estate to see a materialization. "He was a *repairer of solar watches* [my italics] in Boston, and a charming liar" (p. 49). He sells the story of his visit and conversation with Rumfoord to a magazine that Rumfoord reads "Sitting in Skip's Museum under the spiral staircase." He reads "with delight and admiration." Rumfoord has supposedly told Koradubian about "the year Ten Million when there would be a tremendous house-cleaning": "All records relating to the period between the death of Christ and the year One Million A.D. would be hauled to dumps and burned. This would be done, said Koradubian, because museums and archives would be crowding the living right off the earth." So much for Skip's Museum. This then blank period of time would be summed up in history books as "*a period of readjustment.*" Vastly amused, Rumfoord notes the year Ten Million as "A merry time for . . . digging up time capsules" (p. 50). Koradubian, the writer and watch repairer, speaks, in this his only appearance, for the book's omniscient narrator, the Beatrice who authors *The True*

Purpose of Life in the Solar System, and Vonnegut, who all illustrate the writer's ability to readjust a constricting "historical" reality along science-fictional lines by making temporal adjustments.

VII

Hopefully, the preceding analysis, while serving to review many of my concerns throughout this inquiry, does emphasize certain points. It would seem, first of all, that there are works of science fiction that do stand up to and reward the closest critical scrutiny. I should stress, however, that in elaborating a generic continuum that allows one to speak of the "space opera" of E. E. "Doc" Smith and Milton's *Paradise Lost* in the same breath, I wish only to imply a range of potential within a definable form in the interests of indicating the relevant criteria. In discussions of *Paradise Lost,* the matter of the flatness of Milton's characterizations doesn't appear to be the damning criticism it usually is when people talk about science fiction. Vonnegut is the kind of writer who illustrates particularly well the satiric, philosophical, and visionary utopian-to-dystopian range of the apocalyptic imagination in both its science-fictional and non-science-fictional aspects. As a writer whose apocalyptic interests find expression as both science fiction and mainstream literature, Vonnegut is comparable to another American, namely Mark Twain. The American connection is important. Although all apocalyptic writers might be said to inhabit an America of the mind, the central tradition clings to American soil.

Vonnegut's "new world" is essentially, as I have argued, of a visionary or religious nature, and it is this aspect of his work that I wish finally to underline. Because of the distinctions I have drawn between different facets of the apocalyptic imagination, the religious vision traditionally associated with the apocalyptic has often receded in favor of other emphases. But if my distinctions, which do relate only to matters of emphasis, are allowed to disappear, the apocalyptic imagination may be understood as a totality with a movable or fluctuating religious center. The equation between utopian "heavens below" and visionary "heavens above" is only the most direct example of an equation between all new worlds and a visionary reality. To convey—and this is usual—the appreciation of any new world in terms of a sense of "unity," as opposed to the sense of disintegration associated with the old world, is to imply the relevance of a visionary reality. At the same time, philosophical formulations, if not of a direct theological nature, may be viewed as substituting or compensating for or involving the secularization of a religious system of belief. In whatever displaced, disguised, secularized, or antagonistic relationship, the religious element remains a constant identifying characteristic of the apocalyptic imagination.

Index

DATE DUE

DEC 15 1975			